MW00913974

NEW

Total English

Pearson Education Limited
Edinburgh Gate
Harlow
Essex CM20 2JE
England
and Associated Companies throughout the world.

www.pearsonelt.com

© Pearson Education Limited 2012

The right of JJ Wilson and Antonia Clare to be identified as authors of this Work has been asserted by them in accordance with the Copyright, Designs and Patents Act 1988.

All rights reserved; no part of this publication may be reproduced, stored in a retrieval system, or transmitted in any form or by any means, electronic, mechanical, photocopying, recording, or otherwise without the prior written permission of the Publishers.

First published 2012
Fourth impression 2016

ISBN: 978-1-4082-8581-7

Set in MetaPlusBook-Roman
Printed in China
SWTC/04

Acknowledgements

The publishers and authors would like to thank the following people and institutions for their feedback and comments during the development of the material:

Lucia Cortese, Australia; Adriana Lima, Brazil; Jill Fortune, Colombia; Fiona Delaney, France; Eszter Timár, Hungary; Tom Windle, Japan; Witoslaw Awedyk, Hayden Berry, Agnieszka Gugnacka-Cook, Lech Krzeminski, Poland; Maribel Isabel González Ortíz, Spain; Ruth Avison Dang, Switzerland; Alper Darici, Turkey; Anne Cilliers, Rob Turland, Shanel Ali, UK

We are grateful to the following for permission to reproduce copyright material:

Article 1.3 adapted from http://www.nationaldanceawards.com/features/carlos_acosta_04.htm, Mike Dixon is a freelance writer and founder of the Critics' Circle National Dance Awards.; Article 1.3 adapted from http://observer.guardian.co.uk/osm/story/0,1209934,00.html, Mark Rendell @ The Observer; Extract 2.3 from The Rough Guide to Corsica (David Abram) Introduction pages iii-xvi © Rough Guides, 2003; Extract 3. from The Mind-Body Problem ISBN 0140172459, Reprint Edition, Penguin Books (Rebecca Goldstein 1993), Rebecca Newberger Goldstein; Extract 3. from Herzog ISBN 0142437298, Penguin Books (Saul Bellow 1964); Extract 3. Metàmorphosis ISBN 0553213695, Bantam Books / Imprint of Random House (Franz Kafka 1915); Extract 3.2 from The Edge of Day (US) (UK title: Cider With Rosie), 2002, William Morrow and Company, New York/ Random House from Cider with Rosie by Laurie Lee, published by Vintage Books. Reprinted by permission of The Random House Group Limited; Extract 3.2 from The Best Revenge, 1993, New York: Sol Stein / New York: Random House; Extract 3.2 from The Stuntman's Daughter ISBN 1574410091, University of North Texas Press, Denton, Texas (Alice Blanchard 1996); Extract 3.2 from Blister ISBN 0-439-19314-1 by Susan Steve 2001 reprinted by permission of scholastic Inc; Extract 3.2. from Slade, Robert Hale, London (Dyer, Robert 1994) Extracts 4.1.2, 10.1.10a adapted from Focus Magazine, Issue no 141 August 2004 ISBN: 9770966427074; Exhibit 4.3.12 adapted from http://www8.gmanews.tv/story/198528/8-year-old-painting-prodigy-is-new-art-world-star, GMA News/ Jill Lawless 2010; Extract 5.1.10 adapted fromhttp://www.entrepreneur.com/article/0,4621,298643,00.html published on www.entrepreneur.com 1/04/2002, Cliff Ennico, Small business expert, host of the PBS television series MoneyHunt, and author of 15 books on entrepreneurship including 'Small Business Survival; Extract 6.1.4b adapted from Facts and figures from: Mackaness, C. (ed.) 2006, Bridging Sydney, Historic Houses Trust of New South Wales, Sydney., http://architecture.about.com/od/greatbuildings/ig/Stadium-and-Arena-Pictures/Millennium-Dome.htm, Australian Government Culture and Recreation Portal; Extract 7.3.3 adapted from http://www.commondreams.org/cgi-bin/print.cgi?file=/headlines05/0816-03.htm The independent,Maxine Frith / The Independent; Extract 9.3.5 adapted from The bigger picture The Times (travel section), 16/07/2005, 14 (Doug McKinlay)

In some instances we have been unable to trace the owners of copyright material, and we would appreciate any information that would enable us to do so.

The publisher would like to thank the following for their kind permission to reproduce their photographs:
(Key: b-bottom; c-centre; l-left; r-right; t-top)

akg-images Ltd: Anderloni A. Bossi 120tc; **Alamy Images:** Adrian Sherratt 22br, Bubbles Photo Library 55cl, Foto-Zone 130c, Frank Chmura 111cl, Horizon International Images Ltd 66cl, Leonid Plotkin 28cr, Maspix 38br, No Image 73cr, Paul Chauncey 7tl, PhotoAlto 46b, Pictorial Press 84tc, Rob Bartee 41br, Sally & Richard Greenhill 116cr, Simon Curtis 161cr, Steve Sant 66cr, Terry Harris 106tr, 116bl, The Africa Image Library 96t; **albanpix.com:** Alban Donohoe 58cr; **Andrew Tift:** 123tc; **Art Directors and TRIP Photo Library:** Douglas Houghton 39tr, Helene Rogers 41bl, 59tr; **Biaracing.com:** Carsten Horst 14tr, 15tr; **Bridgeman Art Library:** Advertising Archives 35cl, Staatliche Kunstammlungen Dresden 119tl, William Holmes Sullivan / Gavin Graham Gallery 35tl; **Corbis:** 41tr, 49t, Aerial Skelly 133bl, Atlantide Phototravel 119t, Barry Lewis / In Pictures 22tl, Beau Lark 7bl, Bernd Vogel 112tr, Bettmann 22tr, 36tr, 122br, 130tl, 137cr, Bjanka Kadic 77cl, Boris Roessler / EPA 26-27t, C.Lyttle 67tr, Creasource 112tc, David Turnley 8tl, 105bl, James Lauritz 67cr, Joe Toth / BPI 86cl, Jose Luis Pelaez Inc 106cl, Kai Pfaffenbach / Reuters 63t, Kim Kulish 86bl, LWA-Dann Tardif 113br, Matthius Kulka 77t, Murray Close / Sygma 35bl, Naashon Zalk 69bl, Ocean 91t, 133cl, Paul A Souders 22bl, Paul Harris / JAI 63tl, Ramin Talaie 105tl, Richard Lewis / EPA 63cl, Rick Freidman 86br, Robbie Jack 119bl, Ron Nickel / Design Pics 67tl, Rudy Sulgan 21t, Seth Resnick / Science Faction 95b, The Gallery Collection 35t, Toshiyuki Aizawa / Reuters 119cl, Walter Geiersperger 24cr; **Dean Marsh:** 123tr; **Fotolia.com:** Aleksandar Radovanov 49tr, Andrzej Tokarski 49cl, Claude Coquilleau 78tl, DNGood 137tl, Donald Joski 100bl, Felix Mizioznikov 10tc, Lorenzo Verso 152t, Maksym Gorpenyuk 79tr, Noel Moore 95cr, Sergey Galushko 100tc, Wusuowei 144t; **Hanh Nguyen Photography:** 58br; **Robert Harding World Imagery:** Frans Lemmens 21cl; **Getty Images:** Adrian Weinbrecht / Taxi 63cr, AFP 77tl, Alfred Eisenstaedt / Time & Life Pictures 120tr, Andrew Gunners / Photodisc 102, Andrew Watson 91bl, Art Wolfe / The Image Bank 126bl, Bongarts 133t, Caitlin Mogridge / Redferns 72cr, Carl Mydans / Time & Life Pictures 36tl, China Photos 126cl, Chris Jackson 147tr, Cultura RF 82tl, Dan Dalton / Photodisc 73tl, Dan Kenyon / Taxi 116c, David Lees / Iconica 55tr, David Malan / Photographers Choice 53tr, Digital Vision 144cr, Erin Patrice O'Brien / Stone 96tl, Haywood Magee / Hulton Archive 158t, Heath Korvola / Uppercut Images 82cl, James Darrell / Photodisc 81tr, Javier Pierini / Digital Vision 7t, Javier Pierini / Stone 32cr, Jewel Samad / AFP 133tl, Jon Kopaloff / Film Magic 86cr, Kelley & Meyers / Taxi 73br, Kevin Philips / Photodisc 106br, Lawrence Lawry / Photodisc 60b, Maurice Rougemont / Gammo-Rapho 66br, Michael Blann / Stone 21tr, Michael Nagle 77bl, Mike Powell / Stone 144tr, Peter Dazeley 153br, Photolink / Photodisc 60t, Shelly Strazis / Uppercut 109tc, Stephen A. Alvarex / National Geographic 126tl, Steve Granitz / Wire Image 84tr, Steve Niedorf Photography 162tr, Tanya Constantine / Blend 57tl, Thinkstock / Comstock 21bl, 73bl, Universal Images Group / Hulton Archive 12tl, Vincent Besnault / Digital Vision 73tr, Westend61 / Jupiter Images 114b, White Packert / Photonica 106cr, Wides & Hall / Photographers Choice 156tr; **Kobal Collection Ltd:** Marvel / Sony Pictures 50t, Universal / Working Title 43cr, Warner Bros / James David / DC Comics 51tl; **Lonely Planet Images:** Lindsay Brown 116tl; **Masterfile UK Ltd:** Mike Randolph 144br, Peter Griffith 32tr, T Ozonas 159t; **Pearson Education Ltd:** Lord & Leverett 41tc; **PhotoDisc:** 40br; **Photofusion Picture Library:** Paul Ridsdale 114bl, Warren Powell 114br; **Photolibrary.com:** Aflo Photo Agency 74tr; **Photoshot Holdings Limited:** Xinhua 154tr; **Press Association Images:** DPA Deutsche Press Agentur 12cr, James Vellacott / Daily Mirror / PA Pool 8tr, M. Spencer Green / AP 144r; **PunchStock:** Bananastock 71tl, 71tr, Valueline 112cr; **Reuters:** Jeff Christenson 60cl, Robert Galbraith 67c; **Rex Features:** 12tr, 44t, Alexander Caminada 109tr, Everett Collection 42tl, 51tr, Henry T. Kaiser 116br, John Powell 82tr, Kristin Callahan 84tl, Mario Beauregard 25tl, NBCUPhotobank 136tr, Roger-Viollet 43br, Sipa Press 8t, Stewart Cook 153bl, Tony Buckingham 65tl, Wojtek Laski 99tl; **Science Photo Library Ltd:** 11b, Pascal Goetgheluck 60c, Ria Novosti 137cl; **Shutterstock.com:** Adrio Communications Ltd 11tr, Africa924 91tl, Alexander Raths 94tl, Alysta 161br, Ansono618 148, Borislav Borisov 92-93t, Borislav Toskov 106tl, Bylikova Oksana 95bl, Charlie Hutton 29cr, Cheryl-E Davis 164t, Consu1961 163tr, Cora Reed 100t, David Steele 28tr, Dora Modly-Paris 100cr, Elnur 7cl, FrontPage 78tr, Goodluz 81tc, Gorilla 74tc, iPhotos 161tr, Jan Martin Will 105t, Kevin Eaves 157tr, KWest 24tr, Lars Christensen 91cl, Lightpoet 28tl, Maggee 100br, Oblong1 79tl, Pixinity 155tr, Pra-Zit 105cl, Prodakszyn 160tl, Ralph Loesche 29tr, S. Borisov 29br, Smileus 106bl, StockLite 65br, Sunxvejan 78br, Tandem 130tc, Tereshchenko Dmitry 100cl, Valery Kraynov 95tr, Vfoto 74tl, Vladimir Sazanov 80bl, Vladkol 74bl, WillG 79bl, Yampi 79br, YanLev 111tr, Yuri Arcurs 49bl; **SuperStock:** 153tr, Blend Images 38tl, 44b, Corbis 25tr, Prisma 18tr; **The Random House Group Ltd:** 136bl, 136bc; **Tim Okamura:** 123tc; **TopFoto:** 12cl, 116tr, Imageworks 24br, 153tl, Nigel Norrington / Arenapal 147cl; **Wellcome Library, London:** 120tl; **Xerox Ltd:** 130tr

All other images © Pearson Education

Every effort has been made to trace the copyright holders and we apologise in advance for any unintentional omissions. We would be pleased to insert the appropriate acknowledgement in any subsequent edition of this publication.

Illustrated by Beach (Beach-o-matic), Mark Duffin, Sally Newton, Amanda Montgomery-Higham (SGA), Roger Penwill and Lucy Truman (New Division)

Cover photo © *Front*: **Getty Images:** Mark A Paulda

NEW

Total English

ADVANCED

Students' Book

JJ Wilson with Antonia Clare

Contents

Contents

Do you know ...?

1 Read the text and match the parts of speech (a–j) to each <u>underlined</u> word or phrase.

In 1967, Allen and Beatrice Gardner embarked on an (1) <u>experiment</u> to train a chimpanzee to talk. Realising that chimpanzees don't have the vocal apparatus to be able to speak like humans, but that (2) <u>they</u> can use gestures (3) <u>easily</u>, the Gardners decided to train (4) <u>the</u> animal in ASL, American Sign Language. Their subject was a chimpanzee called Washoe. The Gardners (5) <u>brought up</u> Washoe like a child, giving her regular meals and getting her to brush her teeth before sleep. At first Washoe made meaningless hand gestures, similar to the meaningless 'babbling' of baby children learning a language. But after four years Washoe had learned over 150 signs. She (6) <u>could</u> also combine the signs on some occasions, such as when she made the signs for 'water' and 'bird' on (7) <u>seeing</u> a swan on a lake. Linguists and scientists, (8) <u>however</u>, are (9) <u>sceptical</u> about the Gardners' (10) <u>research</u>, and question whether Washoe can really 'speak'. They say that her 'language use' is simply imitation.

a present participle *(ing)* 7
b link word (contrast) 8
c uncountable noun 10
d countable noun 1 *(an)*
e article 4
f phrasal verb 5
g adjective 9
h adverb 3
i pronoun 2
j modal verb 6

2 Find the grammar mistake in each sentence.

future on adverb
1 By this time tomorrow, we will have arrive in Peru. *d*
2 We were hot because we'd run. *had been* *(ing)*
3 If I would have seen you, I would have stopped. *had*
subjunctive
4 It's time we go home. *went*
couldn't
5 It mustn't have been John – John's tall and that man was short.
6 We haven't been knowing her long. *Known*
7 The conference will held in the theatre tomorrow. *be*
8 I had my purse stole yesterday. *was n*
9 She persuaded me buying the car.
10 He climbed up the Mount Everest.

3 a Complete the word maps with words/phrases from the box below.

> half-sister   career path   uncharted territory
> soulmate   culture shock   spending spree
> gamble   be made redundant

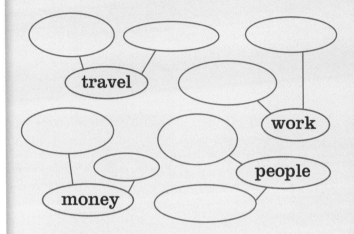

b <u>Underline</u> the main stress in each word/ phrase.

c Add three more words to each word map.

4 a Look at the dictionary extract below from the *Longman Dictionary of Contemporary English*. What does it tell you about each of the following: grammar, pronunciation, use and meaning? *go to page 86*

dead·line \'dedlaın\ *n* [C] a date or time by which you have to do or complete something: [+**for**] *The deadline for applications is May 27th.* | [+**of**] *It has to be in before the deadline of July 1st.* | **meet/miss a deadline** (=have or not have something finished on time) *working under pressure to meet a deadline.* | **set/impose a deadline** *They've set a deadline of Nov 5.* | **tight/strict deadline** (=a deadline that is difficult)

b Complete the dictionary extracts below by writing a definition for each one.

1 over·priced /ˌəʊvəˈpraɪst/ *adj*

_____ :

The food was overpriced.

2 wan·der¹ /ˈwɒndə/ *v* [+**around**] [I, T]

_____ :

We didn't know where to go, so we wandered around.

3 ac·quaint·ance /əˈkweɪntəns/ *n* [C]

_____ : *I don't know her well – she's just an acquaintance.*

4 i·ni·tia·tive /ɪˈnɪʃətɪv/ *n* [U]

_____ : *You need to have initiative to do this job.*

Lead-in

p. 16

1 Look at the photos. Work in pairs and discuss the questions.

1 What types of challenge are shown?

2 Have you ever faced any challenges similar to these? What happened? How did you feel?

2 Look at the sentence beginnings (1–8) and check you understand the <u>underlined</u> phrases. Match them with the endings (a–h).

c 1 I like to <u>set achievable goals</u>,

f 2 It's important to <u>face challenges</u>, but

g 3 She usually <u>rises to the challenge</u>, even if

e 4 If I succeed, it will <u>make my dream come true</u>, because

a 5 I <u>couldn't have done it without</u> help, so

h 6 It was a <u>burning ambition</u>, which

d 7 It's important to <u>have the right attitude</u>, because

b 8 It's quite a <u>daunting challenge</u>, but hopefully

a I'd like to thank my family and my sponsors.

b I can achieve it.

c so, before starting, I always think about my objectives.

d if you are a positive person, it will be easier.

e I've wanted to do this since I was a child.

f you mustn't be afraid of them.

g it's something very difficult.

h I finally managed to achieve.

3 What are your goals (on this course, in your career or studies, or in your personal life)? What challenges do you think you will face?

Reading

1 Work in **pairs** and **discuss** the questions.

1 How many languages do you speak? **W**hy and how did you learn them?

2 Why might the people in the photos need to know different languages? What jobs require several languages?

3 Do you think it is easier to learn a new language when you already know other languages? Why/Why not?

4 Do you know any polyglots (people who speak many languages)?

2 a Read the article and answer the questions.

1 How did Francis Sommer learn his European languages?

2 What advantage did Stephen Wurm have as a learner of languages?

3 According to Kenneth Hale, what type of talent do polyglots have?

4 How is learning new languages sometimes 'easy', according to David Perlmutter?

5 What do polyglots sometimes worry about?

6 What bonuses and problems has Ziad Fazah experienced because of his linguistic abilities?

b Work in pairs and discuss your answers.

3 Work in pairs and discuss the questions.

1 What are the benefits of being a polyglot? Are there any drawbacks?

2 In your opinion, what personal qualities are necessary to become a polyglot?

Great language learners

According to legend, Cardinal Giuseppe Mezzofanti (1774–1849), who spoke 72 languages, once learned a language
5 overnight in order to hear the confession of two condemned prisoners the following morning. While this story sounds too amazing to be true, there are
10 polyglots who have achieved quite staggering feats of language learning.

Arguably the greatest of all was Francis Sommer. Brought up
15 in Germany, Sommer was still a schoolboy when he succeeded in learning Swedish, Sanskrit and Persian. On a trip to Russia, he mingled with the international
20 community and, so the story goes, learned a dozen European languages. He later moved to the United States, where he worked as a research librarian, and by the
25 1920s, had mastered 94 languages.

Another great linguist is Stephen Wurm, Professor of Linguistics at the Australian National University at Canberra. Wurm benefited
30 from the fact that he came from a multilingual family. His father, also a linguist, asked everyone in the family to speak to the child in their own language. This meant
35 that his mother addressed him in Hungarian, his father in English, his grandfather in Norwegian, and his grandmother in Mongolian. Because of Wurm's father's work, the family
40 also lived for periods in Germany, Russia, China, Argentina and Turkey. As a result, Wurm spoke ten languages by the time he was six.

To most of us, the achievements
45 of polyglots seem superhuman, but the polyglots themselves don't see it that way. Kenneth Hale, a linguistics professor who speaks around 50 languages, believes his
50 talent bears similarity to that of

Vocabulary | learning languages

4 Match the words/expressions (1–8) from the article to the definitions (a–h).

1 master (v) (line 25)
2 let (sth) slide (phrase) (line 58)
3 pick up (phrasal verb) (line 70)
4 garble (v) (line 74)
5 information overload (n) (line 88)
6 babble (v) (line 103)
7 unintelligibly (adv) (line 103)
8 dialect (n) (line 107)

a in a way that is impossible to understand
b to neglect something or allow it to get worse
c a form of a language which is spoken in only one area, with its own words/grammar
d to speak quickly in a way that is difficult to understand
e to learn something so well that you have no difficulty with it
f too much to remember
g to learn without consciously studying
h to mix up or confuse words

5 **a** Complete the sentences using words/ expressions from exercise 4.

1 It's easy to _____ foreign languages _____ if you don't use them regularly.
2 In many countries, people can understand the standard form of their language and also a local _____ .
3 The best way to _____ new vocabulary is by reading a lot.
4 It may be impossible to _____ a foreign language completely.
5 For most students, more than ten new words per lesson equals _____ .
6 Many language learners find that native speakers speak _____ – they use lots of idioms and colloquial expressions.
7 When babies _____ , they are imitating adult language.
8 If you know three or more languages, you're more likely to _____ your words.

b Work in pairs. Discuss which sentences you agree with.

---

a musician's. And while talent is one factor, a love of languages is essential. Hale recalls the time when he was learning Navajo:
55 "I used to go out every day and sit on a rock and talk Navajo to myself." Languages became an obsession. "I let everything else slide," he says.
60 David Perlmutter, Professor of Linguistics at the University of California, likens the process of language learning to a puzzle. Mastery, he believes, stems from
65 the joy of solving the puzzle. "If you know English and German," he says, "it's easy to learn Dutch." Therefore, once you know Spanish and another Romance language,
70 you can pick up Portuguese quickly.
But is there any chance that these super-polyglots might get confused? Do they ever get nervous about garbling their languages?
75 According to Kenneth Hale, it does happen. Occasionally, he begins speaking in one language and, without knowing it, finds

that he has drifted into another. It
80 happens especially when it's difficult to distinguish between related languages. "Unless I'm attentive ... I can mix up languages like Miskitu and Sumu, both of which
85 are spoken in Central America and are very similar." Francis Sommer felt the same. Fearing information overload, he gave up learning new languages in later life.
90 Of today's polyglots, Ziad Fazah, a Lebanese living in Brazil, is probably number one. A speaker of around 60 languages, Fazah, unlike many great polyglots, was not
95 born into multilingualism. Besides his native Arabic, he learned only French and English at school, and taught himself the other languages. His astonishing abilities have had
100 some interesting consequences. On one occasion, the Brazilian police stopped an undocumented alien who was babbling unintelligibly. They asked Fazah for help. Fazah
105 realised immediately that the man was from Afghanistan and speaking

a dialect called Hazaras. On another occasion, the US Consulate grew suspicious of Fazah's ability
110 to speak Chinese and Russian. Suspecting that he was a terrorist, they brought him in for questioning. After two hours, however, he was released.
115 Fazah is not widely known, though that may change. In recent years, he has appeared on TV programmes in Greece and Spain, where he was quizzed in multiple
120 languages including Hungarian, Korean, Japanese and Chinese. He passed with flying colours. While this earned him a reputation as a phenomenon, he is still a few
125 languages behind the legendary Cardinal Mezzofanti. Unlike Mezzofanti, Fazah cannot claim to learn languages overnight, but he can apparently learn a thousand
130 words a month – a gift that language students around the world would envy and admire!

Listening

6 a  **1.02 Listen to Mark Spina talking about language learning. Make notes on the questions.**

1 How many languages does he speak?
2 Where/how did he learn them?
3 What special techniques does he use?
4 How does he feel about language?
5 What problems does he have?

b Work in pairs and compare your answers. Then listen again to check.

7 Do you have similar experiences of language learning? Discuss with other students.

Grammar | verbs/adjectives/nouns with prepositions

8 a Look at examples 1–5 in the Active grammar box and underline the prepositions. What type of word does each preposition follow?

b Answer the questions for rules A and B in the Active grammar box.

Active grammar

1 *Sommer was still a schoolboy, when he succeeded in learning Swedish, Sanskrit and Persian.*

2 *Mastery, he believes, stems from the joy of solving the puzzle.*

3 *Wurm benefited from the fact that he came from a multilingual family.*

4 *Do they ever get nervous about garbling their various languages?*

5 *This can happen, especially when it is difficult to distinguish between related languages.*

A Prepositions after verbs, nouns and adjectives always have an object. What is the object in each sentence above?

B When the preposition is followed by a verb, the verb is usually in the *-ing* form. Which of the sentences above use this structure?

see Reference page 19

9 a Complete the sentences with prepositions from the box. Check any new expressions in your dictionary.

> from (x3)   to   in (x2)   about (x2)   for   with

1 Do you think you'll succeed _____ passing your next exam?
2 If you could improve your English by watching DVDs, by living in an English-speaking country or by studying from books, which would you opt _____ ?
3 Do your problems in English stem _____ poor grammar, or are there other problems?
4 Do you feel you are lacking _____ vocabulary?
5 Even at advanced level, some students' spoken English is riddled _____ errors. Does this matter or is fluency more important?
6 What distinguishes your first language _____ English?
7 What types of classroom exercises appeal _____ you?
8 Is pronunciation worth bothering _____ or are you happy to keep your accent?
9 Are you nervous _____ giving presentations in English?
10 How can your vocabulary benefit _____ using the media?

b Match the questions (1–10) in exercise 9a to the possible answers (a–j).

a Some of the vocabulary is similar but the grammar is completely different.
b I always make an effort with the sounds of English, but I know I'll never sound like a native speaker.
c Yes, I think so. I've been studying hard and I really hope I achieve my goal!
d I like class discussions best of all, and also role plays.
e I think accuracy is important, too. It's difficult to listen to someone whose speech is full of mistakes, and it distracts you from the content of what they're saying.
f I'd choose to immerse myself in the language and culture by living in Canada or Australia.
g Listening regularly to the news or looking at websites is good for learning new words.
h Yes. I don't know many idioms, phrasal verbs and informal expressions.
i A lot of the difficulties come from the fact that I can't understand native speakers when they speak fast, but I also need to work on my grammar!
j Speaking in public worries me a little bit, but I think it's a good thing to do in class.

Speaking

10 a Work with a partner. Discuss questions 1–10 from exercise 9a. Are the suggested answers from exercise 9b true for you? If not, why not?

b Tell the class what you found out about your partner.

Vocabulary | knowledge

1 Choose the correct words in *italics*.

1 'Who won the first Oscar?'
 'I haven't *an idea/a clue.*'

2 'What was the first book ever published?'
 'I don't know off the top of my *head/hand.*'

3 'What date did Man first go to the moon?'
 '*I don't know/I'm sure* offhand, but I can look it up.'

4 'Where did Elisha Gray come from?'
 'Who? I've never *heard/known* of him.'

5 'Do you know Paris?'
 'Yes. I lived there for years so I know it like the back of my *head/hand.*'

6 'Which state has the smallest population?'
 'I'm pretty *sure/positive* it's the Vatican.'

7 'Do you know Eliot's poem about cats?'
 'I know it *by/at* heart. I learned it at school.'

8 'What do you know about company law?'
 'I know it inside *in/out.* I have a PhD in it.'

9 'What do you know about Belgian politics?'
 'I know *close/next* to nothing about it.'

10 'Which country has the biggest population?'
 'I haven't the faintest *idea/clue.*'

11 'Are you sure Russia is the biggest country in the world?'
 'I'm fairly *certain/positive* it is, but it might be China.'

12 'Are you sure the Nile is the longest river in the world?'
 'Yes. I'm *positive/fairly positive* it is.'

2 a Complete the How to... box with the <u>underlined</u> expressions from exercise 1.

b How are the expressions different? Which are strongest? Which mean the same?

How to... say how much you know/don't know

I know	*I'm pretty sure*
I don't know	*I haven't a clue.*

Speaking

3 Work in pairs and do the quiz. Try to use expressions from the How to... box.

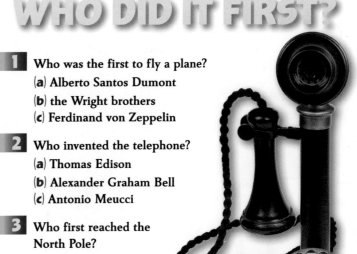

WHO DID IT FIRST?

1 Who was the first to fly a plane?
 (**a**) Alberto Santos Dumont
 (**b**) the Wright brothers
 (**c**) Ferdinand von Zeppelin

2 Who invented the telephone?
 (**a**) Thomas Edison
 (**b**) Alexander Graham Bell
 (**c**) Antonio Meucci

3 Who first reached the North Pole?
 (**a**) Robert Peary
 (**b**) Frederick Cook
 (**c**) Roald Amundsen

4 Who invented the light bulb?
 (**a**) Thomas Edison (**b**) Alexander Graham Bell
 (**c**) Leonardo da Vinci

5 Which country won the first football World Cup (and hosted it)?
 (**a**) Brazil (**b**) Uruguay (**c**) Germany

6 Which country first allowed women to vote?
 (**a**) Switzerland (**b**) New Zealand (**c**) the United States

7 Who was the first woman to sail solo around the world via Cape Horn?
 (**a**) Ellen MacArthur (**b**) Amelia Earhart (**c**) Naomi James

8 Which country first held the Olympic Games?
 (**a**) Italy (**b**) France (**c**) Greece

Listening

4 a 🔊 1.03 Listen to a radio programme and check your answers to the quiz.

b Work in pairs. Listen again and discuss the questions.

1 Which 'famous firsts' do photos 1–4 refer to? What can you remember about them?

2 Did you find anything surprising in the radio programme? What extra information did you learn?

Grammar | passives: distancing

5 a Look at examples 1–6 in the Active grammar box and underline the passives.

b Read rules A–C in the Active grammar box and write true (T) or false (F).

c Why do you think passives are used in these sentences?

Active grammar

1 *Santos Dumont was widely believed to have flown the first plane.*

2 *He's said to be the first person to have owned a flying machine.*

3 *It's commonly assumed that Bell invented the telephone.*

4 *In 2003, files were discovered which suggest that Philipp Reis had invented the phone.*

5 *The cheering of the crowd is said to have been the loudest noise ever heard in Uruguay.*

6 *It is often thought that rugby and sheep are the main claims to fame for New Zealand.*

A We can use the passive to show that a statement is not our own opinion. ☐

B We often use the passive to show that a statement is a personal opinion. ☐

C If we aren't sure that the information is 100% correct, we can use the passive to put 'distance' between ourselves and the statement. ☐

Other verbs for 'distancing' include *It appears/seems that* and *It seems as if/though*.

We can use *appears/seems to have* + past participle to describe a past event.

see Reference page 19

6 Write sentences using structures for distancing with the verb in brackets.

People say that Edison invented more machines than anyone else in history. (say)

Edison <u>is said to have</u> invented more machines than anyone else in history.

1 But the evidence suggests that Edison didn't invent as much as we thought. (seems)

But it _____ though Edison invented fewer things than we thought.

2 People believe that da Vinci invented the helicopter. (think)

Da Vinci _____ invented the helicopter.

3 North American historians assert that the Wright brothers flew first. (assert)

It _____ by North American historians that the Wright brothers flew first.

4 At that time, everybody in the US thought that the Wright brothers were the first to fly. (assume)

It _____ that the Wright brothers were the first to fly.

5 A number of journalists in the late 19th century said that William Dickson had 'invented' the movie. (claim)

It _____ that William Dickson had 'invented' the movie.

6 We think Dutchman Joop Sinjou and Japanese Toshi Tada Doi invented the CD player at the same time. (believe)

Sinjou and Tada Doi _____ invented the CD player simultaneously.

7 Newspapers of the time reported that Felix Hoffman had invented aspirin. (report)

It _____ that Felix Hoffman had invented aspirin.

8 We now think that aspirin was first used by Egyptians. (believe)

It _____ that aspirin was first used by Egyptians.

Listening

7 **a** 🔊 1.04 Listen to some news headlines. What achievements do they talk about?

b 🔊 1.05 Listen only to the headlines and write down exactly what you hear.

c Now look at the headlines in **bold** in audioscript 1.04 on page 88. What problems did you have?

Pronunciation | word stress (1)

8 **a** Look at the headlines from exercise 7c. Which are the content words (nouns, verbs, etc.)? Which are the function words (prepositions, auxiliary verbs, etc.)?

b 🔊 1.05 Listen to the headlines again and <u>underline</u> the stressed words.

c Repeat the sentences, stressing the <u>underlined</u> words.

Writing and speaking

9 Work in pairs. Look at the cartoons and answer the questions.

1 Which story is the most interesting?
2 Which is the most likely/unlikely?
3 What preparation or lifestyle would be required to do these things?

FIRST MAN TO LIVE WITH LIONS

FIRST WOMAN TO SKATEBOARD AROUND THE WORLD

FIRST TWINS TO REACH 125 YEARS OLD

10 **a** Write a news bulletin based on one of the cartoons (about 100–150 words). Use at least two passive constructions for distancing.

b Work in pairs. Practise reading your news bulletins. Concentrate on putting stress on the most important words.

c Read your bulletins to the class.

11 Read the Lifelong learning box. Work in pairs and discuss the questions.

Use the news

❗ Listening to radio news or watching English-language news is a great way to improve your listening and vocabulary. Sometimes it helps to hear the news in your own language before listening to the same stories in English.

1 When and how can you access news programmes in English? Are there any programmes you've seen/heard that you particularly like or recommend?

2 What current news stories would you like to listen to in English?

Lifelong learning

Reading

1 Work in pairs. Look at the activities in the box and discuss the questions.

1 Who generally does each activity better: women, men or neither? Why?

2 Are there any other activities which you think men or women do better?

> driving   cooking   gardening
> doing jobs around the house
> expressing emotions
> looking after children   being alone
> teaching   ballet   tolerating pain
> listening to other people

2 Work in pairs. Read about an ambitious person and make notes on questions 1–5 below.

Student A: read about Bia Figueiredo on page 15.

Student B: read about Carlos Acosta on page 77.

1 What is/was their ambition?

2 To what extent have they achieved it?

3 What challenges have they faced?

4 Who has helped them achieve their ambitions? How?

5 Any other information?

3 Tell your partner about the person you read about. As you listen, make notes. What similarities are there between the two stories?

4 Work in pairs and discuss the questions.

1 Do you think that women have limited opportunities in the world of sport? Is this changing?

2 '... there is a prejudice that ballet is not for boys.' Do you agree? Is it the same in all countries?

3 Do you think sport or dance can help reduce levels of delinquency in teenagers and young people?

4 What do you think of the fathers' behaviour in these two cases? Would you have reacted similarly? Do you believe that parents should influence the ambitions of their children?

Vocabulary | achievement

5 **a** Work in pairs. Find the words/expressions (1–8) in the articles and try to work out the meaning.

1 head (straight for the top)

2 pursue (a dream)

3 deal with (chauvinism)

4 face (barriers)

5 believe in (what you can achieve)

6 have the potential (to do something)

7 persevere (with something)

8 keep pushing someone (to do something)

b Complete the sentences using words/expressions from exercise 5a.

1 It was obvious that Venus Williams had the _____ to become a tennis champion when she was very young.

2 Ralf Schumacher had to _____ with criticism from his colleagues.

3 Ellen MacArthur _____ her dream of sailing solo around the world.

4 McManus is _____ the biggest challenge of his career.

5 If you _____ yourself, you can achieve almost anything.

6 Woods found the course tricky at first, but _____ and came through to the final.

7 If you win this championship, nothing will stop you from _____ straight for the top.

8 Encourage your kids to try new things, but don't _____ them too hard.

Fast female heads for Formula 1

Is Formula 1 ready for its first female star? Matt Rendell travelled to São Paulo to meet Bia, who is tipped to join the ranks of her country's greats – Senna, Piquet, Barrichello. She has already beaten the boys from Brazil at their own game. Now she's ready to take on the world.

As the swarm of go-karts completes its final warm-up lap and hurtles across the starting line, the race is on. Thirty minutes later, when the winner's helmet is removed, a wave of dense dark hair flows freely. For the champion is a girl, Ana Beatriz Figueiredo – Bia, for short – and she is heading straight for the top.

I first met Bia Figueiredo in May 2001. She was 16 and her rivals on São Paulo's kart scene – all male – had been suffering the obvious taunt for eight years: 'Beaten by a girl ... again?'

Now she is in her 20s and still winning. One day soon, the image of her long hair spilling out of her helmet could open motor sport to new audiences, sponsors and perhaps a whole new lease of life. For in Brazil, she is being spoken of as the possible future of Formula 1, the woman to transform an increasingly predictable sport.

The Ayrton Senna Kartodrome in Brazil is a theatre of dreams, and Bia Figueiredo is pursuing hers in the Brazilian Formula Renault Championship. 'The first time I went to the kartodrome,' she tells me, 'I was five or six. I begged my father to take me and fell in love with the noise and the crashes. He told me I had to be seven before I could learn to drive. Somehow, I managed to wait.'

Money pressures are inherent in motor racing, even for a family that is well-off, by most standards. Compared with other drivers at this level, Bia is disadvantaged. Bia's father, Jorge, says that Bia was already dreaming of Formula 1 at the age of six. And having encouraged his daughter's passion, he has accepted the financial burden with good humour. 'I once heard a Formula 1 team boss say it costs $10 million to become a Formula 1 driver. I said to myself, 'OK. I'm only $9,990,000 short!'

Because of the expense, Bia could only do two 50-minute tests before each race, when other drivers did four. She went to one of the best schools in São Paulo, which meant she was doing school work

when other drivers were on the track. 'Given these constraints, she has done very well,' her father says. 'She was born with a forceful personality and, today, she's still forceful and has a caustic sense of humour. I feel a little sorry for anyone in her way!'

Motor racing would not be every father's chosen career for his daughter. 'Yes, it can be dangerous,' Jorge concedes. 'But the element of risk can be controlled. I'm much more afraid of Bia not doing what she loves. By pursuing what they enjoy, I think people have more chance of being happy.'

Yet Bia will have to deal with chauvinism. Not the least of the barriers facing her is whether motor sport is prepared to accept a genuine female contender. 'A beautiful woman is always welcome,' Alex Dias Ribeiro says, smiling and then adds: 'But she will have to be quick and mentally tough, because Formula 1 is a pressure cooker'.

One man who believes in Bia's potential is her mechanic and mentor of nine years, Naylor Borigis de Campos. He has worked closely with most of Brazil's best drivers. He compares Bia favourably with the best of his protégés. 'She's as cool, aware and determined as Rubens Barrichello and as any other driver I've ever worked with.'

As for Bia herself, she believes in the future and in what she can achieve: 'I have a lot to learn, but my temperament is right: I've got plenty of animal instinct. I believe I have the potential to reach Formula 1, and perhaps one day be a great driver.'

Listening

6 Work in pairs and discuss the questions.

1 How difficult do you think it is to do the activities below?

2 What do you think is the best way to prepare for each one?
- run a marathon
- work abroad
- start your own business

7 1.06 Listen and answer the questions.

1 Which activity from exercise 6 has each speaker achieved?

2 What did each person say about their experience?

3 What challenges did they face?

Grammar | perfect aspect

8 Read the Active grammar box. Underline the perfect tense in each sentence (1–3) and complete the name of each tense (*Past Perfect*, *Future Perfect* or *Present Perfect*).

> **Active grammar**
>
> Verbs used in their perfect forms link two times. The perfect aspect is used to refer back from one point to a point in time before that.
>
> 1 *I've always run, but just for myself.*
> (tense: _____)
>
>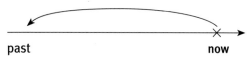
> past   now
>
> 2 *Next week I'll have been here for three months.*
> (tense: _____)
>
>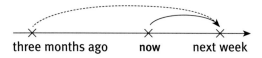
> three months ago   now   next week
>
> 3 *I'd always thought it would be great to cycle across a whole country.*
> (tense: _____)
>
> before that   past   now
>
> Perfect tenses can be used in the simple or continuous forms. Perfect continuous tenses, like other continuous tenses, focus on an event which continues, or is temporary.
>
> *Next March I'll have been playing with the team for five years.*
>
> *I've been doing voluntary work all my adult life.*

see Reference page 19

9 **a** Correct the mistakes.

1 Jake, this is my friend Amy, who I've been knowing for absolutely ages.

2 I asked what had been happened, but nobody could tell me.

3 I chose this school because I'd hear it was the best.

4 He should have finish by the time we get back.

5 Before I came to the US, I never been abroad.

6 I'm so exhausted. I'd been working really hard.

7 By the time she retires, she'll have be working there for more than 50 years.

8 I'll phone you as soon as we will have arrived.

b 1.07 Listen and check your answers.

Speaking

10 Complete the How to... box.

> expect   decided   expectations
> challenge

> **How to... talk about an achievement**
>
> | Background information | *I've always ...*
 I'd never done ... |
> | --- | --- |
> | Details | *We set up ...*
 We (1) _____ to organise ... |
> | Problems | *I didn't know what to (2) _____ .*
 The whole thing was quite a (3) _____ .
 It was very tough. |
> | How it felt | *It exceeded my (4) _____ .*
 We felt we'd accomplished something.
 It was a fantastic learning experience. |
> | Results/ follow up | *I've learnt a lot.*
 I'm planning to ... |

11 **a** Prepare to talk about something you have achieved. Make notes using the headings in the How to... box.

b Tell the class about your achievement.

1 a Read the story below and <u>underline</u> 12 prefixes.

On Saturday Mick Johnson, the multi-talented Londoner – previously a semi-professional basketball player – rescued a sub-standard performance by the unimpressive league leaders. With a superhuman effort, Johnson scored two goals in two minutes against arch-rivals Blackbridge Rovers. Trailing by one goal until the 68th minute, Johnson's overcautious team had looked tired and under-prepared. Johnson, probably the best footballer ever to play for Sidcup United, single-handedly brought his side back from the brink of disaster. Johnson's manager, Paul Deacon, said, 'They outplayed us. I don't know why we misfired so badly, but it's irrelevant. We got the goals and we took home the points.'

b Read the story again and answer the questions.

1 Which prefixes suggest a large/exceptional degree, or amount?

2 Which suggest 'not enough'?

3 Which prefix means 'not wholly' or 'half'?

4 Which can have a negative meaning?

c Work in pairs. What do the <u>underlined</u> prefixes in sentences 1–4 below mean?

1 Johnson had an early chance to score, but was <u>in</u>decisive with his shot.

2 'Winning the league isn't <u>im</u>possible for us,' said Deacon.

3 'Yeah, we won,' said the <u>mono</u>syllabic Johnson.

4 The team looked <u>de</u>motivated.

2 Complete the sentences with the correct form of the words in brackets. Use prefixes.

A: *He's a little bit rude!*

B: *Pardon?*

A: *He's rather <u>impolite</u>. (polite)*

1 A: Our interpretation of the instructions was completely wrong.

 B: Pardon?

 A: We completely _____ the instructions. (understand)

2 A: I didn't know that you were a vegetarian.

 B: Sorry?

 A: I was _____ that you were a vegetarian. (aware)

3 A: I'm 70 years old. I quit my main job but I still work part-time.

 B: Pardon?

 A: I'm _____. (retire)

4 A: We lost the match because they had more players! There were ten of them, and only six of us.

 B: Really? So the numbers weren't equal?

 A: That's right. We were completely _____. (number)

5 A: I must go on a diet. I weigh too much.

 B: What?

 A: I'm _____. (weight)

6 A: My estimate was wrong. I thought there would be ten people here, not 50.

 B: Really?

 A: Yes, I _____ the numbers. (estimate)

3 a Work in pairs. Look at the opposites below. Where do you fit on a scale of 1–5? Tick a box on each line.

1 2 3 4 5

1 super-fit ☐ ☐ ☐ ☐ ☐ totally unfit

2 talented ☐ ☐ ☐ ☐ ☐ untalented

3 imaginative ☐ ☐ ☐ ☐ ☐ unimaginative

4 overpaid ☐ ☐ ☐ ☐ ☐ underpaid

5 political ☐ ☐ ☐ ☐ ☐ apolitical

b Compare your position with other students.

Can do | respond in detail to a questionnaire

1 a Read the questionnaire and choose a, b or c for each situation.

b 🔊 1.08 Listen to someone describing what the answers say about your personality.

c Work in pairs. Discuss your answers and explain why you chose them. Do you agree with the ideas you heard about? Why/Why not?

2 Work with another pair and discuss the questions.

1 Which would be the most difficult/the easiest challenge for you? Why?
2 What preparation would you need for each challenge?
3 Do you think challenge involves being in extreme situations? Or are there more challenges in day-to-day life?
4 Which do you think are tougher: mental or physical challenges? What examples can you think of?

DO YOU LIKE A CHALLENGE?

1 You are climbing a mountain with some friends. It is cold and wet and you are halfway up. You
   a feel like turning round and going home to a hot bath.
   b keep going. Nothing will stop you once you've started.
   c see what your friends want to do. It doesn't really matter if you reach the top.

2 You get an offer to work abroad for a year. But it means you have to learn a difficult new language and live in an isolated place with no cinemas, cafés or nightlife. You
   a refuse politely. Only a madman would live in the middle of nowhere.
   b accept. Who needs nightclubs and cappuccino? And you may love it.
   c ask all your colleagues, friends and family what they think.

3 You are asked to perform in a local play. You will have to learn some lines and act in front of a large audience. You
   a say no. You aren't going to make a fool of yourself in public.
   b jump up on stage and start singing. This is your chance of fame and fortune.
   c find out exactly what you'll have to do, then say you'll think about it.

4 Your friends decide to do a parachute jump for charity. They want you to join them. You
   a refuse, saying you're too young to die.
   b immediately book lessons. What fun! And what a great view you'll have too!
   c find some statistics on the mortality rate of parachutists before committing yourself.

5 You are asked to cook for 15 people. You
   a immediately find out the name of a good takeaway food restaurant, and make sure they'll be able to take your order on the night.
   b start dreaming of the delicious feast you will prepare. It could be a great night.
   c consult your parents' cookery books and work out how much it'll cost.

6 You are offered a place on a sailing boat that will go around the world. You
   a say no. You can't take the time off work and all that sea gets annoying after a while.
   b buy some large rubber boots and a sailing hat immediately. Nothing will stop you!
   c ask about the exact schedule and if there's Internet access on board and what the food will be like.

7 You are asked to be the babysitter for six young children for one evening. You
   a quickly think of a brilliant excuse – for example, you have tickets for a game or you need to wash your hair that evening, so you won't be available.
   b buy a large bag of balloons, chocolate cake and lots of children's games – it's going to be the party of the century!
   c ask for details of the children's behaviour, exact ages, and dietary requirements, then think about it.

8 A magazine wants you to write a piece about your hobby. You
   a explain that you're far too busy doing it, so you don't have time to write about it.
   b jump up and down with excitement, write three different drafts and offer them all to the editor the next day.
   c read previous issues of the magazine to see if you like it, then arrange a meeting with the editor to discuss the piece.

Verbs/adjectives/nouns with prepositions

There are many fixed phrases which use prepositions.

Verb + preposition:

opt **for**, distinguish **from**, succeed **in**, stem **from**, appeal **to**, bother **about**, rely **on**, benefit **from**

Adjective + preposition:

short **of**, riddled **with**, lacking **in**, nervous **about**

Noun + preposition:

to the delight **of**, a new form **of**

Passives: distancing

Passives can be used for 'distancing'. This means that the speaker/writer doesn't want the whole responsibility for the ideas they express. The passive is often used to make a statement less personal and slightly more polite:

We don't allow that. → That **isn't allowed**.

(It isn't the speaker's decision; it is an impersonal rule.)
You must hand in the essay by Friday.
→ The essay **must be handed** in by Friday.

in formal writing, when the focus is on achievements and events rather than the people responsible:

The vaccine **was discovered** by chance.

Here are some common passive expressions to show that we are not certain of a statement:

It is believed that the thief was an ex-employee.

It is said that he was able to speak more than 20 languages, but there is no proof.

It was claimed that the president had not seen the documents before the scandal broke out.

She was thought to have come from Germany originally, but there was little evidence.

He was reported to have been living in Brazil, but there was only one sighting of him.

Perfect aspect

We use the perfect aspect to refer from one point in time to another point in time before that. It shows that the speaker sees one event as: (1) linked to a later event; (2) finished by a certain time.

She**'d lost** her ticket so she missed the show.
By 6.00 I **will have finished** work.

We use the Present Perfect to describe something that happened during a period that includes past and present:

We**'ve been** here since Friday.

in the past but when the exact time isn't relevant to this discussion or isn't known:

She**'s lived** in over 20 countries.

in the past, but has a result or effect in the present:

Oh no! I**'ve lost** my passport.

in the very recent past (especially with *just*):

I**'ve just heard** the news.

We use the Past Perfect to talk about completed actions that happened before another in the past:

He wanted to go to Rome, but I**'d already been** there.

We use the Future Perfect with time phrases with *by* (*by this time next week*, *by the end of the day*, etc.):

By June we **will have finished** the project.

We often use the perfect aspect with *for, since* and *just*:

By January, I **will have been** here *for* a year.
I**'ve just been speaking** to Mickey.

Perfect continuous tenses focus on an event which continues or is temporary:

She**'s been working** as a nurse since 2001.
We**'d been playing** football when it started to rain.

Key vocabulary

Challenges
set achievable goals   face challenges
rise to the challenge   make my dream come true
couldn't have done it without   burning ambition
have the right attitude   daunting challenge

Learning languages
pick up   let (something) slide   master   garble
information overload   babble   unintelligibly   dialect

Knowledge
I haven't a clue   I don't know off the top of my head
I'm pretty sure   I've never heard of him
I know it by heart   I know it like the back of my hand
I know it inside out   I don't know offhand
I know next to nothing about   I'm fairly positive
I haven't the faintest idea

Achievement
head (straight for the top)   pursue (a dream)
deal with (chauvinism)   face (barriers)
believe in (what you can achieve)
have the potential (to do something)
persevere (with something)
keep pushing someone (to do something)

Prefixes
super-fit unfit multi-talented impossible
unimpressive underpaid overpaid apolitical
monosyllabic demotivated arch-rival indecisive
single-handedly outplayed semi-professional
sub-standard misfired irrelevant superhuman
overcautious underprepared

Listen to the explanations and vocabulary.
ACTIVEBOOK

see Writing bank page 81

1 Complete the text with the correct words/expressions (a, b or c).

The language Hawaiian Creole was invented through necessity. In 1880, thousands of immigrants from Europe and Asia went to work for the English-speaking owners of sugar plantations in Hawaii. Among all the other challenges these immigrants (1) _____ , the most (2) _____ was to understand each other, their bosses, and to understand the Hawaiian people. To these immigrants, other ethnic groups must have sounded as if they were (3) _____ . After a short time, they were able to (4) _____ some English, but barely enough to communicate. Instead, they (5) _____ body language and a simple code of sounds.

However, things changed fast, and by 1910 a new language had emerged: Hawaiian Creole. This included words and sounds from other languages, but could be (6) _____ all of them by its different grammar. Hawaiian Creole, a simple dialect, is (7) _____ complex structures. With this new easily understood language, everybody (8) _____ increased communication.

Many years later, Derek Bickerton studied the origins of Hawaiian Creole. He was amazed that within a generation, the immigrants had (9) _____ creating a language that was (10) _____ to all. In fact, in his book *Roots of Language*, he says that the children invented the language while playing together.

1 **a** made	**b** knew	**c** faced
2 **a** daunting	**b** definite	**c** harsh
3 **a** babbling	**b** garbling	**c** cramming
4 **a** discuss	**b** pick up	**c** pick out
5 **a** persisted in	**b** appealed to	**c** relied on
6 **a** riddled with	**b** distinguished from	**c** defined by
7 **a** reminds you of	**b** stemming from	**c** lacking in
8 **a** benefited from	**b** benefited	**c** mastered
9 **a** opted for	**b** succeeded to	**c** succeeded in
10 **a** intelligible	**b** unintelligible	**c** intelligibly

2 Find the mistake in each sentence and correct it.

1 Giant multinational research centre Sci-Corps seems to abandoned its research into cloning after pressure from the government.

2 Ex-President Michael Nkrumah is said be recovering well from the stroke he suffered last Thursday.

3 Michaela Kritzkoff, the explorer who disappeared for a month while canoeing along the Amazon, has been found in a village in Brazil. It believed that she had drowned during a storm.

4 British Commonwealth boxing champion Roderick Bland appears to finally retired, at the age of 46.

5 And finally, it seems if summer really is coming. Sarah Smith reports on tomorrow's weather.

3 Find the mistakes in nine of the sentences and correct them.

I've never seen the man before yesterday, when he knocked on my door.

I'd never seen the man before yesterday, when he knocked on my door.

1 By the time she finishes her degree, she will be at the university ten years.

2 He was delighted when they told him he had got the job.

3 I feel healthier now that I took up kickboxing.

4 Where were you? I've been waited here for at least an hour!

5 It was a shock when I saw him. I would expected to see a big man, but he was tiny.

6 When she got to work, she found out she was fired. Her desk was empty, everything gone.

7 Hi, John! We've just talked about you!

8 It's 9 o'clock. Mandy will land at the airport by now.

9 I've been running for years before I entered my first competition.

10 We'll have use up all the world's oil long before 2100.

4 Write B's replies in the correct order.

A: What is Pelé's real first name?

B: pretty / I'm / Edison / it's / sure / .

I'm pretty sure it's Edison.

1 A: Have you ever been to Prague?

B: Yes, / I / of / the / hand / like / my / back / it / know / .

2 A: How many women have succeeded in Formula 1 racing?

B: I / many / know / not / but / don't / offhand / .

3 A: Can you help me? I need some information about space travel.

B: know / nothing / it / to / next / about / I / .

4 A: When's the best time to go there?

B: far / as / concerned / As / never / I'm / .

5 A: Who's Michael Vaughan?

B: never / him / heard / I've / of / .

6 A: Who's the President of Colombia?

B: head / I / top / tell / off / the / can't / of / my / you / .

Lead-in

1 Work in pairs and look at the photos. Discuss the questions.

1 What types of community are shown?

2 What are the positive/negative aspects of each?

2 **a** Check you understand the <u>underlined</u> words/phrases. Write positive (+) or negative (–) next to each feature (1–16).

1 reasonable <u>cost of living</u> ☐

2 <u>cosmopolitan</u> ☐

3 good transport <u>infrastructure</u> ☐

4 <u>mild</u> climate ☐

5 personal <u>freedom</u> ☐

6 efficient <u>healthcare</u> system ☐

7 high <u>standard of living</u> ☐

8 interesting historical <u>monuments</u> ☐

9 high <u>crime rate</u> ☐

10 high level of <u>unemployment</u> ☐

11 traffic <u>congestion</u> ☐

12 a lot of <u>pollution</u> ☐

13 racial <u>tension</u> ☐

14 <u>no-go areas</u> ☐

15 no <u>cultural</u> life ☐

16 <u>vibrant</u> nightlife ☐

b Work in pairs. Which four features from exercise 2a are the most important to you? Why?

Reading

1 Look at the photos. Work in pairs and discuss the questions.

1 Where do you think each community is?

2 What do you think life is like there?

2 Read the comments (A–D). Who thinks their community is changing for the worse? Who has positive things to say?

A

My family emigrated from Italy to the US 50 years ago. When they arrived, they were penniless and spoke no English. It was the community that helped them get on their feet. Other Italian-Americans got them jobs, lent them money when they couldn't afford to buy groceries, even found the apartment where my grandmother still lives. When my father was thinking of going to college, the elders in the community not only advised him to do it, they also paid some of his fees. It was a real community. The area was full of bakeries and *trattorias* where people from the old country still spoke the dialect and served Italian food. That's all gone now.

Vincenzo, New York, USA

B

There's a very strong sense of community where I live. People don't mind helping others. You see it all the time. Youngsters visit the elderly. People look after each other's children. Everybody knows everybody else. I can't imagine living in a big, soulless city, where you're anonymous and don't know your neighbours, where you avoid going out at night because you're worried about the high crime rate. I know the world is evolving, but we've held onto old values here and I think that's a good thing.

Devin, Cork, Ireland

C

I think our communities are changing fast. For example, the big supermarket chains have driven out local shopkeepers. Personally, I can't stand shopping in those places. I think they damage the local economy, and people don't want to go to five different shops when they can stock up on everything in a supermarket. The schools are closing one by one. Lots of families object to sending their kids to a school six miles away, but what choice do we have? Our hands are tied. The local shop that has been there for a hundred years is going to close. It's a shame, but I guess that's the way the world is going.

Paula, Cornwall, UK

D

Here in Melbourne there is a big, very visible Greek community and I don't think that will change any time soon. You can buy Greek food like tzatziki and baklava everywhere you go, and you still hear Greek spoken in the bars and restaurants. And of course we have the Antipodes Festival, which showcases Greek culture. Community is so important to us. Maybe it's because Greece is made up of lots of little islands, so people live cheek-by-jowl and rely on each other. That has carried over to our communities in Australia.

Kouros Calombaris, Melbourne, Australia

3 Answer the questions. Read the comments again to check.

1 What does Vincenzo say about language and food as part of the Italian-American community?

2 What three examples of a 'strong sense of community' does Devin give?

3 How have things changed for shoppers and families in Paula's community?

4 Why is community important to Greeks, according to Kouros?

4 Work in groups and discuss the questions.

1 Do you agree with Vincenzo that communities are not as strong as they used to be? If so, why?

2 How much contact do you have with your local community? Do you know your neighbours? Do you use local shops and services?

Grammar | verb patterns (1)

5 **a** Look at the extract below and underline three verb patterns (verb + verb). The first has been done for you.

> Other Italian-Americans ... lent them money when they couldn't afford to buy groceries ...
>
> When my father was thinking of going to college, the elders in the community not only advised him to do it, they also paid some of his fees.

b Find six more examples of verb patterns used by Devin and Paula on page 22.

6 Find the mistakes in the sentences (1–15) and correct them.

A

1 I'm thinking to visit the community where I used to live.

2 If you can't afford eating in expensive restaurants, there are lots of cheaper *trattorias*.

3 I can't imagine live in a different community.

4 We look forward to see you.

5 You can avoid to offending people by learning the host country's customs.

B

6 I don't mind to look after my niece and nephew.

7 I don't fancy eat Greek food tonight.

8 She doesn't want that she lives far away from her family.

9 I can't stand to shop in big supermarkets.

10 If you object to pay lots of money for clothes, don't go shopping in Ginza, Tokyo.

C

11 I advise you going to the Antipodes festival.

12 I'd encourage all foreigners try some *baklava*.

13 I'd urge you visiting the different communities in New York.

14 I'd recommend to go to the local restaurant.

15 She persuaded us visit Cork in the spring.

7 Work in pairs and answer the questions.

1 Which group of sentences from exercise 6 (A–C) is connected with recommendations? Which is connected with likes/dislikes?

2 Which underlined verbs in group B have a very similar meaning? Which is/are the strongest?

3 Which underlined verbs in group C have a very similar meaning? Which is/are the strongest?

8 Complete the table in the Active grammar box with the underlined verbs from exercise 6.

Active grammar

verb + *-ing*	verb + infinitive
verb + object + infinitive with *to*	verb + preposition + *-ing*

see Reference page 33

9 Rewrite the sentences (1–8) with the verbs in brackets. Begin each sentence with *I*, *I'd* or *I'm*.

You really must go to the National Gallery. (urge)

I'd urge you to go to the National Gallery.

1 I don't have the money to go to the theatre. (afford)

2 You should go to Brixton Market on Sunday. (advise)

3 I think people ought to use the parks more. (encourage)

4 It will be good to see you next weekend. (look forward)

5 You should buy tickets early for Buckingham Palace. (recommend)

6 It's better not to take Intercity trains because they're more expensive. (avoid)

7 I'd like to take a short trip to Paris. (fancy)

8 I may go to Thailand in February. (think)

Speaking

10 Complete the How to... box with the words from the box.

> wary   were   out   found   value   sure   all

How to... give advice/make recommendations about places

Saying it's good	*It's a must/a must-see.*
	It's good (1) _____ for money.
Saying it's not so good	*It's a bit overrated/overpriced.*
	It's not (2) _____ it's cracked up to be.
	I (3) _____ it a bit dull/touristy.
Recommending	*If I (4) _____ you, I'd go to ...*
	Make (5) _____ you go to ...
	Don't miss .../You should try ...
	I suggest going .../that you go there.
Warning	*Watch (6) _____ for ...*
	One thing to be (7) _____ of is ...

11 a Think of a place with a strong sense of community (customs, food, things to see, etc.). Make notes about what you would/wouldn't recommend about the place.

b Work in groups. Take turns to describe the places you chose. Try to use language from the How to... box.

Listening

12 Work in pairs and discuss the questions.

1 Have you (or do you know anyone who has) lived abroad?
2 What were your/their impressions of the place?
3 What problems might there be living in a foreign country?

13 a ● 1.09 Listen to three people and make notes in the table.

	speaker 1	speaker 2	speaker 3
Where did he/she live?			
What was he/she doing there?			
What did he/she like about the host country?			
Was there anything he/she didn't like, or that was difficult?			
What are his/her favourite memories of the country?			

b Match the speakers (1, 2 or 3) to the things they did (a–j).

a pretended something ☐
b got a few surprises ☐
c was there at the wrong time ☐
d is from a small town ☐
e would like to return ☐
f learned about the culture by talking to the local people ☐
g says the place was multicultural ☐
h has lived in many countries ☐
i doesn't mention the scenery ☐
j describes a special type of cooking ☐

c Listen again and check.

14 Work in pairs. Discuss the questions.

1 In which of the places from exercise 13a would you most like to live?
2 Would you like to live abroad?
3 Why do you think the speakers talk mainly about food, scenery and people? Which is the most important?

Listening

1 Work in pairs and discuss the questions.

1 How often do you use the Internet? What do you use it for?

2 Are there any websites that you use frequently? What do you like about them?

3 Do you trust what you read on the Internet? Why/Why not?

4 Has the increased use of computers and the Internet been a good thing for you, and in general?

2 🔊 1.10 Listen to two people discussing some of the questions from exercise 1. Which do they discuss? Are their views similar to yours?

3 Listen again and tick (✓) the phrases you hear.

1 (it's) *miles easier*
2 (it's) *far easier*
3 (it's) *nowhere near as ... as*
4 (it's) *nothing like as good as*
5 *the less we ..., the less we ...*
6 *the more we ..., the more we ...*
7 (it's) *not quite as ... as ...*
8 (it's) *definitely not as ... as*
9 (it's) *considerably* + comparative (formal)
10 (it's) *marginally* + comparative (formal)
11 (it's) *much the same*
12 (it's) *much* + superlative

Grammar | comparatives (review)

4 **a** Read the rules and examples in the Active grammar box. Then write the phrases from exercise 3 in the table.

b Write the phrases below in the table in the Active grammar box.

> sightly   a tiny bit   far   decidedly

Active grammar

When using comparatives, if we want to be specific about the degree of difference between two people/things, we use modifiers, e.g. *far*, *nowhere near*, *slightly*.

*I'm **slightly** taller than my brother.*
*The green house is **nowhere near** as beautiful as the red one.*

We can use combined comparisons to describe how a change in one thing causes a change in another.

***The longer** you wait, **the worse** it will be.*

1 A big difference	
2 A little difference	
3 *the* + comparative + *the* + comparative	

see Reference page 33

5 Cross out the incorrect words in *italics*.

1 Buying things in shops is *not like/nowhere near/nothing like* as cheap as shopping online.

2 *It's decidedly easier/It's best/It's considerably easier* to write on a computer than doing it by hand.

3 The more you know about computers, *the easier/easier/the simpler* they become.

4 Buying things online is *marginally/extremely/slightly* more risky than face-to-face transactions.

5 It's *a mile/considerably/far* quicker to find information on the Internet than in books.

6 *The more we rely on/The more we use/As much as we use* computers, the more vulnerable we are to hackers and computer viruses.

Speaking

6 **a** Look again at the sentences from exercise 5. How far do you agree with each sentence?

b Work in groups and discuss your views.

Reading

7 Work in pairs. Do you use Wikipedia? If not, what do you think it is?

8 Read the article and match the paragraphs (1–7) to the headings (a–g).

a   Why you can't trust Wikipedia

b   Jimmy Wales

c   The future of Wikipedia

d   Editors who care

e   The wiki

f   Locking out the vandals

g   First stop for fact-seekers

9 Answer the questions.

1   What expression in the article is used to describe groups combining their knowledge?

2   Why, according to the article, is Wikipedia generally reliable?

3   Who is Jimmy Wales and what is he like?

4   What technological innovation led to the popularity of Wikipedia?

10 **a** Read the article again quickly. Is it formal or informal in style?

b Complete the How to... box with headings from the box below.

> Humour   Informal vocabulary   Style (spoken English)
> Ellipsis (omitting words)

How to... recognise features of informal language

(1) _____	*savvy* (paragraph 4)
	guy (paragraph 5)
(2) _____	*Join the gang.* (paragraph 1)
	Short forms: *It's a gang* (paragraph 1), *It'll surely need more* (paragraph 7)
(3) _____	*Want to know the capital of Turkmenistan?* (paragraph 1). The full question = *Do you want to know the capital of Turkmenistan?* *'And the future?'* (paragraph 7)
(4) _____	*One famously compared the site to a public toilet seat: you never know who's used it before you.* (paragraph 2)

c Work in pairs and answer the questions.

1   What are the formal words for 'savvy' and 'guy'?

2   Are there other examples in the text of informal vocabulary, spoken English, or humour?

3   What is the full version of: 'And the future?'

The Internet's largest encyclopaedia

1

Want to know the capital of Turkmenistan? Or how to make chicken fricassee? Or what goes in a Cuban cigar? The first place you probably turn to is Wikipedia. Join the gang. It's a gang that now has access to over 18 million entries in 279 languages. And the striking thing about Wikipedia is that it isn't high-flying professors who are providing the answers. It's amateurs. Wikipedia is a perfect example of 'crowd sourcing'. Anyone can add an entry. Anyone can edit it. No qualifications are necessary. In short, the site uses the masses to pool their information, and the result is the world's biggest encyclopedia.

2

But is it the most reliable? Ask one of its founders, Larry Sanger – who went on to lecture at Ohio State University – and the answer is an unequivocal 'no'. Sanger doesn't let his students use Wikipedia for their research; he knows they can simply invent information, put it anonymously on Wikipedia, and claim it's accurate. Other academics also have their doubts. One famously compared the site to a public toilet seat: you never know who's used it before you. But they are now probably in the minority.

3

If it's so easy to edit, how come, in several recent research studies, Wikipedia has been found to be as accurate as other encyclopedias including the *Encyclopedia Britannica*, which has existed for 250 years? How come, with all the potential 'vandals' keen to rewrite history according to their own ideologies, Wikipedia, it turns out, is generally trustworthy? The answer is that the editors of Wikipedia care more than the vandals. The Massachusetts Institute of Technology (MIT) did a study and found that obscene comments added on Wikipedia were, on average, removed within a hundred seconds. For the vandals, it's about as worthwhile as a graffiti artist using invisible ink.

4

Those who run Wikipedia are also savvy enough to know when a bout of vandalism is going to occur. During the 2004 Bush–Kerry US election, realising that the supporters of each candidate would attempt to smear the opponent on Wikipedia, the company

locked the entries on George Bush and John Kerry.

5 _____

So, in this utopia of crowd sourcing, who exactly is making the decisions? The boss is founder Jimmy Wales. In 2000, Wales was a regular guy looking to combine his two hobbies: nosing through the *Encyclopedia Britannica* and surfing the Internet. Online he found himself discussing all sorts of topics and meeting all sorts of people on obscure mailing lists. He decided he wanted to set up something longer-lasting and fun. 'Fun' is a big word for Jimmy Wales. One of the world's great optimists, Wales has breezed through life enjoying pretty much everything he's turned his hand to, including trading options and futures and founding nupedia, Wikipedia's forerunner.

6 _____

Nupedia didn't have a massive impact. It used 'the old model' of experts writing entries, but then Wales and his co-founder, Larry Sanger, decided to experiment with a relatively new technology: a wiki. The wiki got its name because the inventor had his honeymoon in Hawaii, where you catch the 'wiki wiki' (quick) bus from the airport. The idea of a wiki is that anyone can contribute to a website; it's a pooling of knowledge. With this technology in place, Wikipedia exploded in popularity. Within its first year contributors wrote 20,000 entries in 18 languages.

7 _____

And the future? For most of its short history, Wikipedia has been staffed by a group of volunteers, with only a handful actually getting paid. By 2011 the company's paid employees had grown to over 50. It'll surely need more in the future, as the company tries to expand its popularity in Asia, South America and the Middle East. It's also trying to improve the quality of entries by teaming up with universities to get some expert input and working with museums to supply better images. As the world shrinks and people's thirst for information grows, it's likely that Wikipedia will keep growing, too. As for the capital of Turkmenistan, it's Ashgabat. And if you need proof, you know where to look.

11 Look at techniques 1–4. Are they generally used in formal or informal texts?

1 full verb forms
2 lots of phrasal verbs
3 sentences beginning with *and* or *but*
4 repeated use of the passive

12 Read the two formal emails below. Some language is too informal. Replace it with more appropriate language from the box.

> Regards   attend   don't hesitate to   concerning   following   requested   will be very happy to attend   will be unable to attend   a previous arrangement   we would be grateful if you could   queries   could you please confirm your attendance

1

Dear Mr Fry,

After our telephone conversation, I would like to invite you to the meeting of the Online Encyclopaedia Anglia Group on 15 November at 7.00 p.m. at 24 Bland Street. We will be discussing how to take forward the proposals for a new interactive website. I have attached a preliminary agenda for the meeting, and also a map showing how to get to Bland Street. There will also be a dinner in the evening, to which you are invited.

Let us know if you're coming by 4 November. Bring copies of the sample contract. Feel free to get in touch if you have any questions.

Best wishes,

Mary Johnson

2

Dear Ms Johnson,

Thank you very much for the invitation to come to the meeting on 15 November, about the plan to start a new website. Thanks for the agenda. I can come to the meeting.

As asked, I will bring copies of the sample contract. Unfortunately, I won't be able to come to the dinner because of something I've already organised.

I look forward to seeing you there.

Yours sincerely,

Peter Fry

13 Work in pairs and read the Lifelong learning box. Compare the emails and article on this page and discuss questions 1–6.

Keeping your reader in mind

❗ When you are planning a piece of writing, think about who your readers are and consider the following points.

1 Why are they reading your piece?
2 How much information do they already know?
3 How much do they need to know?
4 What are their expectations?
5 How formal and what length do they expect the piece to be?
6 What is the relationship between writer and reader?

This information will help you to choose the best tone for your piece (formal, informal, academic, etc.), to organise your ideas, and to think about what to include or omit.

Lifelong learning

Corsica

Cape Town

Cali

Speaking and reading

1 Work in pairs and discuss the questions.

1 What do you know about the places in the photos?

2 What do you think they are like?

3 Would you like to visit them? Why/Why not?

2 **a** Work in small groups. Read about a place and make notes on the topics below.

Student A: read about Cali.

Student B: read about Cape Town on page 79.

Student C: read about Corsica on page 80.

- atmosphere
- things to do
- things to see
- food
- the local community

b Use your notes to describe the place to your group.

3 Work in pairs and discuss the questions.

1 Each place is described as a type of 'paradise'. Which aspects sound good to you? What makes them unique?

2 Which place would you prefer to go to? Why?

3 Do you think tourism is good for these three places? What problems might it bring?

Cali

In Cali, they say, even the ghosts dance salsa. Its rhythms, born in Cuba, nurtured in New York and carried on the winds all the way to hot Cali, can be heard in bars, on buses, along the avenues of Juanchito
5 and Plaza Caicedo. And here too, in a taxi moving at the speed of light, taking me to the heart of the bustling city. The driver slows down at a traffic light, turns to me and says '*las calenas*,' (the women from Cali) 'are the most beautiful women in the world!' And we're off
10 again, driving past gangs of *mulato* men laughing in the street. It's no wonder this city is adored by everyone who visits.

My hotel is a run-down old building whose blue skin is peeling in the heat. It has a stunning view from the
15 balcony and I gaze down on the square. The guidebooks tell you to visit the Gold Museum and the Museum of Colonial Art, the churches of San Antonio and La Merced, but there's only one thing on my mind as I leave the key at reception: salsa.

20 The *salsotecas* don't get busy until midnight so instead I stop at a restaurant serving typical Colombian food:

Vocabulary | adjectives to describe places

4 Work in groups. Match the definitions (1–10) to words/phrases from the articles.

1 energetic and noisy, full of life (Cali, line 6; Cape Town, line 25; Corsica, line 29)
2 in poor condition, uncared for (Cali, line 13; Cape Town, line 18; Corsica, line 31)
3 amazingly beautiful (Cali, line 14; Cape Town, line 14; Corsica, line 16)
4 having variety (Cali, line 26; Cape Town, line 43; Corsica, line 19)
5 not damaged in character or atmosphere (Cali, line 30; Cape Town, line 39; Corsica, line 44)
6 next to each other (Cali, line 31; Cape Town, line 21; Corsica, line 22)
7 extremely large (Cali, line 32; Cape Town, line 20; Corsica, line 36)
8 peaceful (Cali, line 34; Cape Town, line 38; Corsica, line 45)
9 in areas people don't normally go to (usually outside the city) (Cali, line 35; Cape Town, line 17; Corsica, line 48)
10 very busy, crowded (Cali, line 44; Cape Town, line 32; Corsica, line 47)

5 **a** Complete the sentences (1–8) with words/phrases from exercise 4.

1 The roof is falling off and the windows are broken. The old house looks very _____.
2 It's hard to find the little villa in the countryside because it's _____.
3 You can hardly move during carnival time because the streets are absolutely _____.
4 There are many different nationalities living there, so the culture is very _____.
5 Huge skyscrapers stand _____ with tiny wooden houses.
6 The Sahara Desert is 9,100,000 square kilometres. It's absolutely _____.
7 We're going to spend a _____ few days camping, far from the noisy city.
8 The town remains _____, even though there are lots of tourists now. It hasn't changed at all.

b Describe the places in photos A–C with the words/phrases from exercise 4.

sancocho – a stew made with chunks of beef, vegetables, cassava (a tropical plant with edible roots) and plantain (a type of banana, but not
25 so sweet) served with rice. Then I must choose from the amazingly diverse selection of Colombian fruit. I settle for guanabana and maracuya and I'm not disappointed. I stroll for a while, tempted by dark smoky cafés, the fans spinning weakly on the
30 ceilings. This is the old, unspoilt Cali, which lives side by side with a newer version, the Cali of junk food, Internet cafés and vast touristy discos. I walk past the trees and sculptures that line the river, and into San Antonio park, a tranquil spot
35 off the beaten track.

Later, on Avenida Sexta – Sixth Avenue – I find what I'm really looking for: a *salsoteca*. Some charming young Colombians teach me a few dance steps and we chat about Cali. They say
40 that when times are tough, they dance away their worries. And I must never forget '*las calenas* are the most beautiful women in the world!' By 2.00 a.m. the salsa is swinging, the drinks are flowing, the place is packed and I know one thing
45 for sure: I've found the Cali that I was looking for – the salsa dancer's paradise.

Speaking

6 **a** Think of places you have been to that match the topics below.

- it has stunning views
- it is off the beaten track
- it is unspoilt despite tourism
- it has modern parts side by side with the old parts
- it is tranquil
- it is bustling at the weekends
- it has some run-down parts

b Work in pairs. Describe the places you thought of to your partner.

Grammar | introductory *it*

7 **a** Read the paragraph below. Is it about Corsica, Cape Town or Cali?

> With its wonderful food, semi-tropical climate, and great nightlife, it appears that the city has everything going for it. Local bartender Juan Hernandez tells me, 'It's no coincidence that the city is growing. We've worked hard to improve everything: the infrastructure, the standard of living, the nightlife. When I think back to 20 years ago, it's surprising how fast things are changing here. We love it when tourists come to stay.' It cannot be denied that the city is on the way up and it's a pity I only have a few days here, but I'll be back!

b Look at the underlined phrases above. What do they have in common? Find another example in the first paragraph of the article about Cali from exercise 2.

c Read rule A in the Active grammar box. Complete examples 2–4 with underlined phrases from the paragraph in exercise 7a.

d Read rule B in the Active grammar box. Complete example 8 with an underlined phrase from the paragraph in exercise 7a.

Active grammar

A We often use introductory *it* when we describe our feelings and opinions. This sounds less direct than using *I think, I believe*, etc.

1 *I thought there would be more tourists.*
   → ***It's surprising that*** *there aren't more tourists.*

2 *I'm sorry to say ...* → _____

3 *I have the impression ...* → _____

4 *There's no doubt, in my opinion, ...* → _____

B We also use *it* in the middle of a sentence (after certain verbs) to introduce a clause.

5 *I could hardly believe **it** when I saw how much the city had changed.*

6 *I'd appreciate **it** if you could send me information about the city.*

7 *I hate **it** when I go to see a tourist attraction and it's closed.*

8 _____

---

8 Match the sentence beginnings (1–8) to the sentence endings (a–h).

1 It's no coincidence that the
2 It's a shame that
3 It shocked me to
4 It cannot be denied that
5 It's no use
6 It's no wonder people
7 It seems strange,
8 It's essential that

a you have to leave this wonderful town.
b the food here is the best in the country.
c see so much poverty in the city centre.
d love this place. It's absolutely perfect!
e you learn the basics of the language before you travel.
f but I actually prefer cold, rainy climates to hot weather.
g complaining about the transport infrastructure. You should walk!
h crime rate is lower. They've doubled the number of police.

9 **a** Complete six of the sentences so they are true for you.

1 It's really wonderful to think that ...
2 It always surprises me when ...
3 It's a pity that ...
4 It's no use ...
5 It cannot be denied that ...
6 It appears to me that ...
7 I always appreciate it when ...
8 I hate it when ...

b Work in pairs and compare your sentences.

see Reference page 33

1 Read the texts below. Would you like to join any of these communities? Why/Why not? Would you like to join them temporarily or permanently?

1
They said it was a passing trend that would never catch on. They were wrong. When I turned up at the Chrysalis Hippy Commune 40 years after I'd left it, nothing had changed. Living here, you can still get by on $50 a week and you'll have no problems fitting in. Everyone is welcome.

2
We decided to do up a small barn in a tiny rural village. No water, no electricity, no Internet! We filled in some forms to get planning permission, and this took months. Then the terrible weather held us up so we couldn't start renovating. Finally, a year later, the house was finished. We knew nobody in the community except John, who had carried out most of the work.

3
I first came across Claudio and the surfing community in São Paulo. I'd never surfed before, but I took to it immediately. Claudio told me they were expecting giant waves at the end of the summer, so I practised every day and saw to it that I was ready. When the big waves came, I got through it OK.

4
I came up with the idea of starting an online book community. It seemed like a good way to keep up with the latest books. Anyone is welcome to write reviews and post them on the site. It really comes down to democratising the process, because we wanted to get away from the idea that you need a degree in order to write and read reviews.

2 Find four phrasal verbs in each text and match them to the correct meanings (a–p).

Text 1
a arrive
b feel comfortable in a social group
c survive financially
d become fashionable

Text 2
e complete paperwork
f restore/redecorate
g delay someone
h put ideas/instructions into practice

Text 3
i finish successfully
j meet/find by chance
k organise/manage
l like something/someone

Text 4
m escape/avoid
n be essentially
o invent/think of
p know about recent developments

3 There are four types of phrasal verb. Match the types (a–d) to the examples (1–4).

a transitive (1)
b transitive (2)
c intransitive
d three-part phrasal verbs

1 The plane took off.
(verb + particle, no direct object)

2 I paid back the money. / I paid the money back.
(verb + particle, with a direct object. If the object is a noun, it can come between the verb and the particle or after the particle.)

3 She looked after me. *NOT:* She looked me after.
(verb + particle, with a direct object that always goes after the particle)

4 I went on a spa break to get away from it all.
(verb + particle + preposition, with a direct object that usually goes after the preposition)

4 **a** Work in pairs and discuss the questions.

1 Did you take to your partner or best friend immediately? Why/Why not?
2 Do you have to come up with ideas at work/school?
3 Have you come across any interesting people/books/places in the last few months?
4 Do you usually turn up early, on time or late for appointments? What does it depend on?
5 Do you do anything special to get away from your daily routine? What?
6 Do you keep up with new developments in your work/hobby? How?
7 When was the last time you filled in a form? What was it for?

b Tell the class one thing about your partner.

5 Read the Lifelong learning box and do the exercise.

Note it down

! When you read/hear phrasal verbs that you think are useful, write them down in context. Note what type of phrasal verb they are (see the four types from exercise 3) and look for patterns in the use of particles.

Circle four phrasal verbs in the paragraph below and add them to your notes. What types of phrasal verb are they?

I visited Sydney, Australia, for a few days so I could catch up with my long-lost cousin. He put me up in his spare room. In the end, he looked after me so brilliantly and we became such good friends that I stayed on an extra month and did all his cooking and cleaning!

Lifelong learning

1 a Read about a club. Do you think the club is silly, funny or a good idea?

THE NOT TERRIBLY GOOD CLUB

In 1976, Stephen Pile formed 'The Not Terribly Good Club'. To qualify for membership, you had to be not terribly good at something and then attend meetings. During these meetings, people gave public demonstrations of things they couldn't do, such as painting and singing, and gave awful presentations on things they knew nothing about. Stephen Pile kept a record of these unsuccessful events and then published them as *The Book of Heroic Failures* in 1979. The stories included epic examples of incompetence, such as the World's Worst Tourist, who spent two days in New York, believing he was in Rome; 'the slowest solution of a crossword' (34 years); and the burglar who wore metal armour to protect himself from dogs – the armour made so much noise that he got caught and it was too heavy for him to run away. Included in *The Book of Heroic Failures* was an application form for membership to 'The Not Terribly Good Club'. Amazingly, within two months of the book's publication, the group had received 20,000 applications to join, and the book appeared on various bestseller lists. As a result of his sudden fame, Pile was kicked out of his own club and the club itself soon disbanded. It had become too successful.

CAN YOU TELL ME THE WAY TO THE COLISEUM?

2 a 🔊 1.11 **Listen to two people describing clubs they belong to. Make notes on the topics below.**

Old boys' club
- the main idea of the club
- other things that it does
- type of meeting
- who can be a member
- problems

Ballroom-dancing club
- number and type of people in the club
- how long she has been a member
- when and where it meets
- problems
- things they have learned

b Work in pairs and compare your notes.

3 Work in groups. You are going to form a club. Think about the following questions.

1 What type of club is it?
2 What events will you organise?
3 How will you know if the club is successful? (What are your goals?)
4 What is the name of the club?
5 Where will you meet?
6 How often?
7 How many people can join the club?
8 What do people have to do to join?
9 What rules will the club have?
10 What will the club's symbol, logo, motto or song be?

b If you were joining The Not Terribly Good Club, what would your presentation be about?

4 Present your ideas to the rest of the class. Which clubs would you like to join?

Verb patterns (1)

When one verb follows another, the second is either an *-ing* verb or the infinitive.

Some verbs which use an *-ing* form are related in meaning. The following verbs all show personal tastes: *adore, fancy, don't mind, detest, can't stand*.

*I **adore living** here.*

Other verbs take an object + the infinitive:

*I **told her to come** here.*

Some of these verbs are related in meaning. The following verbs show one person (or thing) influencing the actions of another: *warn, tell, advise, urge, order, persuade, encourage, force, forbid, allow*.

*I **persuaded her to visit** me.*

Verbs which are followed by a preposition use the *-ing* form:

*I **look forward to meeting** her.*

Some verbs can only be followed by the infinitive or the *-ing* form. See page 23.

Comparatives (review)

There are many expressions we can use to show if the difference between two things is big or small. For a small difference we can use: *slightly, a little bit, a tiny bit, marginally* (formal), etc.

*I'm **slightly taller** than Peter.*

*The population is **marginally larger** than that of Ghana.*

For a large difference we can use: *much, far, miles* (informal), *considerably* (formal), etc.

*They're **miles** better than us at football.*

*The government was **considerably more** corrupt 100 years ago.*

as + adjective + *as* means the two things are equal:

*It took me **as long** to drive to Cardiff **as** it did to travel there by train.*

If we want to say two things aren't equal, we can say:

*She's **not as big as** me. (= she's smaller)*

*The new menu **isn't as nice as** the one they had during the summer.*

There are many expressions with *as* + adjective + *as* which show whether the difference is big or small. For a small difference we can use *not quite as*:

*This bed **isn't quite as comfortable as** the other one. (= It's nearly as comfortable)*

For a big difference we can use *nowhere near, nothing like*:

*He is **nowhere near as good as** me at tennis.*

Introductory *it*

There are a number of set phrases that begin with *it*. These are often used for describing personal opinions. In these expressions, *it* is the subject of the verb.

***It's a shame** you won't be here tonight.*

***It's no use** complaining all the time.*

***It amazes me** to hear you say that.*

There are several set phrases with *it* that refer to general impressions.

***It strikes me** that he's not as good as he was.*

***It appears** as if they aren't coming.*

***It seems** like a hopeless case.*

After certain verbs, *it* can also be used to introduce a clause. In this case, *it* is the object of the verb.

***I hate it** when she does that.*

***We'd appreciate it** if you turned down the music.*

***I'd love it** if we won the league this year.*

Key vocabulary

Communities

cost of living   cosmopolitan   infrastructure
mild climate   freedom   healthcare system
standard of living   monuments   crime rate
unemployment   traffic congestion   pollution
racial tension   no-go areas   cultural life
vibrant nightlife

Adjectives to describe places

off the beaten track   unspoilt   diverse   tranquil
side by side   vast   run-down   stunning   packed
bustling

Phrasal verbs

catch on   turn up   get by   fit in   do up   fill in
hold up   carry out   come across   take to   see to
get through   come up with   keep up with
come down to   get away from   take off   pay back
look after   catch up with   put (someone) up
stay on

 Listen to the explanations and vocabulary.

ACTIVEBOOK

 see Writing bank page 82

1 Complete the sentences with the correct form of verbs from the box (infinitive or *-ing* form). You may need to add a preposition.

> take   pay   spend   apply   consult   hear
> make   wear   buy   live

1 I encouraged the architects _____ the community about their new project.

2 We didn't mind _____ a few days in the town, but we didn't want to live there.

3 I look forward _____ from you soon.

4 We urged them not _____ a house in that area because it's very expensive and noisy.

5 She's thinking of _____ for a job as a tour guide.

6 I object _____ such a high rent in such a horrible part of town.

7 They persuaded us _____ an effort and actually see some of the city.

8 I can imagine _____ here for the rest of my life. I love it.

9 Members of the ski club are advised _____ helmets while skiing, for their own protection.

10 To relieve stress, I recommend _____ a long holiday in the countryside.

2 Complete each sentence with one word.

Chile is _____ pretty as Argentina.

Chile is <u>as</u> pretty as Argentina.

1 You'd be _____ off going to Texas in the spring than in the summer.

2 Paraguay is nowhere _____ as big as Brazil.

3 I _____ sooner go to Cartagena than Bogotá for a holiday.

4 Fiji is nothing _____ as rich as New Zealand.

5 Switzerland is much the _____ as it always has been: safe, clean and expensive.

6 The more cars we use, the _____ polluted our environment becomes.

7 Poland _____ quite as cold as Norway, but its climate is similar in the north-east.

8 Honduras is a tiny _____ bigger than Guatemala.

9 China is by far _____ most populated nation in the world.

10 Rather _____ getting a job in Madrid, why don't you travel around Spain?

3 Complete the text with words/phrases from the box.

> stunning   came up with   come across
> keep up with   side by side   get away from
> turn up   held up   run-down   carried out
> bustling   vast

In 1883, Italian priest Don Bosco dreamed of a futuristic city in the heart of Brazil. Seventy-seven years later, his dream came true. Brasilia was completed in 1960, the construction of this specially designed city (1) _____ in just three and a half years. Brasilia has never forgotten Don Bosco: a cathedral in the city bears his name.

The city was commissioned by President Kubitschek to house the government and its buildings. Brasilia's supporters say the city promotes growth in the whole of Brazil, which is a (2) _____ country (easily South America's biggest), not just on the famous east coast. Its detractors say it was built so that politicians could (3) _____ the high crime rates of Rio and São Paulo and so they wouldn't have to live (4) _____ with the population in (5) _____ areas.

Instead of a (6) _____ city centre full of people, Brasilia seems quite empty and almost like a machine. Its architects (7) _____ a rigidly organised design, with designated areas for government buildings, housing, etc. In the original design, there were no traffic lights; cars would go through tunnels and bridges in the sky, never getting (8) _____ by excess traffic. In order to (9) _____ a growing population, however, Brasilia eventually had to install traffic lights.

It isn't a charming city, compared to other parts of Brazil, as it is very regimented and lacks pretty little streets. But if you (10) _____ in the centre of Brasilia you will (11) _____ some excellent restaurants. You should also pay a visit to the futuristic cathedral built by Niemeyer, the television tower with its (12) _____ views, and the zoo near the airport.

Lead-in

1 Look at the pictures. Work in pairs and discuss the questions.

1 How are the pictures connected?
2 What types of story do they illustrate?
3 Are you good at storytelling?
4 What makes a good storyteller?

2 **a** Work in pairs. Discuss the difference between the pairs of phrases (1–5).

1 a plot/a biographical sketch
2 a fake/a myth
3 a tall story/a fairy tale
4 a legend/an anecdote
5 a punch line/a joke

b Can you think of any examples of the words/phrases above?

3 **a** Check you know the meaning of the underlined phrases.

1 Do you think it's OK to <u>tell a white lie</u> if it makes life easier?
2 What would you do if you heard that someone had been <u>spreading rumours</u> about you?
3 Are you sometimes a <u>bit of a gossip</u>?
4 Have you ever taken part in (or heard about) an <u>elaborate hoax</u>?
5 When you describe things, are you <u>prone to exaggeration</u>?
6 Do you know anyone who is good at <u>making up stories</u>?
7 Did you listen to <u>bedtime stories</u> when you were a child? Which were your favourites?

b Work in pairs. Discuss the sentences from exercise 3a.

Reading

1 **a** Work in pairs. Look at the photos and discuss the questions.

1 Where are the people in the main photo?

2 What do you think they are doing?

3 What do you think their relationship is with Manuel Elizalde?

4 What is a hoax?

b Read the article and check your ideas.

2 Write true (T) or false (F).

1 The Philippines government encouraged thousands of visitors to see the tribe. ☐

2 After losing power, Manuel Elizalde gave some money to the tribe. ☐

3 There have been many hoaxes connected with anthropology. ☐

4 Piotr Zak, Sidd Finch and Nat Tate were all invented characters. ☐

5 The public loved Piotr Zak's and Nat Tate's work, but the critics knew it was a hoax. ☐

3 Work in pairs and discuss the questions.

1 Why do you think people were so excited about the discovery of the Stone Age tribe?

2 Why do you think the people created these hoaxes? Did Elizalde, Shinichi, Plimpton and Boyd have different reasons?

3 What type of person would you need to be in order to create a successful hoax?

4 Why do intelligent people such as journalists and academics fall for hoaxes, (i.e. believe them)?

HOAXES THAT FOOLED THE WORLD

In 1971, while he was working as a government minister in the Philippines, Manuel Elizalde announced a great discovery. He
5 had found a Stone Age tribe living in a remote part of the country. They lived in caves, used stone tools, and ate any food they could find. This isolated tribe, just 27 people,
10 had been living this way for many generations, and in fact they didn't even speak the same language as other people in the area. Journalists arrived from all over the world, a
15 documentary about the tribe was filmed for TV, and thousands of dollars were spent on research trips. The Philippines government, however, not wanting to destroy
20 a way of life that had existed for thousands of years, allowed only a few people to visit them.

It was only years later, when the government (and Elizalde) lost
25 power, that the truth came out. Researchers found the tribe living in villages, wearing Levi's jeans and communicating happily with other people. They explained that they
30 had been pretending all along – Elizalde had paid them to act like a Stone Age tribe. What's more, Elizalde had left the country with all the money.

35 Elizalde's hoax was just one in a long line. Anthropology has been a particularly rich field for hoaxers, with stories ranging from the famous Piltdown Man hoax – a
40 supposedly ancient skull that was actually made of the bones of a medieval human and an orangutan, and chimpanzee teeth – to Fujimura Shinichi, the Japanese archaeologist
45 who faked vital discoveries for years before being found out in 2000.

But perhaps the most interesting hoaxes are those that involve fictitious people. Piotr Zak was a
50 Polish composer. An avant-garde modernist, he was not well-known among the public. At least not until 1961, when the BBC broadcast his piece *Mobile for Tape and Percussion*.
55 Some music critics hailed it as a great work. Unfortunately for them, the piece had consisted of BBC staff making silly noises edited by BBC technicians. It was a classic hoax.

60 Nearly a quarter of a century later, another great hoax was to shake the world of American sports. It was 1 April, April Fools' Day, which is a day for playing
65 practical jokes. *Sports Illustrated* ran an article about Sidd Finch, a truly extraordinary baseball player. The subheading of the article read: 'He's a pitcher, part yogi and part
70 recluse. Impressively liberated from our opulent lifestyle, Sidd's deciding about yoga – and his future in baseball.' Read the first letters of these words again, carefully. They
75 spell out 'Happy April Fools' Day'. On 15 April, the magazine came clean: Finch was an invention. The writer of the article, George Plimpton, then extended his article
80 into a novel, published in 1987.

Just a year later, British writer William Boyd published *Nat Tate: American Artist, 1928–1960*, the tragic biography of a New York painter. A
85 number of prominent critics claimed to remember Tate's work, claiming that he had been one of the greatest artists of the century. He'd never existed. The name Nat Tate is derived
90 from two of Britain's most famous art galleries: The National Gallery (Nat) and the Tate Gallery.

Grammar | narrative tenses review

4 **a** Read the first paragraph of the article again. <u>Underline</u> examples of the Past Simple, Past Continuous, Past Perfect Simple and Past Perfect Continuous.

b Work in pairs and explain the difference in meaning (if any) between the pairs of sentences (1–3) in the Active grammar box. Why might one verb form be more appropriate than the other in this context?

c Complete the rules (A–D) in the Active grammar box with the words from the box below.

> progress   length   chronological   before

Active grammar

1 a) *When the truth came out, Elizalde had already left the country.*
   b) *When the truth came out, Elizalde left the country.*

2 a) *People believed the tribe had been living the same way for centuries.*
   b) *People believed the tribe had lived the same way for centuries.*

3 a) *When researchers arrived, the people from the tribe weren't living in caves any more.*
   b) *When researchers arrived, the people from the tribe didn't live in caves any more.*

A Use the Past Simple for finished actions in the past. Use it to describe a sequence of events in _____ order.

B Use the Past Continuous for actions in _____ when something else happened.

C Use the Past Perfect Simple for actions completed _____ other events in the past. Use it when you are already talking about the past.

D Use the Past Perfect Continuous for progressive actions that started before the main events happened. Use it to emphasise the _____ of the action.

see Reference page 47

5 **a** Read about some famous hoaxes. Complete the paragraphs with the correct form of the verbs in brackets.

> In 1957, a news programme called *Panorama* broadcast a story about spaghetti trees in Switzerland. While the reporter told the story, Swiss farmers in the background (1) _____ (pick) spaghetti from trees. Following this, thousands of people (2) _____ (call) the show, asking how to grow spaghetti trees.

> In 1998, large numbers of Americans went to Burger King asking for a new type of burger. The food company (3) _____ (publish) an ad in *USA Today* announcing the new 'left-handed Whopper', a burger designed for left-handed people. The following day, Burger King (4) _____ (admit) that they (5) _____ (joke) all along.

> Swedish technician Kjell Stensson (6) _____ (work) on the development of colour TV for many years when he (7) _____ (announce) in 1962 that everyone could now convert their black-and-white TV sets into colour. The procedure was simple: you (8) _____ (have) to put a nylon stocking over the TV screen. Stensson demonstrated, and fooled thousands.

> Pretending that it (9) _____ (develop) the product for some time, a British supermarket announced in 2002 that it (10) _____ (invent) a whistling carrot. Using genetic engineering, the carrot grew with holes in it, and, when cooked, it would start whistling.

b 🔊 1.12 Listen and check.

Pronunciation | contractions (1)

6 **a** 🔊 1.13 Listen and write the sentences you hear. Which words are being contracted?

b Work in pairs. Look at audioscript 1.13 on page 90 and practise reading the sentences aloud. Can you hear the contractions?

Speaking

7 **a** Prepare to tell a story about something that happened in your life (e.g. a time you did something funny or learned an important lesson). Think about the topics below.

1 What were you doing when it happened?
2 How long had you been doing it?
3 Where were you? Who were you with?
4 What had happened before this? Why?
5 What happened next? How did you feel?

b Invent some minor details to add to your story.

c Work in pairs and take turns to tell your story. As you listen, think of questions to ask. Guess which details your partner invented.

Vocabulary | synonyms

8 Find synonyms for the words/phrases (1–10) from the article on page 36.

1 tricked (v) (title)
2 alone (adj) (line 9)
3 ruin (v) (line 19)
4 faking (v) (line 30)
5 a big, elaborate trick (n) (line 35)
6 extremely old (adj) (line 40)
7 extremely important (adj) (line 45)
8 freed (adj) (line 70)
9 expanded (v) (line 79)
10 extremely sad (adj) (line 83)

9 **a** Read about four hoaxes. Try to think of possible synonyms for the underlined words/phrases.

1 Footage was supposedly filmed in 1947 of doctors performing an autopsy on an extra-terrestrial. The story goes that the alien crash-landed in Roswell, New Mexico, US. The 17-minute clip since spread around the world on the Internet and even spawned a film, but it turned out that two English businessmen had staged the scene in 1995.

2 In 2009, a large weather balloon floated into the sky. The owners, Richard and Mayumi Heene, panicking, claimed their six-year-old son was in it. After a one-hour journey 2,000 feet into the air, and pursued by US National Guard helicopters, the balloon landed, but there was no sign of the boy. Had he fallen out? No. He was hiding in the family garage, as his parents had ordered him to.

3 In 2008, a film poster appeared heralding the arrival of a new superhero film. Titled *Gundala*, its hero was based on an Indonesian comic book. The film had its own Facebook page and website, with photos of the film in production and even a Wikipedia entry. However, it was a hoax perpetrated by Indonesian digital artist Iskandar Salim.

4 Actor/director Orson Welles's 1938 radio production *The War of the Worlds* conned thousands of Americans into thinking they were in the middle of a full-scale Martian invasion. The fake 'news bulletins' about the invasion sounded so genuine that many listeners thought they were real.

b Match the words from the box below to the underlined synonyms from exercise 9a.

> announcing   allegedly   appearance   attack
> authentic   carried out   chased   deceived
> doing   instructed   led to   rose

10 **a** Read the Lifelong learning box. Then rewrite the underlined words in sentences 1–5.

In your own words

! When learning new words it can be useful to keep a note of synonyms.

Using synonyms can help us to:

1 avoid repeating a word we have just used.
2 make what we say and write more interesting and memorable.
3 be more specific about the things we are describing.

Lifelong learning

1 Advertisers use a lot of tricks to trick people into believing that a product is exactly what they need.
2 Many so-called authentic products look authentic but when you examine them closely you can see they are counterfeits.
3 Instead of being extremely old artefacts, discoveries that are said to be extremely old often turn out to be modern fakes.
4 Destroying the environment will destroy our children's future, but some people insist that global warming is a hoax.
5 Hoaxes perpetrated on the public are very serious – the perpetrators should be punishable by imprisonment.

b Work in pairs. Do you agree with the sentences from exercise 10a? Give reasons and examples.

photo 3.1

3.2 A good read

Vocabulary compound words

Can do describe a person in detail

Vocabulary | books

1 Work in pairs and discuss the questions.

1 What sort of books do you like reading?

2 What three books would you take to a desert island?

3 Would you like to be a writer? Why/ Why not?

2 a Match the sentence beginnings (1–8) with the sentence endings (a–h).

1 I was

2 It's very

3 The story

4 I found the

5 The characters

6 It's based on

7 I'm a real

8 It's a

a is gripping.

b best-seller.

c story quite moving.

d readable.

e bookworm.

f a true story.

g are one-dimensional.

h hooked.

b Match the sentences from exercise 2a to the sentences below.

1 I'm an avid reader.

2 I couldn't put the book down.

3 The story really holds your attention.

4 It depicts real events.

5 It has a nice, easy style.

6 It has sold a lot of copies.

7 I was emotionally involved in it.

8 They didn't really come alive for me.

3 Complete this book review with the correct words (a, b or c).

I love Stieg Larsson's trilogy *The Girl With the Dragon Tattoo*, *The Girl Who Played with Fire* and *The Girl Who Kicked the Hornet's Nest*. The series is absolutely (1) _____ and I was (2) _____ after just a few pages. Although a lot of the characters are quite (3)_____ dimensional, the heroine, Lisbeth Salander, is fascinating. To see her journey from sulky cyber-geek to superwoman avenger is the main reason I couldn't (4) _____ the book down. Although not exactly a (5) _____, I've always been an (6) _____ reader of crime fiction, and Larsson's work is among the best in the genre. The style is very (7) _____, which is one reason why teenagers like the books. The heroine's story, although full of violence, is actually very (8)_____ because she has to overcome so many personal problems just to function successfully in the world.

1	a interesting	b moving	c gripping
2	a hooked	b gripping	c hooking
3	a one-	b single-	c mono-
4	a leave	b put	c drop
5	a book worm	b bookworm	c well-read
6	a appreciated	b interesting	c avid
7	a readable	b understanding	c alive
8	a emotionally involved	b moving	c movable

4 a Work in small groups. Make a list of books which could be described by the words from the box.

> gripping   based on a true story   moving
> a best-seller   readable

b Discuss the books on your list.

The Da Vinci Code is a best-seller. It's very readable and quite gripping.

Listening

5 **a** 🔵 1.14 Listen to three people answering some of the questions below. Which questions do they answer? Make notes on what they say.

1 Who is your favourite fictional character?
2 How do you visualise them (what do they look like)?
3 What personal traits (characteristics) do they possess?
4 What memorable things do they do?
5 What problems do they overcome?
6 Do you know anyone like them in real life?

b Listen again and check.

6 **a** Make notes on your own answers to the questions in exercise 5a.

b Work in small groups and discuss your favourite fictional characters.

Reading

7 Read the book extracts (1–6). Decide which extract describes the types of character below (a–f). There may be more than one possible answer.

a a dangerous character
b a middle-aged and not very handsome character
c a character who is probably very bossy and talkative
d a very active child
e a character who probably has a tough job outdoors
f a character who is old but has a youthful mind

8 Work in small groups. Read the extracts again and discuss the questions.

1 What type of person is being described in each extract?
2 What physical details are included? Do they show the people's character?
3 What actions are described? How do these reveal the people's character?
4 Do any of the people sound attractive? Why/Why not?
5 What type of book do you think it is from (funny, serious, etc.)?
6 Which person do you think is the most/ least attractive? Why?
7 Would you like to read any of the books?

(1)

For one thing he was unlike any other man we'd ever seen – or heard of, if it came to that. With his <u>weather-beaten</u> face, wide teeth-crammed mouth, and <u>far-seeing</u> blue eyes, he looked like some wigwam warrior stained with suns and heroic slaughter.
(*The Edge of Day* – Laurie Lee)

(2)

My father is still living, but less and less. Judge James Charles Endicott Jackson … that tall, lean, <u>hollow-cheeked</u> man who had made such a religion of the law, preached from the head of our dining-room table each evening of my young life.
(*The Best Revenge* – Sol Stein)

(3)

Nola is a tomboy, a <u>hell-raiser</u>, a maverick, and she's captured my heart like no other. She's got the broad choppy legs of an athletic boy and the scowl of an old maid. No matter how many baths she takes, she manages to smell unwashed. She stands in the sunlight, an amber specimen in a glass jar, still as an Indian or a stone. Then quick as an insect, she sparks into action, running down the hill where the wasps won't follow, stepping on the dried brown grass.
(*The Stuntman's Daughter* – Alice Blanchard)

(4)

He was 55, but he could have been ten years either side of that. Thin sandy hair, a big awkward mouth. Bad teeth, crooked and dark when he smiled, jug-handle ears. As a <u>self-conscious</u> boy he'd tried different things with those ears. He'd made an elasticised band with elaborate leather flaps to flatten his ears while he slept. He'd tried his hair short. He'd tried it long. He'd tried all kinds of hats. Eventually he'd grown the moustache as a kind of diversionary tactic, and he'd kept it.
(*The Idea of Perfection* – Kate Grenville)

(5)

Her grandmother was small and thin, with tiny hands and feet – <u>fast-moving</u> feet the size of a child's – and <u>washed-out</u> red frizzy hair that she dyed the colour of Red Delicious apples. She had disappearing lips, painted large, twice their size, the colour of plums. All her life, she'd been a dancer, every kind of dancer. Even now, at 75, she'd put on tights and a leotard and tutu, and do her ballet exercises in front of the long mirror on Alyssa's bedroom door.
(*Blister* – Susan Shreve)

(6)

He was just a <u>hot-headed</u>, 20-year-old kid at the time, but he was greasy-fast with a gun. The problem was that he was spoiling for a fight and got it. At over six feet and 190 pounds, he was a big boy and he had set out to prove to everyone that he was a man to reckon with.
(*Slade* – Robert Dyer)

Vocabulary | compound words

9 Work in pairs. Look at the <u>underlined</u> compound words in the extracts and answer the questions.

1 All of the extracts on page 40 except one contain compound adjectives. Which one contains only a compound noun?

2 Which compound adjectives describe someone's character? Which describe something physical?

3 Sometimes we can guess the meaning of compound adjectives. Which compound adjectives in the extracts are easy to guess because they have a literal (non-idiomatic) meaning?

4 What compound adjectives do you think would describe people with the characteristics below?

> work hard   keep an open mind
> look good   think freely   love fun

10 a Read sentences 1–8 below. Work in pairs and explain in your own words what the <u>underlined</u> compound adjectives mean.

1 He's <u>single-minded</u>. It took him ten years to learn the violin and he never gave up!

2 She's very <u>self-sufficient</u> for a child. She makes her own food and entertains herself for hours.

3 Writers have to be <u>thick-skinned</u>. Lots of people criticise their work, but they try not to get upset.

4 He's so <u>kind-hearted</u>. He always helps everybody even if he's busy.

5 They can be rather <u>stand-offish</u>. At the party they refused to talk to anybody.

6 He's very <u>career-orientated</u>. He even reads about law when he's on holiday.

7 They're really <u>level-headed</u>. Even when they won all that money they didn't get too excited.

8 I'm a bit <u>absent-minded</u>. I keep forgetting where I put my glasses.

b Are the compound adjectives positive, negative or neutral?

Speaking

11 a Look at the photos and write down compound adjectives to describe each person.

b Work in pairs and compare your opinions of each person.

12 Read the How to... box and prepare to write a short description of someone you know well. Make notes about first impressions, physical details, character, etc. Use compound words.

How to... describe people

First impressions	*She comes across as ... (adjective) ... but once you get to know her, she's ... (adjective)*
	The thing that strikes you about ... is that ...
Character – good things and bad things	*The thing I (don't) like about ... is ...*
	What I (don't) really like about ... is ...
	He's so + (adjective)
	He's such a (+ adjective) + person/man, etc.
	He can be a bit ... (negative adjective)

13 Describe your person to the rest of the class. Did any of the descriptions sound similar?

Reading

1 Work in pairs and discuss the questions.

1 Do you have any favourite comedians?

2 Which comedians are famous in your country?

3 Have they made any films?

2 Read about Groucho Marx. Guess the answer to the question at the end of each section.

1 Julius Henry Marx was born in New York into a poor but loving family on 2 October 1890. His father worked at home as a tailor and his mother, Minnie, worked as a promoter for her brother, comedian Al Shean. Growing up with a comedian in the family would have important consequences later. But, as a child, Groucho's first love was reading. He was also an extremely good singer.

What happened next?

a He became a singer.

b He wrote a book.

c He started performing with his uncle.

Go to 4 to find out.

2 Groucho became host of a radio show called *You Bet Your Life*. It was so popular that they moved it to TV. Groucho would interview the contestants and ad-lib jokes. Some of the more memorable questions included: 'What colour is the White House?' and 'Who is buried in Grant's Tomb?' Returned now to national prominence, Groucho embarked on his solo film career, with a string of films throughout the 50s and 60s. But by now he was entering his 70s.

What happened next?

a Groucho went to live in the Bahamas, for health reasons.

b Groucho started writing fiction.

c Groucho returned to fame in the Seventies.

Go to 8 to find out.

3 Desperately attempting to win some money, Groucho met Irving Thalberg, a big name in Hollywood, during a card game. Thalberg, impressed with his new friend's act, helped the Marx Brothers to get established in the movie business. In the 30s and early 40s, the brothers made their most famous films: *A Night at the Opera* (1935) and *A Day at the Races* (1937).

What happened next?

a Groucho got sick and then retired.

b The Marx Brothers disbanded.

c The brothers set up their own production company, which made them rich.

Go to 5 to find out.

4 At the age of 14, he began singing with the LeRoy Trio. His first tour wasn't a great experience. Having been left behind in Colorado, Groucho had to work his way back home. At this stage he wanted to become a doctor, but his mother had other plans for him.

What happened next?

a He ran away to study medicine.

b Groucho and his brothers formed a musical act.

c Groucho won a TV competition.

Go to 7 to find out.

King of the Jokers

5 Following a film called *The Big Store* (1941), the Marx Brothers disbanded. It seemed as though Groucho was going to fade into obscurity, when suddenly another opportunity arose.

What happened?

a He started a radio show.

b He became a politician.

c He was invited to perform in front of the British royal family.

Go to 2 to find out.

6 After suffering a severe stroke, Minnie died. Then the stock market crashed, signalling the beginning of the Great Depression. After hitting the heights of fame and fortune, suddenly Groucho and his brothers had lost everything. Depressed by the situation, Groucho began to suffer from insomnia, a condition that would plague him for the rest of his life.

How did the Marx Brothers recover in the 1930s?

a They invested in property.

b They toured the world, playing in small theatres.

c They started making films.

Go to 3 to find out.

7 Groucho and his brothers, encouraged by their ambitious mother, formed a group called The Six Mascots. Having been no more than a moderate success, one day they suddenly started cracking jokes on stage. The audience loved it. Being funny came naturally to them. Soon the Marx Brothers were performing in the best venues all over the country. Groucho, with his fast-talking characters, chicken-walk, painted-on moustache, big glasses, and a cigar that he never smoked, was the star. Then everything changed in 1929.

What happened in 1929?

a The brothers' mother died and Groucho lost all his money.

b Groucho went to live on a Pacific island.

c The brothers argued about money and split up their act.

Go to 6 to find out.

8 Groucho made a comeback in the 1970s, with a live one-man show. But with his health failing, he retired. He died of pneumonia in 1977 at the age of 86, three days after Elvis Presley. Voted the fifth greatest comedy act ever by his fellow comedians in a 2005 poll, Groucho lives on, at least in memory. His films may not be watched much these days, but everyone recognises those famous glasses with the fake nose and moustache.

THE END

3 **a** Do you think the following statements about Groucho Marx are true? Write D (definitely), P (probably), PN (probably not) or DN (definitely not).

1 He had a hard life. ☐
2 He had a great relationship with his mother. ☐
3 He had a great relationship with his brothers. ☐
4 He had a long career. ☐
5 He was a lucky man. ☐
6 His type of humour is still funny today. ☐

b Work in pairs and compare your answers. Give reasons.

4 **a** 🔊 1.15 Listen to someone describing Groucho Marx's life. What mistakes does she make?

b Work in pairs and compare your answers.

Grammar | participle clauses

5 **a** Read rule A in the Active grammar box and find an example of a past participle and a present participle in section 3 of the article on page 42.

b Read rule B and find an example of *Having* + past participle in section 7 of the article.

c Read rule C and find an example in section 6 of the article.

d Read rule D and find an example in section 1 of the article.

Active grammar

The article on page 42 contains several examples of participles and gerunds. There are two types of participle: past participles (*-ed* forms) (for regular verbs) and present participles (*-ing* forms).

A We often use participles to add extra information to the idea in the sentence. The past participle sometimes acts as an adjective. The present participle sometimes gives background information.

Returned now to national prominence, Groucho embarked on his solo film career ...

B *Having* + past participle shows the cause of a second action (or a sequence of actions).

Having been left behind in Colorado, Groucho had to work his way back home.

C We often use the *-ing* form after conjunctions (*after*, *before*, *when*) and prepositions.

After suffering a severe stroke, Minnie died.

D We can use the *-ing* form as the subject of the sentence.

Being funny came naturally to them.

---

see Reference page 47

6 **a** Find the mistake in each sentence and correct them with participles.

1 When tell a joke, timing is very important.
2 Work as a comedian must be a great job because you make people laugh.
3 Have become famous, comedians usually get depressed.
4 Making to look out of date by modern comics, old comedians like Chaplin and Groucho Marx are not funny these days.
5 Tell jokes in a foreign language is extremely difficult.
6 On been told a joke, you should laugh even if you don't think it's funny.
7 After to watch Mr Bean and Chaplin, etc., I think physical humour can be as funny as verbal.

b Work in pairs. Do you agree with the statements in exercise 6a?

Vocabulary | humour

7 **a** Match the types of humour from the box to the people or ideas in sentences 1–8. Use your dictionary to check any words you don't understand.

> farce   puns   cartoons
> black humour   surreal
> irony   exaggeration
> satire

1   bizarre (very strange) humour
2   a series of things go wrong, and the situation gets funnier and funnier
3   Tom and Jerry
4   jokes about death and other serious issues
5   word play
6   not saying exactly what you mean, or saying the opposite of what you mean
7   saying something is much more than it is (sometimes for comic effect)
8   laughing at politicians and 'important' people

b Work in pairs and discuss the questions.

1   Do you know any famous actors/comics/writers/films associated with these types of humour?
2   Which types of humour do you like?
3   Do you ever tell jokes in your own language or in English?
4   In your country, are there any special days when people play jokes on each other? What happens?

Pronunciation | speech units

8 **a** 🔘 1.16 Cover the text below and listen to someone telling a joke. Do you find it funny?

b Why do you think the speaker pauses at certain moments? Listen again and read the joke. Mark the pauses with / /.

Three colleagues, a photographer, a journalist and an editor are covering a political convention. // One day, during their lunch break, they walk along a beach and one of them sees a lamp. He picks it up and rubs it and a magic genie suddenly appears. The genie says 'You can each have one wish.' So the photographer says, 'I want to spend the rest of my life in a big house in the mountains with a beautiful view, where I can take photographs.' Bazoom! Suddenly the photographer is gone to his home in the mountains. Then it's the journalist's turn. 'I want to live in a big house in the countryside with an enormous garden where I can sit and write for the rest of my life.' Bazoom! The journalist is gone. Finally, the genie says to the editor, 'And what about you? What's your wish?' So the editor says, 'I want those two back before lunch. We've got a deadline at 6.00 tonight.'

Speaking

9 **a** Work in groups of three. You are going to tell a joke. Read your joke and try to memorise it. Think about where you will pause.

Student A: turn to page 79.
Student B: turn to page 80.
Student C: turn to page 78.

b Tell the joke to the other students in your group. Whose joke was the funniest? Who told it best?

1 **a** Look at the picture. Work in pairs and discuss the questions.

1 What kind of relationship do the people have?

2 What do you think is happening?

b Read the story and answer the questions.

1 Who is the narrator describing?

2 What made them the way they were?

Top chefs aren't known for their <u>warm personalities</u>. Assistants who overcook the pasta by ten seconds usually <u>struggle</u> to get out of the kitchen alive. My father was a top chef. We'd had a <u>stormy relationship</u>, but I decided to <u>follow in his footsteps</u> anyway, and train as a chef. It was better than the <u>dead end</u> I'd reached with the job I'd been doing.

After three years I became head chef in a restaurant called The Tortoise. As the boss, I <u>called the shots</u>, but if anything went wrong, I was the one <u>in the firing line</u>. Experiencing the sweaty kitchens, the egos, the closeness, I learned why my father was the way he was. When I began, I didn't <u>have my sights set on</u> anything much – I just wanted a regular job – but soon I realised my career <u>was taking off</u>. The rich and famous started to visit the restaurant and eventually I <u>reached a crossroads</u>: I could either open my own restaurant or go and work for one of the big ones. Then destiny intervened. My father retired and I got his job.

On my first day, I received a <u>frosty reception</u>. No one would talk to me. What was worse, I was <u>feeling under the weather</u> – I had a cold, and my hands were shaking as I went into the kitchen. I held my breath, stood up in front of everyone and said, 'My name is Leah Kleist. You all know my father. Whether you loved him or hated him, I don't care. He is the past. Now let's get to work.' And we did.

2 Match the <u>underlined</u> metaphors from the story with the definitions below.

Describing life as a journey

1 do the same things someone did before you

2 with no progress possible

3 start to become successful

4 a time when you have to decide about your future

Describing character/feelings as weather

5 friendly character

6 with arguments and strong feelings

7 unfriendly welcome

8 ill

Describing business as war

9 fight

10 make the important decisions

11 responsible if something goes wrong

12 have a goal/an objective

3 Complete sentences 1–8 with the metaphors from the story.

1 I went to the doctor because I was feeling a bit _____ the _____ .

2 We tried to develop the project, but soon we'd reached a _____ _____ .

3 They're always shouting and screaming at each other. They definitely have a _____ _____ !

4 I'm the chief executive and major decision-maker, so I have to _____ _____ shots.

5 My career began to _____ _____ when I landed a role in a TV series.

6 As the manager, you are _____ the _____ line when things go wrong.

7 She had her sights _____ _____ fame and fortune so she went to Hollywood.

8 Will you follow _____ your mother's _____ or work in a different field?

4 Work in pairs. Talk about the topics below.

• something you struggled to do

• a dead-end job you'd hate

• something you have your sights set on

• someone whose footsteps you'd like to follow in

• someone who'd get a frosty reception in your home

5 **a** Write metaphors for the things below. They can be metaphors you know, or you can make up your own.

> a good/bad person
> a good looking man/woman
> a problem   a boss   life
> an easy task
> a husband/wife   a city

a good person – an angel

b Work in pairs. Take turns to read your metaphors. Your partner guesses what it describes.

Can do | tell an extended story

1 Work in small groups. Read the openings to some pieces of fiction (1–8) and discuss the questions below.

1 What can you guess about each story? What type of story might it be?

2 Which extracts make you want to read more? Why?

3 Look at the ideas below for how to write a great opening line for a story. Which story openings (1–8) match the ideas in the notes?

present an unusual situation

show someone in a lot of trouble

catch the reader's attention

introduce a fascinating character

jump straight into the action

first-person narration ('I')

third-person narration ('he'/'she')

establish the narrator's voice

humorous/informal/'spoken' style

serious/formal/literary style

2 **a** You are going to write a story called 'Truth and Lies'. Think of an opening sentence for your story and write it down.

b Pass your sentence to another student. Write a continuation of the story.

c Check your story. Does it continue logically from the opening line? Does it have a beginning, middle and end?

d Work in small groups. Take turns to read out your stories. Which was the best opening line? Which was the best story? Why?

1 All happy families are alike; each unhappy family is unhappy in its own way.
(*Anna Karenina* – Leo Tolstoy)

2 I'm often asked what it's like to be married to a genius. The question used to please me …
(*The Mind-Body Problem* – Rebecca Goldstein)

3 In my younger and more vulnerable years, my father gave me some advice I've been turning over in my mind ever since.
(*The Great Gatsby* – F. Scott Fitzgerald)

4 It is a truth universally acknowledged, that a single man in possession of a good fortune must be in want of a wife.
(*Pride and Prejudice* – Jane Austen)

5 As Gregor Samsa awoke one morning from uneasy dreams, he found himself transformed in his bed into a gigantic insect.
(*Metamorphosis* – Franz Kafka)

6 All children, except one, grow up.
(*Peter Pan* – J.M. Barrie)

7 Someone must have been telling lies about Joseph K, for without having done anything wrong he was arrested one fine morning.
(*The Trial* – Franz Kafka)

8 He was an inch, perhaps two, under six feet, powerfully built, and he advanced straight at you with a slight stoop of the shoulders, head forward, and a fixed from-under stare which made you think of a charging bull.
(*Lord Jim* – Joseph Conrad)

Narrative tenses (review)

We often use narrative tenses together in order to make the order of events in a story clear.

Use the Past Simple to talk about completed actions in the past:

*We **went** to Paraguay last year.*

The Past Simple can be used for short actions, long actions or repeated actions.

Use the Past Continuous to talk about actions in progress at a particular time in the past:

*We **were talking** about her when she walked in.*

We often use the Past Continuous to set the scene in a narrative:

*The sun **was shining** and the children **were playing** in the garden. Suddenly ...*

Use the Past Perfect Simple to talk about completed actions that happened before another action in the past. The Past Perfect Simple is only used when we refer to two actions/moments in the past:

*She took out a DVD, but I**'d already seen** it.*

We <u>don't</u> need the Past Perfect when we are describing past events in chronological order:

*We **ordered** the food, **ate** and **paid**.*

Use the Past Perfect Continuous to talk about actions or situations which continued up to the moment in the past that we are talking about:

*Before he gave up, he**'d been smoking** for years.*

The Past Perfect Continuous is often used to show the reasons for a situation:

*He was angry because he**'d been waiting** for ages.*

Participle clauses

We can use participle clauses in many ways.

As reduced relative clauses. Instead of complete verbs, we use a participle clause:

*I recognise the man **who is sitting** over there.*
*→ I recognise the man **sitting** over there.*

We can use participle clauses like full adverbial clauses, expressing cause, result, conditions, etc. Adverbial participle clauses sound formal and are more common in writing than speech.

***Feeling hungry**, he bought a cake.*
*= **Because he was feeling hungry**, he bought a cake. (cause)*

Having + past participle is a special form that shows the cause of a second action/a sequence of actions.

***Having run the marathon**, he was exhausted.*
*= **After running the marathon**, he was exhausted.*

We can use participle clauses after many conjunctions and prepositions, e.g. *as, after, before, since, when, once, without, in spite of.*

***Before leaving**, he gave me a present.*

*He swam **in spite of having** a sore arm.*

We can also use participle clauses as the subject of the sentence.

***Talking** is the best therapy.*

The subject of the participle clause is usually the same as the subject in the main clause.

***Running** around till they were tired, the kids had fun.*
(= the kids ran and the kids had fun)

NOT: ~~*Waiting for hours, the day seemed to Tom as if it would never end.*~~ *(Tom was waiting; the day wasn't.)*

Key vocabulary

Tales

plot   biographical sketch   fake   myth   tall story
fairy tale   legend   anecdote   punch line   joke
tell a white lie   spread rumours   a bit of a gossip
elaborate hoax   prone to exaggeration

Books

it's very readable   I was hooked
it was quite moving/gripping   bookworm
the characters are one-dimensional   a best-seller
based on a true story   avid reader   depict
emotionally involved   come alive
I couldn't put (it) down

Compound words

single-minded   self-sufficient   thick-skinned
kind-hearted   stand-offish   career-orientated
level-headed   absent-minded

Humour

farce   puns   cartoons   black humour   surreal
irony   exaggeration   satire

Metaphors

follow in his footsteps   reach a crossroads
a career takes off   a dead-end job   frosty reception
feel under the weather   stormy relationship
warm personality   a struggle   have your sights set on
call the shots   in the firing line

ACTIVEBOOK

Listen to the explanations and vocabulary.

 see Writing bank page 83

1 Find seven mistakes with narrative tenses in the article and correct them.

In April 2000 journalists at *Esquire* were deciding that life at the magazine was getting a bit boring. So they published an article about FreeWheelz, an Internet company that gave customers free cars which were covered in advertising. The article had claimed that FreeWheelz 'will transform the auto industry more than Henry Ford did'. The company didn't yet become famous but it would 'on 1 April, when FreeWheelz launches on the web for real'. Readers who were seeing the website, which had been created by the author of the article, were impressed. Within days, the site had been receiving over a thousand hits and messages from other entrepreneurs who claimed they had been planning similar businesses. The website contained a questionnaire for potential clients which was including a number of bizarre questions such as 'Does hair loss concern you?' In the following edition, the magazine owned up, explaining that the article had been an April Fools' hoax. The magazine prepared to forget all about it when suddenly an offer for the domain name FreeWheelz came in. The author of the article sold the name for $25,000, splitting the profits with the owners of the magazine. The conclusion? Never trust a strange story which contains the date 1 April.

2 Rewrite the sentences so that they have the same meaning. Use participle clauses with the correct form of the verb in brackets.

Because we couldn't find our way, we had to turn back. (lose)

Lost, we had to turn back.

Robbie ate all the cherries and then he was sick. (have/eat)

Having eaten all the cherries, Robbie was sick.

1 Life's biggest pleasure is when you do things for other people. (do)

2 Anyone who wishes to take the exam must register in June. (wish)

3 Most of the dead animals that were found after the earthquake were domestic pets. (find)

4 Because she felt sleepy, Luisa went to bed. (feel)

5 When you swim, it is compulsory that you wear a bathing cap. (swim)

6 He had been famous for years, and he finally wanted some peace and quiet. (have/be)

7 As they were banned from exhibiting their paintings in the national exhibition, they decided to set up their own. (ban)

8 David woke up early as usual and looked out of the window. (wake up)

3 Put the underlined letters in order.

Posted by Nico

I am a complete bookworm and I'm particularly (1) ivda reader of Spike Davies's fiction. I found his latest book, *Charms*, a real (2) eapg-eutnrr. It's full of (3) albkc uhroum, which made me laugh aloud. I was absolutely (4) odehko.

[posted 16:41, viewed 10 times]

Posted by Nina J

Whilst I'd say that *Charms* is very (5) rbadlaee, I thought that the characters were a bit (6) oen-idsilanomne compared to normal. His previous book, which was (7) edbsa on a true story, was very (8) ggniprpi – in fact I (9) ulcdno't tup ti dnow. I wasn't surprised it became a (10) sebt-lelres. But *Charms* seems a bit self-conscious. There are too many weak (11) sunp and it lacks the clever (12) ynior of his best work.

[posted 17:22, viewed 8 times]

Posted by Olivier

His first novels were very (13) ogmniv – I cried about five times when reading *Brain Food* – but those were (14) siildecafntoi accounts of things that really happened to him. His recent novels don't (15) etdipc the same type of characters or situations. They all have (16) rlsuare plots that don't make sense and aren't funny. I've lost interest in his work.

[posted 20:05, viewed 3 times]

4 Complete the dialogues by adding one word.

A: He's the new boss, isn't he?

B: Yes, he _____ the shots.

Yes, he calls the shots.

1 A: How are you?

B: I'm feeling a bit under _____ weather, actually.

2 A: How are Julia and Antonio?

B: Well, they seem to have a very stormy _____ .

3 A: In 1988 you became Head of Exports. Is that right?

B: Yes, that's when my career really took _____ .

4 A: So are you going to become a carpenter too?

B: No. I really don't want to follow in my father's _____ .

5 A: I don't know whether to get a job or continue with my education.

B: It seems you've _____ a crossroads in your life.

6 A: So she takes responsibility for all the decisions?

B: Yes, she's the one in the _____ line.

Lead-in

1 Look at the photos, which all show types of progress. Work in pairs and discuss the questions.

1 What types of progress are shown in the photos?
2 What developments have there been recently?
3 What developments might there be in the future?

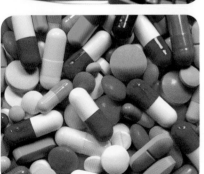

2 **a** Match the news headlines (1–4) to a photo.

1 Resistance to antibiotics on the increase
2 New virus destroys global computer systems
3 Human cloning to make spare parts for children
4 Space mission in danger as budget crisis grows

b Match the words/phrases from the box to the news headlines in exercise 2a.

> network   cell   crash a system   organ   hacker   skin tissue   gene
> test tube   software   strain   microchip   mission   firewall   orbit
> scan   shuttle   genetic engineering   superbug   launch   analysis

c ⬤ 1.17 Listen to the four news stories and check.

3 Check the meaning of the <u>underlined</u> words/phrases. Then work in pairs and answer the questions.

1 Would you describe yourself as a '<u>computer nerd</u>' or a '<u>technophobe</u>'?
2 Are you <u>up-to-date</u> with the <u>latest technology</u>? Are there any new <u>gadgets</u> you would like to buy/own?
3 Do you enjoy reading scientific <u>journals</u> or watching <u>documentaries</u>? Which scientific areas interest you most? Why?

HOW TO BE A

Speaking

1 Work in pairs. Read the facts and then answer the questions (1–3).

> **Bigger.** In the developed world in the 17th and 18th centuries, men were 165 cm tall, on average. Today the average is around 173 cm.

> **Faster.** In 1896, the world's fastest sprinter ran 100 metres in 11.8 seconds. In 2009, Usain Bolt ran it in 9.58 seconds. The 'impossible' feat of running a mile in four minutes was first achieved by Roger Bannister in 1954. Since then, dozens of runners have done the same, and the record is three minutes 43 seconds.

> **Longer.** In the developed world, life expectancy has doubled in 150 years. In 1850, people were expected to live until their late 30s. The age is now the late 70s.

1 Do you think these changes represent progress? If so, what type of progress is it?
2 In the future, do you think people will get bigger, stronger and faster? Will we live longer?
3 What powers do the superheroes in the pictures have? Will normal men and women ever have these powers? What role might science play and why might governments work with scientists to develop 'supermen' and 'superwomen'?

Got what it takes to become a superhero? For most of us, the answer is a resounding 'no' – things that are part of the day-job for world-savers are beyond the reach of mere mortals. But that hasn't stopped scientists from trying to recreate super powers artificially. And you might be surprised at how successful they have been.

Wall climbing
Gecko lizards are so good at this that they can hang upside down from a glass surface by a single toe. The secret lies in the millions of tiny hairs which are on the gecko's skin. Scientists at Manchester University are developing a material covered with similar hairs that would enable a person to walk on a ceiling or up a wall. One square centimetre of the tape holds a million artificial hairs and could support a kilogram of weight. There is every chance that this system could allow people to walk up walls.

Teleportation
Just as superhero Nightcrawler can teleport, scientists in Australia have discovered how to teleport matter for real – even though it is only on a tiny scale. The researchers have succeeded in transmitting information about small particles across space and using this information to reassemble copies of the original particles. It is unlikely that this method could be used for larger objects because of the vast amounts of information involved.

Regeneration
Both Superman and the X-men's Wolverine can regenerate tissue instantly. * Doctors at a children's hospital in Boston have pioneered a similar way of helping terminally ill patients to re-grow healthy organs. There is every likelihood that the procedure could eventually be used to grow organs for transplants.

Super-strength
No matter how many steroids you take, you don't stand a chance of achieving the strength of the Incredible Hulk. However, there is a distinct possibility that genetics could help those seeking a Hulk-like physique. Scientists at Johns Hopkins University have created Mighty Mouse – a genetically modified mouse. They are normal in every respect, except their muscles are two to three times

SUPERHERO

larger than normal,' says molecular biologist Se Jin-Lee. * Presumably, it'll also help scientists to better understand muscle-wasting diseases.

Force field

Superman's hideaway, the Fortress of Solitude, is protected by a force field. The Defence Science and Technology Laboratory run by the UK Ministry of Defence has developed a similar force field to protect tanks from grenades. *

Web-shooter

The US army has developed a device for the New York police which acts like Spider-Man's web shooter. The nets are designed to restrain people without causing serious injury and are shot from a type of gun. The victim caught in the net stands no chance of escape as the nets come in three varieties: a regular net, one that can give an electric shock, and, most fittingly of all, one that becomes sticky on contact with air. *

X-ray vision

Everyone would love to have Superman's ability to see through walls. * This works just like an X-ray but without the harmful effects. While the odds are against the general use of X-rays because they are dangerous, and repeated exposure to them is bad for your health, researchers are developing terahertz imaging for defence and medical purposes.

Flying

* Researchers are looking into the possibility of using spinning discs to cheat gravity. The original research was carried out by a Russian working in Finland in 1996 but so far, no other researchers have managed to reproduce his results. It is doubtful that we will be able to achieve this in the foreseeable future.

Invisibility

The Invisible Woman is part of the Fantastic Four. Now a virtual-reality expert in Japan has created a 'see-through' coat, which appears to make the wearer's body disappear. It is done by coating the material with microscopic reflectors that work like a cinema screen. A tiny video camera is then attached to the back of the coat. The image from the back of the coat is projected onto the front of the coat, which makes observers think that they can see through it.

Reading

2 Read the article and check your answers to question 3 in exercise 1.

3 The article has sentences missing where there is a * symbol. Complete the article with sentences 1–6 below.

1 The solution could be 'terahertz imaging'.
2 Once shielded by the force field there is very little chance that the tanks can be destroyed.
3 Superman, who first appeared in 1932, has the ability to fly without the aid of wings or rockets.
4 These crime-stopping devices are bound to cause some sticky problems for New York criminals!
5 They can be hit by a bullet and recover in seconds.
6 'They look like Schwarzenegger mice.'

4 **a** Read the article again quickly. Tick (✓) the research which you think is important. Write (✗) next to research which is less important and write (!) next to any information which worries you.

b Work in small groups. Compare your views.

Grammar | future probability

5 Look again at the article on page 50 and the sentences from exercise 3. Underline phrases used to talk about future probability and write them in the Active grammar box.

Active grammar

To talk about future probability we can use special phrases, as well as modal verbs like *will*, *could*, *may* and *might*.

Sure to happen	*It definitely will …* *will presumably …*
Very likely to happen	*It almost definitely will …* *There is a strong possibility …* *The chances are that …*
Likely to happen	*It may/might well …*
Unlikely to happen	*There's a slight/remote possibility that …* *I doubt whether …* *It probably won't …*
Impossible	*You haven't a hope of …* *It is inconceivable that …*

---

see Reference page 61

6 **a** Choose the words in *italics* which are not possible.

1 There is no *chance/option/doubt* that we'll make it to the laboratory on time.
2 It's *hopeless/doubtful/possible* that I'll see you again before I go into hospital.
3 They haven't a *hope/doubt/chance* of finding life on Mars.
4 There is a *remote/chance/slim* possibility that the virus will spread.
5 The experts are *bound/sure/hope* to agree with what you have said.
6 There is every *doubt/likelihood/chance* that Superman will kiss the girl at the end.
7 There is *every likelihood/a distinct possibility/ any chance* that the antibiotics will work.
8 Is there any *chance/hope/doubt* of you getting the results back earlier?

b What is the difference in meaning (if any) between the two correct options?

7 Rewrite the sentences with the words in brackets so that the meaning is the same.

There is no chance that I'm lending her my laptop. (stand)

She doesn't stand a chance of me lending her my laptop.

1 It's highly unlikely that they will make a breakthrough in the near future. (doubtful)
2 It is vaguely possible that we'll be able to travel to Mars by 2050. (inconceivable)
3 I'm sure they'll notice it's missing. (bound)
4 We can't be entirely confident that the family haven't already been informed. (chance)
5 We're being met at the airport so we don't need train tickets. (presumably)
6 Unfortunately, he doesn't stand a chance of getting the job. (hope)
7 China has a good chance of winning the space race. (distinct)
8 There doesn't seem to be much hope that the relationship will improve. (doubt)

Speaking

8 Work in pairs. Discuss the chances of events 1–5 happening in the next 20 years.

1 We will be able to have holidays in space.
2 There will be a cure for cancer/AIDS.
3 Nuclear energy will have been abolished.
4 Parents will routinely be able to choose the sex, hair, eye and skin colour of their babies.
5 All foods will be genetically modified.

Listening

9 **a** 🔊 1.18 Listen to an interview with Stan Lee, the creator of Spider-Man. Put the questions (a–d) in the order he answers them.

a Will there ever be real superheroes? ☐
b Why make him a scientist? ☐
c How did you think of Spider-Man? ☐
d Are you at all scientific? ☐

b Listen again. What does he say about the topics from the box below?

Fantastic Four a fly a scientist
science-fiction a 'dummy' diseases wars
Mars genetics

10 Work in pairs and discuss the questions.

1 Do you agree with what Stan Lee says about diseases, going to Mars and genetics?
2 Do you think that 'anything will be possible'?

Grammar	future forms (review)
Can do	talk about plans and arrangements

Vocabulary | arrangements

1 Work in pairs and discuss the questions.

1 How do you keep in touch with your family/ friends?

2 Do you agree with the quotation below? Do you think communications technology has made our lives better or worse?

> 'Modern communications technology is designed to keep us too busy to actually see anyone.'
> (*Paul Mendez, psychologist*)

2 Read the emails below. What is Tom trying to do? What happens in the end?

Hi Maz and Bobby,
I don't know what <u>you're up to</u> this Sunday, but if you're <u>at a loose end</u>, come over to my place. We're going to have a barbecue.
Tom

Hi Tom,
Thanks mate, but I'm completely <u>snowed under</u> at the moment. I have to write an essay by Monday afternoon, so I'll be working all weekend. I've got nothing <u>lined up</u> for the following weekend though, so maybe we can meet then? I'll call you later.
Bobby

Dear Tom,
Like Bobby, I'm a bit <u>tied up</u> tomorrow. Unfortunately, I have to go to my great uncle's house for a family lunch. He was ill so we thought it might <u>fall through</u>, but it looks as if it will <u>go ahead</u>. I really can't <u>get out of</u> it because it's his 60th birthday and most of the family will probably be there.
Maz

OK guys,
I think I should <u>call off</u> the barbecue. Judging from the grey sky, it's going to rain all weekend anyway. Maybe you'll have done your various duties by the end of the evening and we can go for a drink instead! If you want to <u>wind down</u>, I'll be in The Hart, a pub on King Street. Gloria and I are meeting there at about 8.30, as long as nothing else <u>crops up</u>! Don't forget it closes at 10.30 on Sundays.
OK, time to <u>put my feet up</u> and take it easy!
Later,
Tom

3 Read the emails again and match the <u>underlined</u> words/phrases to the definitions (1–12).

1 you're doing
2 happens unexpectedly (a duty or problem)
3 busy
4 planned/arranged
5 relax (usually at home)
6 avoid
7 cancel
8 extremely busy
9 not happen/take place (a plan)
10 proceed as expected (a plan)
11 bored because you have nothing to do
12 become relaxed

4 Complete the sentences below with one word.

1 The match was ruined by rain and eventually we had to call it _____ .

2 _____ your feet up – you deserve a break.

3 If you aren't _____ to anything this afternoon, why don't you come over here?

4 She's finished it so now she's _____ a loose end.

5 A problem has cropped _____ : the printer is broken.

6 I'm tied _____ all of January, but I'll have some free time in February.

7 We've got a good band lined _____ for tonight.

8 I went to the beach in order to wind _____ .

9 Despite the rain, the festival _____ ahead.

10 She can't come tomorrow because she's absolutely _____ under with work.

11 My mum says I have to clean my room now and I can't get out _____ it.

12 Their wedding plans fell _____ when she realised she didn't love him.

5 **a** Work in pairs. Answer the questions below.

1 What are you up to this evening?
2 When do you usually put your feet up?
3 What do you have lined up for next weekend?
4 What do you do when you're at a loose end?
5 Are there responsibilities you'd like to get out of?
6 Have any problems cropped up at work/school?

b Predict what the answers might be for two other students in the class. Ask them and see if you were correct.

Grammar | future forms (review)

6 **a** Look again at the emails on page 53. Which different verb forms are used for talking about the future?

b Match the beginning of explanations 1–8 with the correct endings a–h in the Active grammar box.

Active grammar

1 Use the Present Simple: _e)_
   *Don't forget it **closes** at 10.30 on Sundays.*

2 Use *will*: _____
   *I'll **call** you later.*

3 Use *will*: _____
   *Most of the family **will probably be** there.*

4 Use *be going to*: _____
   *We're **going to have** a barbecue.*

5 Use *be going to*: _____
   *Judging from the grey sky, it's **going to rain** anyway.*

6 Use the Present Continuous: _____
   *Gloria and I **are meeting** there at about 8.30.*

7 Use the Future Continuous: _____
   *I'll **be working** all weekend.*

8 Use the Future Perfect: _____
   *Maybe you'll **have done** your various duties by the end of the evening.*

a) for predictions you make because of present evidence.

b) for something that will be finished before a time in the future.

c) for immediate decisions made at the same time as you speak/write.

d) for something you think, guess or calculate about the future.

e) for fixed timetables, schedules and arrangements.

f) for something that will be in progress during a period of time in the future.

g) for fixed plans or arrangements.

h) for a personal intention or arrangement.

---

see Reference page 61

7 **a** Complete sentences 1–12 with future forms of the verbs in brackets.

1 She looks terrible. I think she _____ (faint).

2 You've dropped your pen. It's OK, I _____ (pick (it) up).

3 We _____ (get) married in July.

4 Oh no! The train is delayed. We _____ (be) late.

5 Do you think you _____ (retire) by 2030?

6 Sorry, you can't borrow the car tonight. I _____ (use) it.

7 This time next month, we _____ (lie) on a beach in Thailand!

8 What do you think you _____ (do) in ten years' time?

9 She offered to help us at 9 o'clock! That's useless. We _____ (finish) by then!

10 The play is at the Olivier Theatre and it _____ (start) at 7.30.

11 I _____ (write) to you as soon as I can.

12 We can't get there until late. By the time we arrive they _____ (eat) all the food.

b Work in pairs and compare your answers. Which sentences can use more than one future form? Why?

8 Complete the questions using *will (do)*, *will be (doing)* or *will have (done)*.

In a year's time …

1 Do you think you _____ (still study) English?

2 Do you think you _____ (have) the same lifestyle?

3 Do you think you _____ (live) in the same place?

4 Do you think your country _____ (have) a different government?

In ten years' time …

5 Do you think you _____ (change) much?

6 Do you think you _____ (have) the same hobbies?

7 Do you think you _____ (have) the same close friends?

8 Do you think you _____ (see) more of the world?

Pronunciation | auxiliary verb *have*

9 **a** Read the sentences below. In which sentence is *have* an auxiliary verb? In which sentence is *have* the main verb? How are these pronounced?

1 Do you think you'll have changed your job?

2 Do you think you'll have the same standard of living?

b ● 1.19 Listen and check. Repeat the sentences.

c ● 1.20 Listen to the questions from exercise 8. Apart from the auxiliary verb *have*, which other words are contracted?

d Listen again and repeat the questions, paying attention to contractions.

10 a Work in pairs. Discuss the questions from exercise 8.

b Tell the class two things you learned about your partner.

Listening and speaking

11 🔊 1.21 Listen to two telephone conversations. What is the speakers' relationship? What plans are they trying to make?

12 We use vague or imprecise language when we don't want to (or can't) give details. Listen to the conversations again and complete the phrases in the How to... box.

How to... be vague/imprecise

Give imprecise information about how often something happens	(1) *once in a blue* _____ (2) *from time to* _____
Give imprecise information about quantity, time and/ or numbers	(3) *more or* _____ (4) _____ *of mistakes* (5) *about* _____ *-ish* (6) *in an hour* _____
Give imprecise information about things you do/have been doing	(7) *bits and* _____ (8) *that kind of* _____
Give imprecise answers to direct questions	(9) *sort of/* _____ *of* (10) *in a* _____

---

13 Put the words in order.

1 We / go / time / to / to / that / still / time / from / café / .

2 We / to / before / bits / various / leave / pieces / going / do / and / we / are / .

3 I'm / pushed / weekend / time / sort / this / for / of / .

4 Her / job / solving / thing / that / kind / whenever / crop / involves / problems / up, / of / .

5 They'll / less / or / here / more / a / for / month / stay / .

6 Because / I'm / a / in / busy, / I / moon / see / my / sister / once / only / blue / .

7 By / time / loads / next / new / I'll / have / this / of / met / year, / people / .

8 We're / ish / at / about / hoping / meet / four- / to / .

9 I'll / at / or / arriving / so / ten / be / .

10 In / home / a / at / I / prefer / on / staying / nights / way, / Saturday / .

14 a 🔊 1.22 Listen to six questions. Write short answers. Try to make your answers imprecise or vague.

b Work in pairs and compare your answers.

15 Work in pairs and play 'Twenty questions'. Follow the instructions below.

Think of a famous person. Don't tell your partner who it is.

Try to find out who your partner is thinking of. Take turns to ask questions.

You have 20 questions each and you can only ask yes/no questions. However, you can add imprecise or vague information to your answers, if you like (provided it doesn't make it too easy for your partner to guess who you are thinking of). The first to guess the identity of the famous person wins.

A: Does your person appear on TV?

B: Yes, I suppose so, from time to time. Is your person middle-aged?

A: Yes, sort of ... he/she is 50-ish, I think.

Vocabulary | special abilities

1 Work in pairs. What can children usually do by the time they reach the ages below?

- two years old
- five years old
- ten years old

2 Match words/phrases 1–7 to synonyms a–g.

1	gifted	a	for the future
2	in the making	b	difficult
3	prodigy	c	abnormal
4	adulation	d	talented
5	peers	e	admiration
6	demanding	f	genius
7	freak	g	contemporaries

Reading

3 Look at the photo and words/phrases 1–7 from exercise 2. What do you think the article is about?

4 Read the article quickly. Were any of your predictions correct?

5 Read the article again and answer the questions.

1 Why were Son's parents surprised?
2 What does Son think of his gift?
3 According to the article, what problems do child prodigies face?
4 What is the 'big question' about child prodigies?
5 What answer does the article suggest?

6 Work in pairs and discuss the questions.

1 Have you heard any stories about other child geniuses?
2 How do you think society treats them?
3 What might be the benefits and drawbacks of having a child prodigy in the family?
4 Do you know any children who have a special gift for something?
5 Do you think child prodigies are 'born' or 'made'?

HOW TO MAKE YOUR CHILD A GENIUS

They compose operas aged six, become chess grandmasters when barely out of nappies, and paint masterpieces when their peers can't even hold a pencil. According to educator Maria McCann, 'They are our beautiful freaks'. They are child prodigies, and increasingly they are coming out of Asia, a hotbed of mathematical and musical excellence.

Take Nguyen Ngoc Truong Son. Living in a run-down home in the Mekong Delta, Vietnam, the toddler would watch his parents play chess for hours on end. Before he was three years old, he asked them if he could join in. Fully expecting the pieces to end up on the floor, they let him play. Not for one minute had they imagined what would happen next. Not only did the boy set up the pieces correctly, but he also began playing according to the rules. Within weeks he was beating his parents. Within months he was playing in national tournaments against opponents who were twice his age and twice his size. He became world under-10 champion in 2000 and was a grandmaster at 14.

For Nguyen Ngoc Truong Son's parents, it was nothing short of a miracle. They were teachers who took home less than $100 a month combined. They had not trained their boy to be a chess prodigy. In fact, they hadn't even taught him the rules of the game. For Nguyen, it just came naturally. No sooner had he started playing than he was able to adopt complex strategies. 'I just see things on the board and know what to do,' he said.

How do child prodigies become what they are? The subject has been a constant source of mystery to both the public and scientists. These gifted children have been showered with adulation, labelled as overly demanding, treated as money-making machines, and scrutinised like lab rats. Rarely have they been understood.

Perhaps the key question is whether they are born or made. Numerous studies have looked at the inheritability of intelligence. Overall, they confirm that it can be handed down through the generations of a family, but the studies do not confirm the link between intelligence and the particular traits of prodigies. Prodigies are not smart in any general kind of way; they are able to master highly specific activities and skills. Their reasoning may be no better than average, but they can think like computers, grasp complex mathematical structures, or develop fully realised worlds.

There is one thing that the experts are beginning to agree on, however: the importance of upbringing. Taiwanese educator Wu Wutien says, 'Prodigies are half born, half made.' Only if they are in a stimulating home environment will their natural talents flourish. When parents have a house full of books and interesting objects, read to their child from an early age, take them on outings to museums and places of natural beauty, these all stimulate the child. Parents of prodigies also, typically, allow their kids to be independent. This lets prodigies in the making discover things for themselves such as the way music works or the way the parts of a car engine fit together or even, in the case of Nguyen Ngoc Truong Son, the rules of chess.

Grammar | inversion

 a Look at the examples of inversion (1–3) in the Active grammar box. Find two other examples of inversion from the article on page 56.

b Match rules C–F with examples 4–7 in the Active grammar box.

Active grammar

We use inversion to emphasise the adverbial phrase in a sentence and to add variety to a text. Inversion is often used in more formal texts.

1 *Not for one minute had they imagined* what would happen next.
2 *Not only did* the boy *set up* the pieces correctly, but he also began playing according to the rules.
3 *Rarely have they been understood*.

A We put a negative or adverbial expression at the start of a sentence (*never*, *nowhere*, *not only*, etc.) followed by an auxiliary verb + subject.
He plays football and tennis. → *Not only does he play football, but he also plays tennis.*
He arrived and we left immediately. → *No sooner did he arrive* than we left.

B We do not use auxiliary verbs when the main verb is *to be* or a modal verb.
He is a great singer and can also dance. → *Not only is he* a great singer, but he can also dance.

C We use inversion after phrases with *not*.

D We use inversion after negative adverbs which emphasise a time relationship.

E We use inversion for general emphasis with phrases that use *only*.

F We can use inversion with *no way* in informal speech.
4 *No way am I going to sing in public!*
5 *Only if we start to play more intelligently will we win this game.*
6 *Not since I was a child have I enjoyed myself so much.*
7 *No sooner had I arrived than I had to go out again.*

see Reference page 61

8 Read the pairs of sentences (1–6) and tick (✓) the correct option (a or b).

1 a Not since Mozart there has been a greater genius.
  b Not since Mozart has there been a greater genius.

2 a Only after three did she begin to show her gift.
  b Only after three she did begin to show her gift.

3 a Nowhere do the rules say you can't teach advanced subjects to children.
  b Nowhere the rules say you can't teach advanced subjects to children.

4 a Only later did we understand the truth about our gifted child.
  b Only later we understand the truth about our gifted child.

5 a Not only did he able to write poetry when he was five years old, he also played the violin well.
  b Not only was he able to write poetry when he was five years old, he also played the violin well.

6 a No sooner had we given her a paintbrush than she produced a masterpiece.
  b No sooner had we given her a paintbrush, she produced a masterpiece.

Pronunciation | word stress (2)

9 1.23 Listen to the answers to exercise 8. Which words are stressed? Check in audioscript 1.23 on page 91.

10 **a** Complete the sentences.
1 No way would I want to …
2 Rarely do I go …
3 Not only can I …, but I can also …

b Work in pairs. Practise saying the sentences. Pay attention to word stress.

Listening

11 **a** You are going to listen to an expert on gifted children describing an unusual case. Before listening, read the notes. What kind of information is missing?

People involved
The case involved twins called (1)_____ .
Physically they were (2)_____ & wore thick glasses. At school, people (3)_____ at them.

Their gifts
They could tell you (4)_____ in the past & future 40,000 yrs.
They could remember long sequences of (5)_____ .
If you asked them about a day in their lives, they could remember (6)_____ .

Conclusions
Their ability = mathematical & (7)_____ .
Asked how they do it, they reply, '(8)_____ .'

b 🔊 1.24 Listen and complete the notes.

c Work in pairs and discuss the questions.

1 In which jobs would the twins' abilities be useful?
2 How else could they use these abilities?

12 **a** Look at the notes from exercise 11a again. Are they easy to understand? Why/Why not?

b Read the Lifelong learning box and follow the instructions.

Taking notes – get organised!

❗ We take notes for different reasons (recording what was said in a meeting, summarising academic lectures, or writing down instructions so we don't forget them). The purpose of notes is to have a written record which we can review and understand later.

Match techniques 1–6 with explanations a–f.

1 Use underlined sub-headings.
2 Use symbols and abbreviations.
3 Make use of space.
4 Summarise the information.
5 Personalise the information.
6 Use more than just words.

a Don't write everything. Only write the most important points, so your notes are concise.
b Draw diagrams, graphs or pictures if this will help you remember the information more easily.
c Don't write whole words if it isn't necessary. This will help you write your notes quickly.
d Start a separate line for new ideas. Grouping ideas makes your notes easy to understand.
e Divide the information into smaller sections. This makes the notes easier to follow.
f Transform the information by interpreting it and using your own words. This makes it more memorable.

Lifelong learning

---

c Look at the notes from exercise 11a again. Which of the techniques from the Lifelong learning box are followed?

Speaking

13 **a** Work in pairs. You are going to tell your partner about a child prodigy. Read about the child and take notes following the advice in the Lifelong learning box.

Student A: look on page 78.
Student B: look on page 79.

b Use your notes to tell your partner about the person you read about. Discuss the questions below.

1 What do the two boys have in common?
2 Which story do you think is the more interesting? Why?
3 Which type of ability do you think is more commonly associated with child prodigies: musical or artistic?
4 If you could have one special ability (e.g. memorising numbers or words, being able to learn many foreign languages quickly), what would it be? Why?

Kieron Williamson

Nathan Chan

1 **a** Work in pairs. Read the sentences below. Do you agree? Can you give examples?

1 Now and again, an amazing invention, for example the Internet, accelerates the world's progress.

2 By and large, life is probably better now than it was 100 years ago.

b Underline the two-part expressions in each sentence from exercise 1a. What do you think they mean?

c Match the underlined two-part expressions in sentences 1–10 to definitions a–j.

1 A country cannot make progress if it doesn't have law and order.

2 The city is developing rapidly according to the facts and figures.

3 I learned most of what I know about computers through trial and error.

4 I'm sick of all their petty rules and regulations.

5 Apart from the usual aches and pains she felt all right.

6 These are tried and tested security procedures.

7 Most teenagers would rather be out and about with their friends.

8 When the doorbell rang he was ready and waiting.

9 Let's settle this once and for all.

10 I'm sick and tired of your excuses.

a testing different methods in order to find which one is the most successful

b slight feelings of pain that are not considered serious

c a situation in which people respect the law and crime is controlled by the police

d a method which has been used successfully many times

e official instructions saying how things should be done/what is allowed

f prepared for what he was going to do

g angry or bored with something that has been happening for a long time

h deal with something completely and finally

i in places where you can meet people

j the basic details and numbers concerning a situation or subject

2 Work in small groups. Close your books and test your partners on the expressions from exercise 1c.

A: *Trial?*

B: *and error. Law?*

C: *and order.*

3 Cover exercise 1 and complete the sentences.

1 The police have a tough job keeping _____ in the run-down parts of the city.

2 The documentary confused me with all those _____ .

3 We eventually found the answer by means of _____ .

4 I hated being in the army because of all the _____ .

5 I must be coming down with flu. I am all _____ .

6 If you like the cake, I'll give you my _____ recipe.

7 He won't be at home now. He's always _____ .

8 We really need to make a decision about this _____ .

9 Has Martina arrived yet? Yes, she's _____ .

10 I am _____ of always having to do his work for him.

4 Work in pairs. Discuss the questions.

1 What do you think of the current state of law and order in your country? Do you think anything should be done about it? If so, what?

2 Is there anything that you are sick and tired of? If so, what could be done to make the situation better?

3 Are there any rules and regulations you have to abide by (at home/school/work)? Do you think they are good/reasonable rules and regulations?

4 Can you think of anything that you learned by trial and error? How long did it take you to learn?

5 What sort of things do you do only now and again?

6 Can you think of a decision you would like to make (or would like someone to make) once and for all?

7 Are there any facts or figures you have read recently which you find interesting or surprising?

5 **a** Write three questions using expressions from exercise 1.

b Work in pairs and ask and answer your questions.

1 🔊 1.25 Listen to four speakers talking about important discoveries/inventions. Make notes on what they say.

2 Listen again and tick the expressions from the How to... box that you hear.

> ### How to... present a case for something
>
> *It changed ... completely*
> *It paved the way for ...*
> *It's made a massive difference to ...*
> *It's revolutionised ...*
> *We shouldn't underestimate ...*
> *It has had a huge impact on ...*

3 Work in small groups and discuss the questions.

1 Can you think of any other important discoveries/inventions?

2 How have they changed our lives and/ or made the world a better place?

4 Read about three areas of research (A–C) and answer the questions.

1 Is each area of research valid/likely to succeed/likely to affect your life?

2 Would you contribute money to further research in this area?

3 How could you raise funds to support it?

5 **a** Work in groups. You are going to present a case for research funding. Discuss questions 1–4 in relation to your area.

Group A: present a case for research into space travel.

Group B: present a case for research into how robots can help mankind.

Group C: present a case for research into genetic engineering.

1 What important discoveries do you think might be made in this area in the future?

2 What do you think is needed to make this research possible?

3 How do you think the research should be funded?

4 How will the research affect people's lives?

(A) Space travel/exploration

NASA spend billions of dollars every year to send professional astronauts to the moon, Mars and beyond. Now Virgin Galactic is offering to take private citizens into space. They have already collected $6 million in deposits. For $200,000, the paying public will fly 70 miles above the Earth, see the planet's curvature, and experience weightlessness for at least six minutes.

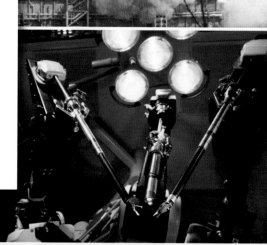

(B) Robots

Various domestic robots are available which can do your ironing or mow the lawn, etc. Now, some hospitals in the UK are experimenting with 'robo-docs' so that doctors can 'visit' their patients from a distance (another ward, or even another country). Also, scientists are improving robots for space exploration.

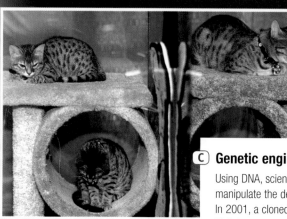

b Decide how you are going to present your case for research, and rehearse your arguments. Use language from the How to... box.

c Present your group's ideas to the rest of the class. Which group makes the strongest/most convincing case?

(C) Genetic engineering

Using DNA, scientists can now manipulate the development of life. In 2001, a cloned cat called 'Little Nicky' was sold to a Texan woman for $50,000. Now scientists are researching the use of DNA to predict hereditary illnesses in unborn babies. The scientists could then potentially alter the babies' genes to prevent the illnesses. Many people worry that the techniques will be used commercially, for example, to manufacture 'superchildren' with unnatural physical advantages.

Future probability

Use *will* to talk about something that is definite or a very strong probability.

Use *could*, *may* or *might* to talk about something that is possible but not certain.

There are many other phrases for describing possibility.

Adverbs/adverbial phrases:

it will almost definitely, it almost definitely won't, presumably it will

Verb phrases:

it may well, it might well, I doubt

Adjectives/adjectival phrases:

bound to, certain to, sure to, unlikely to

Noun phrases:

the chances are that, there's a strong/slight possibility, you haven't a hope of -ing

Future forms (review)

Use the Present Simple to talk about timetables.

*The plane **departs** at 14.30 from Warsaw.*

Use *will* to talk about a decision made at the time of speaking (including offers and promises):

*I **don't think I'll have** a coffee, thanks.*

Use *going to* to talk about a plan or intention (maybe details haven't been decided yet):

*I'm **going to work** in finance.*

Use the Present Continuous to talk about a future arrangement (details such as time and place have been decided):

*I'm **playing** tennis at 4.30 with Zara.*

Use *will* to make predictions based on what you know/believe. We often use *think, hope, believe*, etc. with *will* in this case:

*I think Mike **will be** a good manager.*

Use *going to* to make predictions based on what you can see/hear/think/feel now:

*I think I'm **going to** be sick.*

Use the Future Continuous to talk about something in progress at a definite time in the future:

*This time next year I'**ll be living** in France.*

We can use the Future Continuous to ask about someone's plans, especially if we want something or want them to do something:

***Will you be working** late tonight?*

Use the Future Perfect with time phrases with *by* (*by that time, by this time next week, by the end of February, by the end of the day*, etc.):

*By June we **will have finished** the project.*

Inversion

We use inversion to emphasise the adverbial phrase in a sentence. Inversion is usually used in more formal or literary texts.

The form is negative adverb + auxiliary verb + subject. Note: the word order is the same as the question form.

*Not once **did she** look up from her book.*

We do not use auxiliary verbs when the main verb is the verb *to be* or a modal verb.

*Not only **is he** a great musician, but he can also teach.*

Inversion can be used after restrictive words like *never, rarely, little, hardly*, etc.

*Never before **had he seen** such a beautiful vase.*

We also use inversion with phrases beginning with *only*. These emphasise the first clause.

*Only when I heard her speak **did I** remember her.*

We use *no way* + inversion to show that something is impossible or that the speaker doesn't want to do something. This is informal.

*No way **would I** do a bungee jump!*

Key vocabulary

Progress

antibiotics   virus   human cloning   space mission   network   cell   crash a system   organ   hacker   skin tissue   gene   test tube   software   strain   microchip   mission   firewall   orbit   scan   shuttle   genetic engineering   superbug   launch   analysis

Arrangements

be up to   at a loose end   snowed under   lined up   tied up   fall through   go ahead   get out of   call off   wind down   crop up   put my feet up

Special abilities

gifted   in the making   prodigy   adulation   peers   demanding   freak   abnormal   talented   admiration   genius

Two-part expressions

law and order   facts and figures   trial and error   rules and regulations   out and about   by and large   tried and tested   once and for all   now and again   ready and waiting   sick and tired   aches and pains

---

Listen to the explanations and vocabulary.

ACTIVEBOOK

see Writing bank page 84

1 Rewrite the sentences in three different ways with the words in brackets. There may be more than one answer.

1 We expect the weather to improve in the coming months. (chance/distinct/well)

2 I doubt if they will succeed in contacting us. (remote/probably/slim)

3 We will almost certainly move house in the spring. (likelihood/chance/bound)

4 I don't believe they will offer him the job. (hope/chance/distinct)

5 The organisers are confident that attendance will be high this year. (presumably/bound/strong)

6 There is a slight chance that Thompson could score a goal. (inconceivable/odds/possibly)

2 Choose the most appropriate words in *italics*.

1 Max *retires/is retired/will retiring* soon, so we*'ll be looking/look/will be look* for a new manager.

2 Wait a moment. I*'m just coming/will come/will be coming*.

3 By this time next year, he*'s going to be/'ll be/is* at school.

4 Will you *going to see/have seen/be seeing* Jade this week?

5 Don't worry if you haven't finished. *I'm working/'m going to work/work* on it later.

6 I'm sure he*'ll make/makes/will be making* a great recovery, whatever the doctors *say/will say/will be saying*.

3 Choose the correct option (a, b or c).

1 No sooner _____ left the airport than I realised I had picked up the wrong suitcase.
   a did I   b had I   c would I

2 No _____ should you be made to pay the difference.
   a means   b cases   c way

3 Not _____ did they think it would be possible.
   a for once   b for one moment   c for ever

4 On no _____ should I be disturbed during the meeting.
   a way   b time   c account

5 _____ that I am asked such a difficult question.
   a Not often it is   b Not is it often
   c It is not often

4 Complete the text with suitable words.

A new problem has arisen in the school. No (1) _____ can teachers afford to lose their temper with pupils at any time. It has been noted recently that some pupils are using their mobile phones to film angry teachers. (2) _____ now (3) _____ we discovered what these videos are being used for. (4) _____ only are the videos sent to friends for amusement, but in some cases teachers' heads have been superimposed on another body to make them look stupid. Little (5) _____ we know that the resulting images had also been posted on Internet sites. (6) _____ no (7) _____ can this behaviour be allowed to continue. In order to curb the problem, all teachers are to ensure that mobile phones carried into the classroom are switched off. (8) _____ before has it (9) _____ so important to exercise patience and maintain high standards at all times.

5 Complete the sentences with the prompts in brackets and phrases from the box.

> put my feet up   more or less   in a blue moon
> time to time   cropped up   fell through   up to
> snowed under   bits and pieces   at a loose end

1 I see her once _____ . (very occasionally)

2 I have to do a few _____ . (things)

3 I'm _____ . (have nothing to do)

4 What are you _____ tomorrow? (doing)

5 I've _____ finished. (nearly)

6 A few problems _____ yesterday. (appeared)

7 I still go to that café from _____ . (not regularly)

8 I just want to _____ . (relax)

9 I am absolutely _____ at the moment. (very busy)

10 The dinner _____ . (was cancelled)

6 Complete the text with suitable words.

In the future, there will be a number of new developments in healthcare to add to tried and *tested* procedures. The development of (1) _____ engineering will be important, not only for curing our everyday aches and (2) _____ , but for repairing skin (3) _____ damaged in accidents. Another development will be the insertion of (4) _____ into the human body. These tiny devices will carry medical information about the person. Machines will simply (5) _____ the individual to find out his or her genetic history instantly.

Scientists will continue looking for ways to cure common illnesses (6) _____ and for all. New (7) _____ will be discovered, to add to penicillin and others, but unfortunately new (8) _____ will also evolve to attack the body. New rules and (9) _____ will be necessary to stop the increasing use of human (10) _____ .

Lead-in

1 **a** Work in pairs and discuss the questions.

1 How many ways can you think of to earn a fortune?
2 Which are the easiest/most risky/quickest?

b Check you understand the meaning of the <u>underlined</u> words/phrases in sentences 1–8.

1 She <u>came into a fortune</u> when her mother died.
2 He <u>haggled</u> to get a good deal.
3 The <u>stock market</u> is a little unpredictable at the moment.
4 The employees have asked for a <u>rise</u>.
5 The taxes will affect <u>high-income</u> families.
6 Warhol's paintings are <u>priceless</u>.
7 The sales team is <u>paid on commission</u>.
8 He's been in a bad way since his business <u>went bankrupt</u>.

c Discuss which ones could be used to describe the photos.

2 Work in small groups and discuss the statements.

1 Art belongs to everyone. Priceless paintings should be available for all to see.
2 It's rude to haggle when you buy something. You should pay the asking price.
3 Paying people on a commission basis makes them work hard.
4 High-income families should pay higher taxes.
5 Gambling on the stock market is a sure way to go bankrupt.
6 The best way to get a rise is to be nice to your boss.

Grammar	emphasis
Can do	talk about professional relationships

Vocabulary | business

1 **a** Read the proposal below. Is it a good idea or not? Why?

Your task is to help a group of six people <u>launch a company</u> from which they hope to <u>make a living</u>. Here's the catch: the group members are all ex-criminals and a TV crew will film your every move. The employees will <u>be recruited</u> on a voluntary basis and they will need to be team players because the business will be a <u>profit-share</u>. You must provide <u>hands-on work experience</u> to prepare them for the business world. The TV company will provide <u>start-up funds</u>, and one of the <u>fringe benefits</u> for workers is that they will have some TV exposure to help with <u>publicity</u>. However, the business has to <u>make a profit</u> or at least <u>break even</u>, as the TV company will not <u>bail them out</u> if the business fails.

b What do you think the <u>underlined</u> expressions mean?

c Complete sentences 1–8 with <u>underlined</u> expressions from exercise 1a. You may need to change the verb form.

1 We were going to go bankrupt, so I had to ask my father to _____ us _____ .

2 The new company needs _____ - _____ _____ to buy equipment.

3 It's not easy to _____ a _____ as an actor. Many actors have other jobs.

4 The biggest _____ _____ of my job is the free food.

5 After a year, if the company still hasn't _____ _____ , we'll stop subsidising you.

6 We're going to _____ a new _____ in June. It'll sell web apps.

7 Our company is a _____ - _____ . We only get paid if the whole organisation is doing well.

8 The spy was _____ from our embassy in Iceland.

Reading

2 Read the article about what really happened when the programme was filmed and answer the questions.

1 What type of business was it?

2 What problems were there?

Starting up and starting over

One of the world's most innovative florists, Paula Pryke had written numerous books about flowers, founded a school dedicated to floral design, and taught floristry for the best part of two decades. She was the leader in her field (or garden!) and her life was – excuse the pun – a bed of roses. Then she was given a challenge too big to refuse.

A group of ex-convicts arrived at her door. They'd been recruited through advertisements in cafes, snooker halls and launderettes and Paula's task was to train them to become florists. The whole process was to be filmed for a new television show called One Last Job.

Paula was not in the least bit alarmed by working with criminals. The reason she could be so calm was that she'd deliberately avoided finding out what crimes they'd committed. Happily oblivious, she gave them eight days' training. All six of the ex-convicts were hardened criminals, but what they reminded her of was the children she used to teach in a British comprehensive school. The ex-cons fidgeted in their seats, talked at the wrong times, and couldn't concentrate, but according to Paula, "they did know an awful lot about credit card fraud". At least, unlike the schoolchildren in her care, they didn't set fire to the school.

After their training, they were given some hands-on work experience, and then they launched a company called 'A New Leaf' in Islington, London. It was, naturally, a flower shop. In the spirit of teamwork, A New Leaf was a profit-share, owned and run by its staff. Its initial financial goal was to break even. Although Channel 4 had provided start-up funds, the TV company stipulated that it would not bail out the company if it went bankrupt.

All six of the ex-convicts wanted to turn over a new leaf – start their lives again, free from crime – but the project was by no means easy. During the training, Paula noted their unreliability. The thing that amazed her was that they all wanted to be on TV but didn't always appear for the filming. Once the shop opened, even with the advantage of TV publicity, it proved very difficult indeed to make a profit. Two of the owners dropped out and two were bought out of the business by the remaining two, Judith and Cliff, who became sole owners. Paula was not surprised. Six people trying to make a living from one shop was never likely to work. "It was obvious," she says, "that we would end up with only those who really wanted their own shop."

While Judith and Cliff are becoming more independent, Paula says that when an emergency strikes – for example, they have to make a fancy bouquet for the first time at 5.30 p.m. on a Friday – "it's me they call". But the company has survived and, just like flowers, keeps growing and growing.

3 Write true (T) or false (F).

1 The ex-convicts volunteered to be retrained as florists for the TV programme. ☐

2 Paula used to be a schoolteacher. ☐

3 The group started immediately with hands-on work experience. ☐

4 The group always came to work because they wanted to be on TV. ☐

5 There are only two employees left out of the original six. ☐

6 The group phones her every day at 5.30 p.m. ☐

Grammar | emphasis

4 **a** Read rule A in the Active grammar box and find an example of each type of emphasis in the article on page 64.

b Read rules B and C in the Active grammar box and find examples of cleft sentences and a *what* clause in the article.

Active grammar

A We can add emphasis by including certain words.

1 *own* – to intensify possessive adjectives.

2 *very/indeed*

3 emphasising negatives: *in the least bit/at all*

4 adjectives/adverbs to add emphasis: *actually/by no means/even*

5 Auxiliary verbs: *do/did*

B We can use cleft sentences (sentences split into two clauses) for emphasis.

*The **reason why** we left the party early **is** ...*
*The **thing that** most annoys me about it **is** ...*
*The **person who** I most admire **is** ...*
***It was** Simon **who** asked ...*

C We can also use *what* clauses for emphasis.

***What you need is** a cup of coffee ...*

see Reference page 75

5 **a** Rewrite the sentences to add emphasis, with the words in brackets.

1 He can't complain. It's his fault he lost the money. (own)

2 We're not certain that it isn't the same man committing the crimes. (by)

3 I really miss having enough time to spend with friends. (what)

4 They didn't understand what we wanted. (all)

5 He didn't stop at the red light. He just drove straight through. (even)

6 The costs were very high. (indeed)

7 Sammy always got into trouble. (it)

8 Keith wasn't annoyed when we cancelled the meeting. (least)

9 We came home early because it started raining. (reason)

10 I find those pop-up ads annoying. (thing)

b 🔵 1.26 Listen and check.

Pronunciation | emphasis (1)

6 🔵 1.26 Listen to the sentences in exercise 5a again. Which words are stressed? Practise saying the sentences.

7 Work in pairs and discuss the questions. Use emphasis where possible.

1 What are the three most important elements of a successful business?

2 Would you consider starting your own business. Why/Why not?

3 Who would/wouldn't you choose for a business partner? Why/Why not?

Listening and speaking

8 **a** You are going to listen to five extracts from a radio programme about choosing a business partner. Before you listen, look at the notes below. What information do you think is missing?

The speaker warns against doing business with
(1) _____ .

The only way to get rid of a bad business partner legally is to (2) _____ .

Successful partnerships will combine two types of people: (3) _____ and (4) _____ .

It's a good idea if partners have complementary
(5) _____ .

One may be good in the area of product design, the other in marketing. If your business is lacking in a particular area, you may need to (6) _____ .

Good (7) _____ is essential to ensure that arguments do not interfere with the business.

Ideally, your business partner will be committed to the
(8) _____ success of the business.

b 🔘 1.27 Listen and complete the notes.

9 **a** Listen again. Notice how the speaker uses the phrases below and check you understand the meaning.

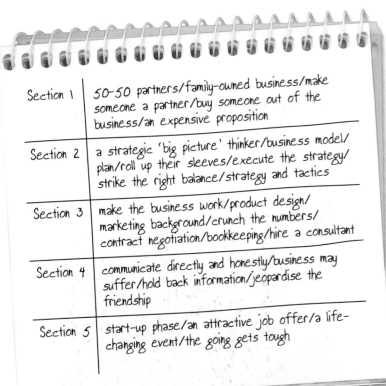

Section 1	50-50 partners/family-owned business/make someone a partner/buy someone out of the business/an expensive proposition
Section 2	a strategic 'big picture' thinker/business model/plan/roll up their sleeves/execute the strategy/strike the right balance/strategy and tactics
Section 3	make the business work/product design/marketing background/crunch the numbers/contract negotiation/bookkeeping/hire a consultant
Section 4	communicate directly and honestly/business may suffer/hold back information/jeopardise the friendship
Section 5	start-up phase/an attractive job offer/a life-changing event/the going gets tough

b Work in pairs. Take it in turns to reconstruct what the speaker says in each section using the notes from exercise 9a.

10 Work in pairs and discuss the questions.

1 Do you agree with what the speaker says? Do you know people in successful/unsuccessful partnerships? Why do you think the relationship does/doesn't work?

2 Are you a 'visionary' or an 'operations' person? What skills, experience and qualities would you bring to a business partnership? In which areas are you lacking? Would you work well with the other students in your group?

Grammar	conditional sentences
Can do	discuss financial decisions/regrets

Reading

1 Work in pairs. Look at the photos above and read the statements (1–3). Which do you agree/disagree with?

1 The most contented people are often those with the least amount of money.

2 Whoever said money can't buy happiness simply didn't know where to go shopping.

3 Money is only a tool. It will take you wherever you wish, but it will not replace you as the driver.

2 Work in pairs. Read an article and make notes on the topics below.

Student A: read the article on this page.

Student B: read the article on page 78.

• What type of childhood did the person have?

• How did they make their money?

• Did they invest the money? In what?

• How is their family connected to their story?

• What do they do today?

3 Tell your partner about the person in your article using your notes.

4 Work in pairs and discuss the questions.

1 Do you know any similar stories involving either rich people who became poor or poor people who became rich?

2 What personal qualities do you think are necessary for successful businesspeople like Zhou Xiaoguang?

Riches to rags

Leon Spinks had it all – money, fame and the physique of a Greek god. Then he lost it. The former heavyweight boxing champion had the world at his feet when he took the title from Muhammad Ali in 1978, but his life began spiralling out of control soon afterwards. A combination of bad deals and 'friends' who stole his money meant that within a few years his fortune was gone.

Today, Spinks has some balance in his life. The boxing gloves he wore in his glory days have been replaced by cleaning gloves: he works as a janitor at a YMCA. Spinks earns just a few dollars an hour, supplemented by his other work – unloading trucks at McDonald's. "I get 50% off Big Macs," he says.

The public perception of Spinks is that he partied away $5 million in the time it takes to pop a champagne cork. But that doesn't tell the whole story. If his lawyers hadn't tricked him, things might have been different. "I gave [them] power of attorney," he says. He went into the ring for a rematch with Ali, expecting to earn $3.75 million. He never saw a penny.

Spinks' luck is in stark contrast to that of his brother, Michael, though they were both boxers. They won Olympic gold medals in Montreal and when Michael defeated Larry Holmes in 1985, the Spinks boys became the first brothers to become world heavyweight champions. Michael invested his money in a $5 million estate in Delaware and secured his future. Leon says they're close, and that he could always ask Michael for help, but that's not his style. "I can make it myself," he says.

Spinks wishes things had gone differently, but he's a hero to the locals. In Chicago, he hands out food, drink and clothes to the homeless. Even if he had never been heavyweight champion of the world, they would still love him. The fact is that, after his tough childhood, he might have been one of them if he hadn't taken up boxing. Local children come up to him all the time, thrilled to be in his presence. It makes everything worthwhile for Spinks. "I tell them I was heavyweight champion and if they eat healthy, stay off drugs and grow up real strong, maybe one day they might become the champ, too."

Grammar | conditional sentences

5 **a** Read examples 1–7 in the Active grammar box. Are they about Leon Spinks or Zhou Xiaoguang?

b Match examples 1–7 to descriptions a–g in the Active grammar box.

c Find three or four sentences with conditionals or *wish* in the final paragraphs of the articles on pages 67 and 78. What type of conditional are they?

Active grammar

1 *If he/she hadn't trusted others, he/she wouldn't have lost so much.*

2 *If it hadn't been for his/her large family, he/she might not have needed to work when so young.*

3 *He/She might still be producing cheap goods today if he/she hadn't seen the industry's potential.*

4 *He/She probably wishes that he/she had saved some of the money.*

5 *If he/she happens to meet some children, he/she tells them about past glories.*

6 *Should he/she be travelling by night, he/she probably won't catch a night train!*

7 *Supposing his/her family offered financial help – he/she wouldn't accept.*

a) *wish* (or *if only*) + Past Perfect to talk about regret

b) Third Conditional to talk about a hypothetical situation in the past

c) Third Conditional with *if it hadn't been for* to talk about how a negative result would have occurred without an event or a certain person's actions taking place

d) Mixed Conditional to talk about a hypothetical present result of a past action

e) *should* (+ somebody/something) used in formal sentences as a replacement for *if*

f) Other phrases (*supposing, provided, as long as,* etc.) can be used as a replacement for *if*.

g) *if* + *happen to* (or *should happen to*) used with First Conditional sentences to emphasise that something is unlikely to occur or will occur by chance

Other words/phrases can be used instead of *if* in conditional sentences, e.g. *provided that, as long as, supposing.*

***Supposing** you could start a new company, what type of business would you choose?*

---

6 Rewrite the sentences (1–8) so the meaning is the same. Use the words in brackets.

I'll renew the contract if the conditions stay the same. (provided)

Provided that the conditions stay the same, I'll renew the contract.

1 Would we get to the bank in time if we left immediately? (supposing)

2 I failed the exam because the last question was so difficult. (if the last question ... passed the exam)

3 I didn't have my credit card with me, so I didn't buy any presents. (I would ...)

4 The business isn't doing well because there is so much competition. (if only ... better)

5 You can call me if you have any problems. (should)

6 Thanks to Dr Hyde, I survived the operation. (if it ... might not)

7 They fell out over money and their marriage broke up. (if they ... married now)

8 In case you arrive late, just ask for me at the desk. (should you ...)

Pronunciation | contractions (2)

7 **a** ● 1.28 Listen to sentences 1–3. Which words are represented by the underlined contractions: *have, had* or *would*?

1 If I'd gone to university, I'd 've probably got a better job.

2 I'd probably be happier now if I'd moved to Australia.

3 If I hadn't got this job, I'd 've probably got into debt.

b Listen again and repeat. Pay attention to the contractions.

Speaking

8 Work in pairs and discuss the questions.

1 What would you do if only you had more time?

2 If you happened to find £100, what would you do with it?

3 Supposing you could do any job in the world, what would you do?

4 Is there anything which you wish you had done when you were younger?

5 How might things be different now, if you had made a different decision at some point in your life?

see Reference page 75

Vocabulary | finance and philanthropy

9 a Read the definition of *philanthropy*. What philanthropists do you know about?

> **philanthropy** (*n*) [U] the practice of giving money and help to people who are poor or in trouble

b Read the article below. Which of the philanthropists have you heard of?

Great philanthropists

John D. Rockefeller once said, 'Giving away money intelligently is more difficult than making it.' He should know – he <u>gave $530 million to charity</u> in his lifetime. Rockefeller's entrepreneurial spirit blossomed early. Aged 12, he lent $50 to a farmer. The following year he got the money back, and <u>charged interest</u>! Decades later, when his three-year-old grandson died of scarlet fever, Rockefeller began <u>investing heavily in</u> medical research. He founded the Rockefeller Institute in 1901, and later his doctors flew around the world providing vaccines for children.

The best-known philanthropist today is Bill Gates, whose foundation has <u>dedicated billions of dollars to</u> projects in over 100 countries. While Gates gives away more money than anyone else in the world, there are many other great but lesser-known philanthropists. Marcos de Moraes, chairman of Brazilian drinks company Sagatiba, <u>funds programmes</u> to keep children off the streets. His Instituto Rukha, founded in 2004, <u>aims to eradicate</u> child labour. Texan oil heiresses Helen and Swanee Hunt <u>make large donations to</u> women's causes. They ask rich women across the US to write million-dollar cheques which are then fed into numerous causes such as <u>promoting welfare</u> for women. On the other side of the world, Indian businessman Sunil Mittal has <u>amassed a fortune</u> in the telecoms industry and is now <u>putting it back into</u> the fight against illiteracy. He has opened over 200 schools and invested in teacher-training and community libraries. His catchphrase is: 'give back what you take'.

10 Work in small groups and discuss the questions.

1 Do you admire the actions of any of the people in the article? Why/Why not?

2 Do you think that, as in Rockefeller's case, tragedy sometimes inspires generosity?

3 Do you believe in giving money to charity? Which causes do you/would you support and why?

11 Work in pairs. Look at the <u>underlined</u> expressions from the article. What do you think they mean? Which expressions have a similar meaning?

12 a Complete each sentence with one word.

1 Anyone who amasses _____ fortune is probably either a genius or a criminal, or both.

2 Dedicating millions of dollars _____ a cause is great, but real heroes dedicate their lives.

3 The trouble with _____ money to charity is that most of it never gets to the people who need it.

4 Philanthropists who _____ huge donations set a great example to the developed world.

5 It's better to invest _____ local causes where you can see the results more easily.

6 The rich should _____ their money back into the community, where it came from.

b Work in pairs. Which statements from exercise 12a do you agree with?

13 Read the Lifelong learning box and do the exercises.

Words that are verbs and nouns

! Many words connected to business and finance can be verbs and nouns.

fund   charge   launch   experience   profit recruit   share   benefit

Complete the sentences below with a word from the list above.

1 a The new _____ was excellent at his job.
b It's getting harder to _____ workers for this business.

2 a He's the philanthropist who will _____ our organisation.
b She donated money to the _____ for disabled war veterans.

3 a The new law will _____ everyone in this business.
b The biggest _____ of the job is that we get free healthcare.

Use the other five words from the list above to write pairs of sentences with gaps (one with a noun and one with a verb). Give your sentences to another student to complete.

Lifelong learning

Grammar	sentence adverbials
Can do	express priorities

Vocabulary | describing a job

1 Work in pairs. What is important in a job? Make a list of the five most important things for you.

2 Check the meaning of the words/phrases from the box. Did any appear on your list?

> job satisfaction   recognition   good salary
> promotion prospects   travel opportunities
> supportive colleagues/boss   pension plan
> freedom/autonomy   flexible working hours
> professional/personal development
> perks and benefits   working environment
> convenience of location   challenging tasks

Speaking

3 Complete the How to... box using words from the box below.

> about   absolutely   could   main   do   really

How to... express priorities

Saying it's very important	My (1) _____ priority is ... The essential thing for me is ... This is (2) _____ vital! I couldn't (3) _____ without ...
Saying it's not important	I'm not (4) _____ bothered/ concerned (5) _____ this. This isn't a major priority. I (6) _____ do without ...

4 Work in pairs. Discuss which things from exercise 2 are priorities and which are not. Try to use language from the How to... box.

Reading

5 Read the article and answer the questions.

1 How does *Fortune* magazine get the results for its annual list?

2 What makes the winners special?

3 What is Wegmans' philosophy?

4 Why does a manager say that the company is run 'by 16-year-old cashiers'?

100 BEST COMPANIES TO WORK FOR

Every year, *Fortune* magazine publishes a list of the '100 Best Companies to Work For'. How does the magazine choose the companies? Firstly, it uses a survey: 350 employees answer 57 questions about their company. Secondly, *Fortune* looks at important features of companies: for example, pay, benefits, and communication between workers and management. Finally, the magazine compares the results to find its Top 100.

To a certain extent, the results are guesswork, but the companies on the list, by and large, have many things in common: they pay their employees well, they allow workers to make decisions, and they offer a comfortable workplace. Broadly speaking, however, the winners tend to offer something above and beyond the norm. J.M. Smucker, a jam company, gives its workers free muffins and bagels for breakfast; at Griffin Hospital, employees get free massages; a bank called First Horizon National gives its employees time off to visit their children's classrooms. Wegmans Food Markets sent one worker on a ten-day trip to London, Paris and Italy to learn about cheese. This is not unusual for the New York-based company, which is well-known for the scholarships it gives its employees to further their education. At W.L. Gore, workers decide on their colleagues' salaries. Surprisingly enough, the most important thing for employees is not money. It is freedom to develop ideas. Timberland offers a six-month paid sabbatical for employees who have 'a personal dream that benefits the community'.

Let's not forget that all these companies are businesses whose priority is making money. They have to make a profit. And do they? Seemingly, the answer is a big 'yes'. The number one company, Wegmans, makes a fortune. The company, which has a motto, 'Employees first, customers second', is one of the 50 largest private companies in the US, with annual sales of $3.6 billion, according to *Forbes* magazine. Apparently, being good to your employees is no obstacle to making money.

How much of Wegmans' success is due to the company's policies? 'Up to a point, the success is because of the freedom they give us,' says one employee. 'On the other hand, no company gets rich just by being nice. Wegmans has great marketing strategies and it's well-positioned within the community. I've been here for 15 years. Looking back, I'd say that the company's innovations for customers, such as the Shoppers' Club electronic discount programme in the 1990s, have been just as important as the benefits to staff.'

But the employee benefits are striking. Fundamentally, Wegmans believes in professional development. As well as scholarships, the company gives its employees business opportunities. For years, one employee made delicious cookies for her colleagues. Eventually, she started selling the cookies in Wegmans. 'I just asked the manager,' she says. 'With hindsight, I should have asked earlier. I could have made more money!'

The staff's freedom to make decisions is another thing you won't find everywhere. Essentially, Wegmans wants its workers to do almost anything to keep the customers happy. Believe it or not, an employee once cooked a Thanksgiving turkey in the store for a customer because the woman's turkey, bought in Wegmans, was too big for her oven. One manager says, 'We're a $3 billion company run by 16-year-old cashiers.'

Grammar | sentence adverbials

6 **a** Read the article on page 70 again. What purpose do the <u>underlined</u> sentence adverbials serve?

b Choose the correct options in rules A and B in the Active grammar box.

c Complete the table in the Active grammar box with the <u>underlined</u> sentence adverbials from the article.

d Add any other adverbial phrases that you know to the table.

Active grammar

A Sentence adverbials show how the sentence fits in with the rest of the text and frequently go at the <u>beginning/ middle/end</u> of a sentence. This makes the link to the previous sentence clear, though adverbials can go in other positions.

B Sentence adverbials show the speaker's attitude and feelings, and are usually separated from the rest of the sentence by a <u>full stop/comma</u>.

Adverbial functions	Examples
Basic ideas	*fundamentally essentially*
Unexpected points	
Generalisations	
How something appears	
Contrast	
Reflection on the past	
Partial agreement	

---

see Reference page 75

7 Choose the sentence adverbial in *italics* which does not fit the context.

We want our workers to be happy. Fundamentally/Essentially/With hindsight this means helping them to foster a sense of pride in their work.

1 We believe in giving our employees as much autonomy as possible.
Broadly speaking/Apparently/By and large, we try not to interfere unless really necessary.

2 Our employees don't complain if they have to work at weekends.
On the other hand/Seemingly/However, they do expect to be paid overtime for this.

3 We believe in second chances, because employees learn from their mistakes. *Believe it or not/Surprisingly enough/Broadly speaking*, our company has never dismissed a worker.

4 Employees like to set their own system *up to a point/apparently/to a certain extent* but we don't let workers pay themselves huge amounts.

5 Some employees' salaries were getting too high too fast. *Believe it or not/Looking back/With hindsight*, we should have introduced a pay cap earlier.

6 We studied some large companies. It is *apparently/seemingly/surprisingly enough* difficult, but not impossible, to change the whole culture of a company.

Speaking

8 Work in pairs and discuss the statements below.

1 It's a good idea for employees to set their own salaries.

2 Employees shouldn't have to wear uniforms.

3 Employees should be allowed to evaluate their bosses formally.

4 In future, everyone will work flexitime.

5 Working at weekends will become normal for every profession.

Listening

9 Work in pairs and discuss the questions.

1 Do you know any companies with particularly favourable/poor working conditions?

2 What effect do/did they have on the employees and on the company results?

10 a 🔘 1.29 Listen to an interview with a company director. What do you think of the conditions he describes?

b Listen again and make notes on the topics below.

- type of business
- staff
- incentives
- salaries
- atmosphere
- personal involvement

c Work in pairs and compare your notes.

11 Work in small groups and discuss the questions.

1 What do you think of the ideas introduced at Piranha Recruitment? Would you like to work for the company? Why/Why not?

2 If you were the director of a new company, what ideas would you introduce to help retain your staff?

Vocabulary | expressing quantity

12 a Complete the phrases (1–10) with words from the box.

> most   many   plenty   majority   awful
> handful   few   much   deal   bit

1 as _____ as (a surprisingly large number)
2 a little _____ more (a little more)
3 a great _____ of energy (a lot of energy)
4 _____ of benefits (lots of benefits)
5 not _____ of an expert (not really an expert)
6 for the _____ part (generally)
7 an _____ lot of time (a surprisingly large amount of time)
8 the vast _____ (most of)
9 quite a _____ staff (a considerable number of staff)
10 only a _____ of people (very few people)

b 🔘 1.30 Listen and check.

c Listen again. Mark the stressed words. Which words are pronounced as weak forms?

d Practise saying the phrases, paying attention to stress and weak forms.

13 Rewrite the sentences below using the words in brackets.

1 The government spends a lot of money on defence. (The government ... great)

2 Not as many people turned up to see the race as had been expected. (Surprisingly ... few)

3 The customers generally appreciate our top-quality service. (For ... most)

4 It isn't a huge fee if you consider the amount of work involved. (It ... much)

5 There are more than enough bottles on the rack. (There ... plenty)

6 Three or four people asked questions at the end. (Only ... handful)

7 Most of the workers joined the strike. (The vast ...)

8 The crowds were huge. (There ... awful)

14 a Complete the sentences below using phrases from exercise 12a.

> I'd like to ... this course by ...

I'd like to get the most out of this course by doing a little bit more homework.

1 I think the government wastes ... on ...

2 ... of people in this country ...

3 ... of road accidents could be avoided if ...

4 There are ... women in top management positions because ...

5 I spend ... my time ...

6 There are not ... as there used to be.

b Work in pairs and compare your sentences.

5 | Vocabulary | Idioms (1)

1 Read the dialogue below. What are the two meanings of *fortune*?

A: Thanks to my good <u>fortune</u>, I picked the correct lottery numbers.

B: Yes, you won a <u>fortune</u>, didn't you?

2 Match the <u>underlined</u> phrases (1–9) to <u>underlined</u> phrases with a similar meaning (a–i).

1 I could never afford that watch. It <u>costs a fortune</u>.

2 He's got six cars and a yacht! You know, he's <u>worth a fortune</u>.

3 If you're careful you <u>can live on</u> £150 a week, even in London.

4 I'm not <u>well off</u> but I still have a good lifestyle.

5 That shirt only cost me £15. It was <u>a bargain</u>.

6 I had a rather expensive holiday. Now I'm <u>broke</u>.

7 Great meal! Shall we <u>split the bill</u>?

8 It's my birthday so I <u>treated myself to</u> a bottle of champagne.

9 That business closed down. The owners were always <u>in debt</u>.

a That house was <u>dirt cheap</u>. It's really spacious and it only cost £150,000.

b I'm not <u>rich</u>, but I get by on my salary.

c Neither of us have much money so let's <u>go halves</u>.

d He can't <u>afford</u> a holiday. He's a bit hard up.

e We're <u>in the red</u> at the moment, but the company's finances will improve in June.

f I'm glad you like my new car. It <u>cost me an arm and a leg</u>.

g She's <u>splashed out on</u> new clothes. Look at her!

h You should have let him pay! He's <u>rolling in it</u>!

i I can't go out tonight. I'm <u>skint</u>.

3 Work in pairs and discuss the questions.

1 Which phrases from exercise 2 are generally more colloquial: 1–9 or a–i?

2 Are phrases 1–9 more formal or more neutral?

3 Do you have similar phrases in your language?

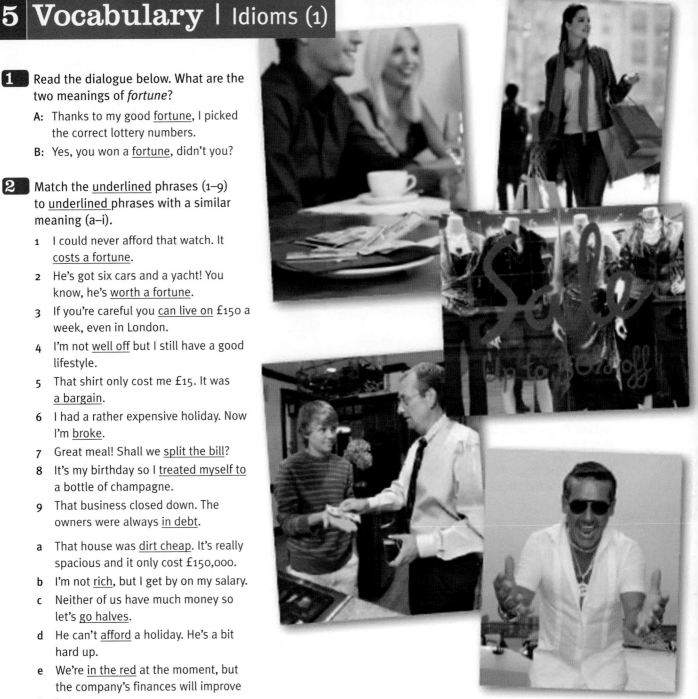

4 Look at the photos above. Which phrases from exercise 2 could you use to describe them?

5 a Work in pairs and discuss the questions.

1 In your home town, how much money does a person need to live on per month?

2 When was the last time you treated yourself to something?

3 What would you splash out on if you suddenly got some money unexpectedly?

4 Do you know anyone who has been in debt or skint? What happened?

5 Where's the best place to look for bargains in your opinion?

6 Which businesses in your home town are worth a fortune?

7 Do you usually go halves when you go out with people? Are there ever any occasions when you don't go halves? What does it depend on?

8 Are most students in your country hard up? Why?

b Compare your answers with other students.

1 **a** ⊙ 1.31 Listen to two people discussing what they would do if their company suddenly had a fortune ($1,000,000) to spend. What ideas do they have?

b How are the speakers' characters different? Listen again and check.

2 **a** Work in small groups. What would you suggest if your company/university/school suddenly had a fortune to spend?

b Compare your ideas with other groups. Which group has the best ideas?

3 Read the profile of Fortune Foods below and answer the questions.

1 What are the company's main strengths?

2 What are the main problems for employees?

4 **a** Work in two groups. Fortune Foods has just received a donation of $2,000,000 from a philanthropic ex-employee! Read the instructions below and decide what the company should do with the money.

1 Group A: you represent the employees. Read the information on page 78.
Group B: you represent the company management. Read the information on page 80.

2 Prepare your arguments and what you would like to negotiate with the other group.

3 Work with the other group and discuss what the company should do. Try to reach a joint decision.

b Discuss the questions with your group.

1 How did the negotiations go?

2 What did you decide to do in the end?

3 Was everyone happy with the decision?

Company Profile

The company: Fortune Foods

Produces: quality food for parties.

Strengths: the company has an excellent reputation and is growing. The clients are rich businesses.

Problems: workers often stay late at night to finish preparing food. They are stressed. The factory is in a part of the city with poor roads and heavy traffic. It is difficult to reach.

Financial Situation: Fortune Foods made a profit last year.

Emphasis

Passive constructions can be used to emphasise information at the beginning of a sentence:
*The suspect **was arrested** by police.*

'What' clauses

You can change the order of a sentence to put a clause at the beginning which would not normally be there:
***What she thinks she's doing**, I don't know!*

Cleft sentences

Sentences introduced with *what* can be used to emphasise different parts of the sentence:
***What annoys me is** her selfishness.*

We can also use introductions with *it is/it was* to emphasise a later part of the sentence:
***It was me** who spotted the mistake.*

Adding words/phrases for emphasis

*She used her **own** ingredients.*
*We were **very** pleased indeed.*
*They aren't **in the least bit** scared.*
*I haven't thought about it **at all**.*
*Some people were **even** asking for discounts.*
*It was **utterly** pointless us being there.*

Conditionals (review)

To talk about something that is always true, use
if + Present Simple + Present Simple:
*If you **go** into business with relatives, it **tends** to put a strain on your relationship.*

To talk about a possible, real situation in the future, use *if* + Present Simple + modal verb:
*If we **find** a bank, we **could change** some money.*

To talk about a hypothetical or unlikely situation in the future, use *if* + Past Simple + modal verb (*would, might, may, could, should*):
*If they **asked** me to go back, I **wouldn't hesitate**.*

To talk about a hypothetical past situation, use
if + Past Perfect + modal verb (*would have, could have, should have, might have*):
*If he **had taken** his phone, I **could've called** him.*

To talk about regrets, use *if only/I wish* + Past Perfect:
*If only I **hadn't told** him about Johnny.*
*I **wish** I'd thought of looking it up on the Internet – it would've saved so much time.*

Mixed conditionals

These may express a hypothetical present result of a past action:
*If we **hadn't answered** the ad, we **wouldn't be** here now.*

Other phrases can be used with, or instead of, *if* in conditional sentences:
provided that, as long as, if only, should you happen to, supposing, if it hadn't been for

Sentence adverbials

These are adverbial phrases which comment on part of a sentence. They can be used to: show the speaker's attitude towards a subject; organise information; rephrase information; change the subject; summarise or generalise information, etc. They are usually separated from the rest of the sentence by a comma.
***Broadly speaking**, we all agree.*

Common adverbials: *fundamentally, essentially, broadly speaking, however, surprisingly enough, seemingly, apparently, up to a point, on the other hand, looking back, with hindsight, believe it or not*

Key vocabulary

Fortunes
come into a fortune   haggle   stock market
high-income   rise   priceless   pay on commission
go bankrupt

Business
launch a company   make a living   recruit
profit-share   hands-on work experience
start-up funds   fringe benefits   publicity
make a profit   break even   bail (something) out

Finance and philanthropy
philanthropy   philanthropist   give (money) to charity
charge interest   invest in (something)
dedicate (billions of dollars) to a cause
make a donation   promote welfare   amass a fortune
put (money) back into (something)

Describing a job
job satisfaction   recognition   perks and benefits
promotion prospects   supportive colleagues/boss
travel opportunities   freedom/autonomy   salary
professional/personal development   pension plan
flexible working hours   convenience of location
working environment   challenging tasks

Expressing quantity
as many as   a little bit more   a great deal of
plenty of   not much of   for the most part
an awful lot of   the vast majority of   quite a few
only a handful of

Idioms (1)
cost a fortune   worth a fortune   live on
well off   bargain   broke   split the bill
treat myself to   in debt   dirt cheap   get by
go halves   hard up   in the red   rolling in it
cost an arm and a leg   splash out on   skint

 Listen to the explanations and vocabulary.
ACTIVEBOOK

 see Writing bank page 85

1 Rewrite the sentences with the correct words in brackets. There may be more than one possible answer.

He was offered the job but he didn't accept. (*surprisingly enough/broadly speaking*)

He was offered the job but <u>surprisingly enough</u>, *he didn't accept.*

1 They explained how the project would be too difficult to manage and I agree. (*on the other hand/to a certain extent*)

2 They didn't know who I was talking about. Georgia left the company years ago. (*Principally/Apparently*)

3 I decided to leave and change careers. I'm not sure that I made the right decision. (*Essentially/With hindsight*)

4 The new arrangements have worked out well. (*By and large/Primarily*)

5 The new minister was faced with an impossible task. (*however/seemingly*)

2 Complete the sentences with the correct clauses (a, b or c). There are two possible answers for each sentence.

1 If he'd planned to give the money back, why ...
   a didn't he contact the police?
   b hadn't he contact the police?
   c would he contact the police?

2 Supposing you lost your job tomorrow, ...
   a what are you going to do?
   b what would you do?
   c you could call me.

3 He can come with us provided that ...
   a he pays for his own meals.
   b he would pay for his accommodation.
   c he doesn't drive the car.

4 If you happen to find my bag,
   a could you call this number?
   b just put it on the side.
   c I'd be really surprised.

5 If it hadn't been for Mary, ...
   a you will still be waiting.
   b we would never have found you.
   c everything would have been fine.

3 Rewrite the sentences to be more emphatic using the words in brackets.

1 We weren't at all surprised to hear that she got the part. (bit)

2 I couldn't believe it when they told me to leave! (what)

3 It was very hot soup. (indeed)

4 I think it is surprisingly warm here. (actually)

5 She makes a lot of her clothes. (own)

6 It is not certain that the game will take place. (means)

7 Rachel complained about the service. (it)

8 They have done nothing to put the problem right. (all)

4 Rewrite the <u>underlined</u> words correctly.

1 Those charity workers are always <u>etsegpirn</u> me for money.

2 Handling the takeover was one of the most <u>glanhingcel</u> tasks of his career.

3 The head of department's duty was to <u>cuexete</u> the strategy.

4 Increasing sales has to be our main <u>trioripy.</u>

5 The job has excellent <u>morotipon</u> prospects.

6 Come on! Let's <u>salhps</u> out on an expensive hotel.

7 I'm sending her some money. She's a bit <u>drah</u> up at the moment.

8 Why don't you <u>retat</u> yourself to something nice?

9 Within a few months of opening, he had declared <u>kracynpbut</u>.

10 He doesn't worry about money. He's <u>ginlorl</u> in it!

5 Complete the text with words from the box.

> vision   charity   mind   remarkable   wealthy
> worth   design   fortune   venture   founded

Anita Roddick, who (1) _____ The Body Shop, kept her promise to give away her entire £51 million (2) _____ to (3) _____ . One of the UK's best-known and most (4) _____ entrepreneurs, she started her business (5) _____ in 1976 with her husband. Their strategy, (6) _____ and excellent product (7) _____ meant that the business, selling body scrubs and ethical beauty products, was a fantastic success. Dame Anita was soon (8) _____ a huge fortune. Later she said she had found business life 'boring' and hoped to achieve peace of (9) _____ by sharing her good fortune with those who had not been so lucky. 'The worst thing is greed,' she once said. 'I do not know why people who are extraordinarily (10) _____ are not more generous. I don't want to die rich. Money doesn't mean anything to me.'

Lesson 1.3 | Ex. 2, page 14

Carlos Acosta ★ a Cuban dream

Dressed anonymously in black trousers and roll-neck, Carlos Acosta sits awkwardly in a red armchair in the interview room of the Royal Opera House. As we shake hands he winks, not confidently, but shyly. But when he starts to speak, although he talks softly, the aura of power seems to grow ...

Carlos Acosta was born in Cuba in 1973. After an incident-filled childhood featuring brushes with crime, he reluctantly took up dancing, at his father's insistence, at the age of ten. His early years were full of ambivalence towards dance as he trained at the National Ballet School of Cuba. Unusually for a great male dancer, his teacher was a woman, Ramona de Saa, who persevered with him. Her training bore fruit and in January 1990 Acosta won the Gold Medal at the Prix de Lausanne. In November 1990 he won the Grand Prix and Gold Medal at the Paris ballet competition. They were to be the first of many competitions and prizes where Acosta attained the highest honours.

Asked about which award meant most to him, he answers unhesitatingly that it was the Prix de Lausanne, his first competition. 'I was the 127th competitor, the last one, entered at the last moment. My greatest hope was to reach the final. I never dreamed of winning. There were a lot of talented people in the competition who I admired.' This was the first time that Acosta realised just how talented he was in world terms. 'I knew that I had something special because in Cuba I would skip class for two months and I was still at the same level as everyone else when I returned, something my teacher commented on many times.' The Lausanne win was tinged with sadness because he couldn't share it with his parents. They were in Cuba and his only means of communication was by letter. 'My family is not of the art world. I tried to explain the importance of the Prix de Lausanne. They were pleased but they didn't really understand.'

It is a poignant irony that Acosta's greatest triumphs as a dancer have still been unwitnessed by his mother and father. Without his father's influence the young Carlos might have been lost to the world of ballet, and might even have been killed in the dangerous milieu of street gangs. 'At the age of ten I was mixing with people who were stealing, and the chances were that I would become a delinquent. My father thought that I might end up shooting somebody. With his eyes on the future he realised that there would be trouble. We lived in a suburb of Havana where it could be pretty rough. I wasn't in a gang. We didn't do drugs. But we didn't go to school either.' Astonishingly, Carlos' father decided to enrol him in the National Ballet School.

'My father had always liked ballet but in his youth, as a black man, he could not practise it. He thought it would be good for me as a career. It would have been nice of him to ask me what I wanted to do' ... (he pulls a comic face) ... 'but thank God he made the right decision. My father was always a strong hand. When the school threw me out, he went there to speak for me. He could have said that he was tired of running around after me and just given up. He could have taken me out of the ballet and put me in a regular school but he just kept pushing me. I did not like the idea of ballet. At the beginning, I didn't even know what it was! Then there was what my friends would say, because there was prejudice that ballet was not for boys. It was embarrassing. I would always rejoin the school with black eyes after fist-fights with boys who teased me. I was treated like the neighbourhood clown. But I was curious about dancing. I was always very physical and did a lot of sport, especially football. But we are all born to do one thing and you can't go against destiny.'

Communication activities

Lesson 4.3 | Ex. 13a, page 58
Student A

The British press has nicknamed him 'mini Monet'. Buyers from all over the world want his work. He has been hailed as a once-in-a-generation artistic prodigy. Meet Kieron Williamson, an eight-year-old with the world in his hands.

It all began when five-year-old Kieron, on a family holiday in Cornwall, UK, asked his parents for pencils and paper. He amazed them by producing an outstanding picture of boats in a harbour. 'We don't know where it comes from,' his mother said later. 'But when your child has got such a gift and a talent, you have to support him.' Kieron soon moved onto depictions of the local landscape in Holt, UK, where they live.

His parents showed his sketches to a local artist, Carol Pennington, who was immediately impressed. She arranged for him to spend an hour a day at her studio, and he blossomed. Soon he was exhibiting his work at local galleries. One exhibition of 33 watercolours sold out in 27 minutes for £150,000.

The work itself has been described as neo-Impressionism: landscapes in pastel colours, huge skies, winding streams. What marks out Kieron's his work is his extraordinary sense of composition, and his mastery of the basics of perspective and colour. He says cows are the easiest things to paint, because 'you don't have to worry about doing so much detail. Horses are harder because you have to get the legs right'.

Despite his gift, Kieron is a normal little boy. He attends school, plays in the football team, and watches TV. He advises aspiring painters: 'Never give up. Try and keep your buildings straight. And don't do a plain blue sky.'

Lesson 3.3 | Ex. 9a, page 44
Student C

A woman goes to a doctor, complaining of pain.
'Where does it hurt?' asks the doctor.
'Everywhere,' says the woman.
'Could you be more specific?'
So the woman touches her knee with her finger.
'Ow!' she says. Then she touches her nose. 'Ow!'
Then she touches her back. 'Ow!' Finally, she touches her cheek. 'Ow!'
The doctor tells her to sit down, takes one look at her, and says, 'You have a broken finger.'

Communication 5 | Ex. 4a, page 74
Group A

You belong to the workers group. You want:

- to build a gym and swimming pool for workers to use at lunch or after work.
- free buses to and from work.
- a free phone in the factory for workers to call home.
- to redecorate the workers' changing rooms.

Which issues are very important, or not so important?

Decide how you will argue for what you want.

Lesson 5.2 | Ex. 2, page 67
Student B

Rags to riches

Sixteen-year-old Zhou Xiaoguang hauled a 50kg bag of trinkets over her shoulder and ascended the steps of the night train. Too poor to pay for a seat, she crouched on the floor for three days and nights, assailed by the stench of the nearby toilets and unable to lie down for lack of room. There she tried – and usually failed – to sell her goods to assorted travellers. It was a humiliating experience, but not the first humiliation she had faced. As a schoolgirl, she was constantly being removed from class because her parents couldn't pay the school fees. Her reluctant entrance into the retail industry was borne of the need to help feed her little brother and five sisters.

Fast forward three decades and multi-millionaire Xiaoguang sits in her own office in Yiwu, Zhejiang Province, China, head of the world's biggest fashion and costume jewellery company. Neoglory, which she founded in the mid-1990s, has nearly 1,000 stores in China alone, employs over 6,000 people, and has a sales force in 70 countries. She has diversified into property holdings, fine wine and other investments, but jewellery is her main business. How did she go from rags to riches?

Her story is a tale of hard work and determination. In the early days, Neoglory was a low-cost manufacturer of cheap bracelets, rings and necklaces. It might have stayed that way if Xiaoguang had not seen the potential of the industry. Gradually she built up the brand by employing professional designers to give the jewellery its own distinct appeal, so that by the mid-2000s, Neoglory was using over 300 designers to produce more than 100 new designs per day. Of her beginnings in the business, she says that she wishes she had not needed 'to become a vendor at such a young age'. But she also acknowledges that if she hadn't experienced those difficult times, she would not have become the extraordinary businessperson that she is today. She still travels all over the world looking for ideas on design, research and investment. It's a safe bet that she doesn't use the night train.

Lesson 2.3 | Ex. 2a, page 28
Student B

Cape Town

The first thing I can tell you about Thabo, my South African guide, is that he is the world's worst driver. From the airport to the heart of the city, he does 100 km per hour, swerving around
5 lorries, motorbikes and taxi-vans crammed with people. The second thing is that he knows everybody and everything about Cape Town. This is good, because I am trying to complete Mission Impossible: see Cape Town in just three days.

10 On the first day, Thabo takes me to the posh areas: suburbs with unpronounceable names – Tamboerskloof and Oranjezicht – from where you can watch the sun go down on Africa. The views are stunning. 'This is all very pretty,' I tell him
15 that evening, 'but show me a community. Show me something the tourists never see.' So the next day, we go off the beaten track to Cape Flats, the run-down township where the buildings are made of cardboard and corrugated iron. It is the poorest
20 part of the city and it is truly vast – nearly a million people live here, side by side. Skinny dogs slide out of the way as Thabo zooms along roads of mud and rotting rubbish. Some people wave, others stare. Children run barefoot by the car.

25 Later that night we walk around the bustling Victoria and Alfred Waterfront, Cape Town's most fashionable area. The contrast from the township could not be greater. As we stroll, the smells of cooking drift up from the kitchens – Asian,
30 French, Italian and of course the wild animals of South Africa that end up on your plate. The bars and restaurants are packed, and I soon find out why. Cape Town is a paradise for gourmets, seafood-lovers and people like me, who just like
35 eating. We go into a charming little bistro, and Thabo tells me I can't leave Cape Town without trying some Cape seafood, so I do. It's delicious.

On my final morning, we spend a tranquil hour sitting outside a café. I gaze at Table Mountain,
40 which forms the backdrop to the city, while Thabo shouts greetings to everyone that passes by. Then we are driving again, experiencing the diverse landscape – sandy beaches, mountain slopes and green valleys unspoilt by tourism. It's
45 a great way to say goodbye to a place I've known only too briefly. I promise myself, and Thabo, that I'll be back.

Lesson 3.3 | Ex. 9a, page 44
Student A

An artist has been displaying his paintings in an art gallery. He asks the gallery owner if anyone has bought his work.

'I have good news and bad news,' says the gallery owner. 'The good news is that a man asked if your work would be worth more after your death. I told him it would and he bought all ten of your painting.'
'That's wonderful,' says the artist. 'What's the bad news?'
'The man was your doctor ...'

Lesson 4.3 | Ex. 13a, page 58
Student B

Nathan Chan has music in his genes. His mother, a classical pianist, and his father, a violinist, took him to concerts when he was a baby. By the age of two, Nathan had begun 'air-conducting'. As seen on many amusing YouTube clips, the little boy would wave his arms around while watching music videos, even splashing water on his face to represent the conductors' sweat. In fact, his mimicry was so accurate and perfectly timed with the rising and falling cadences of the music that it caught the attention of Sara Jobin, assistant conductor at the San Francisco Opera. At the age of three, Chan was invited to conduct the San Jose Chamber Orchestra. That day, they played the works of the most famous musical prodigy of them all: Wolfgang Amadeus Mozart.

A year later, Chan conducted the Palo Alto Philharmonic Orchestra. Then when he was five, his parents decided it was time for him to learn an instrument. He wanted to play the double bass, but as the instrument was about three times bigger than him, he began playing the cello instead.

Since then, Chan has forged a reputation as an outstanding cellist. He has won numerous prizes, played with some of the world's greatest orchestras, recorded CDs, and appeared on several TV programmes about musical prodigies. At the same time, he has managed to maintain a balanced life, attending school, playing badminton and table tennis, and, like teenagers everywhere, enjoying computer games.

Communication activities

Lesson 2.3 | Ex. 2a, page 28
Student C

Corsica

'Day in, day out, they're always watching: the shepherd on the hillside, the road workers resting under the shade of a tree, the old man on the bench in front of his house, his wife airing the
5 sheets at the window, the boules player next to the war memorial. They hardly move their heads but they see everything. It's a survival instinct moulded out of two thousand years of dangers coming from across the sea.'

10 The stereotypical Corsican community is introverted, family-based, dignified and shy. The truth behind the stereotype is that Corsicans love Corsica so much that they don't want the outside world to ruin it. Tradition is important;
15 Corsica is one of the last McDonald's-free zones in Europe. It is also simply stunning; the ancient Greeks called it 'Kalliste', meaning 'the most beautiful one'.

The island is famed for its diverse landscape.
20 You can find magnificent mountains, long stretches of Mediterranean coastline, and thick forest almost side by side, as well as charming villages, perfect for long, slow days in the sun. The island belongs to France but it has an
25 atmosphere all of its own.

A good place to start is Ajaccio. In this charming town, you can sit outside the cafés and watch fishermen mending their nets, or stroll in the bustling market which sells delicious seafood and
30 Corsican specialities: macchia honey and brocciu cheese. Old run-down houses stand proud on the side of the hill, overlooking modern yachts and wooden boats. Stroll along the streets and you will notice something interesting as you gaze at
35 the monuments, the street signs and restaurant names: the town stands in the vast shadow of its greatest son, Napoleon Bonaparte. His influence is everywhere, and in the Musée Napoléonien you can see his baptism certificate and his death mask.

40 Although Napoleon is at the heart of Corsican history, it is Corsica's natural beauty that you'll remember. Fishermen, surfers, sailors and hikers all find everything they need here. And for the less energetic, there is always the pleasure of a wander
45 along some of Europe's most tranquil scenery. Despite the tourists, the island is unspoilt. You won't find any packed nightclubs here, but there are plenty of cosy bars off the beaten track, where you can taste the atmosphere of Europe's own
50 natural paradise.

Lesson 3.3 | Ex. 9a, page 44
Student B

The Queen is on a trip abroad when she decides that she wants to drive. The chauffeur gets into the back of the car and the Queen gets into the front and starts driving. She goes too fast and a police officer stops the car. One minute later, the police officer calls headquarters.

'I can't make an arrest,' he says. 'This person is too important.'

'Who is it?' asks the police chief. 'The mayor?'

'No. Someone more important.'

'The governor?'

'More important.'

'The President?'

'No. More important.'

'Who can possibly be more important than the President?' asks the Chief.

'I don't know, Chief, but he has the Queen as his chauffeur.'

Communication 5 | Ex. 4a, page 74
Group B

You represent the management. You want:

• to build a new café with better food. The workers want a gym and swimming pool. You think the café is more important. You can't build both.

• to arrange buses for employees to come to work, but the employees should buy a subsidised (cheaper) ticket every day.

• to install some modern art in the reception area. This is to impress visitors.

The workers also want a free telephone in the factory. You are worried about the cost of phone bills.

Which issues are very important, or not so important?

Decide how you will argue for what you want.

1 | A leaflet or brochure

Can do write a promotional leaflet

1 Read the leaflet and answer the questions.

1 What is the leaflet advertising?
2 When and where can you study?
3 How old is the company?
4 Who are the teachers?

2 **a** Which of the following doesn't a leaflet usually do?

a advertise a place, event, product or service
b provide information about 'what', 'where' and 'when'
c give the company's background in brief
d explain how to get more information
e discuss the latest trends in the field

b Read the leaflet again. Which parts of the leaflet match the points in exercise 2a?

3 Read the How to... box and find more examples in the leaflet.

How to... write a promotional leaflet/promote something

Use a clear layout with subheadings for the key points	*Language and Culture courses*
Write clearly and concisely and use lists	*LinguaLife offers language and culture courses all over Europe.*
Use positive language	*leading provider* / *highest quality*
Include a slogan	*Courses that change your life!*
Include recommendations/ testimonials	*The market leader in language courses*
Give reasons why the product/service/event is special	*We have been delivering programmes ... for over 20 years.*
Include contact details	*Tel: 0207 7816653*

4 **a** Think of a course or event for the public – it can be real or imaginary. Make notes about the 'what', 'where' and 'when'. Then write a leaflet for the course or event, with language from the How to... box.

b Work in pairs. Take turns to read each other's leaflets. Does the leaflet make you interested in the course or event? Why/Why not?

LinguaLife

Courses that change your life!

About us

LinguaLife is the leading provider of language and culture courses in Europe. We have been delivering programmes of the highest quality for over 20 years. Based in London, UK, we have branches in 18 major cities in Europe.

Language and Culture courses

LinguaLife offers language and culture courses all over Europe. You can learn Italian language and culture in Rome, Spanish language and culture in Madrid, Russian language and culture in Moscow, and many more.

Courses include: language lessons for all levels of proficiency from Basic to Advanced; lectures on art, architecture, literature and customs; cooking demonstrations; field trips to museums and places of historical interest; concerts and theatre performances.

Dates

Courses begin on the first Monday of each month.

Staff

Our outstanding staff consists of a group of dedicated teachers, lecturers and historians, all of whom are accredited, with an average of 15 years' experience in the classroom.

Prices

For a full list of our prices, please visit our website LinguaLifeLondon.com.

What they say about us

"*The market leader in language courses*" Education Weekly Inc.
"*An excellent service to students all over Europe*" Learning Solutions magazine
"*Simply the best value for money in language and culture courses*" NGD Journal

Contact

Tel: 0207 7816653 **or email:** languageculture@LL.org
Website: LinguaLifeLondon.com

2 A formal email

1 Read the emails and answer the questions.

1 Why is Demetri Leopoulos writing? Who is he?

2 What two things does he need from Ms. Foong?

3 What information does Ms. Foong provide in the body of the email? What does she send in an attachment?

4 What is Ms. Foong's official position in her company?

2 Match informal expressions 1–6 to formal expressions in the emails.

1 I'm happy to tell you

2 We want you to come to

3 Can you tell us ...?

4 to go in the ...

5 We'd love to come

6 you asked for

3 Complete the How to... box with words from the box. Which phrases are not included in the emails?

> take   grateful   accept   pleased   find

How to... write a formal email

Giving good/ bad news	I am (1) _____ to inform you that ... I regret to inform you that ...
Inviting	We would like to invite you to ... You are formally invited to ...
Responding to an invitation	We are happy to (2) _____ your kind invitation. I am afraid I am unable to attend.
Making a request	We would be (3) _____ if you could ... Would you (also) be able to ...
Responding to a request	Please (4) _____ attached the document you requested. We would be happy to (send the document that you requested). I am afraid we are unable to (forward the document that you requested).
Including additional information	The event will (5) _____ place ... The venue is located ...

4 **a** Write an email inviting your partner to a formal occasion. It could be a dinner party, a conference, etc. Include an additional request (to make a speech, bring or send something) and additional information (how to get there or where to stay). Use language from the How to... box.

b Exchange emails with your partner.

c Write your response.

d Exchange emails with your partner and read their reply. Which formal expressions have they used?

Dear Ms Foong,

I am pleased to inform you that your company has been shortlisted for Website of the Year by WIA. We would like to invite you to attend the awards ceremony. The event will take place at Turpiric House, 136 Curtain Road, London EC2A 3AR on 4 August at 7 p.m. The venue is located a short taxi ride from Old Street tube station. This year the evening will consist of a formal dinner and entertainment before the official ceremony.

We would be grateful if you could let us know by 4 July how many of your team will be attending. WIA can host up to four people from each shortlisted company. Would you also be able to send a 150-word history of your company for inclusion in the programme?

We look forward to hearing from you.

Yours sincerely,

Demetri Leopoulos

Head of Judging Panel

Web Innovations Awards

Dear Mr Leopoulos,

Thank you for this great news. We are happy to accept your kind invitation. We will bring four members of our team to the awards ceremony: myself, Aisha Holder, Praveen Shastri and Kathleen Smith.

Please find attached the document you requested. If there is anything else you need from us, please don't hesitate to ask.

We look forward to seeing you on 4 August.

Regards,

Sze Foong, M.A.
CEO, magnumlove.com

3 | A story

Can do | write a detailed narrative

1 Look at the photo and the title of the story. Where do you think the story is set? What might happen?

2 Read the story and answer the questions.

1 How old do you think the narrator is?

2 Who do you think 'the man from the sky' is? Where might he really be from?

3 What can we guess about the narrator's character from his actions?

3 Complete the How to... box with the words/ sentences from the box below.

> lush grass   "Back to the sky"
> spewing orange flames
> His hands were the size of Yorkshire hams

How to... write fiction with style

Use metaphors (describing something by referring to it as something different)	*He was a giant.* *Darkness began to fall.*
Use similes (comparisons that often use *like* or *as* + adjective + *as*)	*He had a jaw like a bucket.*
Use personification (describing an inanimate object as if it were human)	*the plane's outstretched arms*
Use adjectives	*dazed cows*
Use dialogue	*"I need water," he said.*
Use a variety of sentence lengths	*I looked around. From the hill you could see fields and cows and clumps of trees and the box-like buildings of the farm.*

4 **a** Prepare to write a short story. Choose one of the titles below or write a story you already know. Make an outline of the story.

- A Family Tale
- A Dream Come True
- The Secret
- 24 Hours

b Write your story. Include the techniques in the How to... box.

c Work in small groups. Take turns to read each other's stories.

1943: The Man from the Sky

I would never forget him: the smell of his burned-out plane, the colour of his eyes, the way the apple disappeared in his hand. Pilots, along with everything else, seem smaller these days.

A trail of black smoke cut through the clouds. The plane was burning as it dropped. We saw it land roughly and bounce over Mowbray Hill. Then we chased it, me, Ronald, Arthur and Sue, haring across the green fields while the dazed cows barely turned their heads. Arthur, six years old and the youngest of us, tripped in the lush grass, but we kept going.

There, over the hill, the plane had stopped, spewing orange flames, its outstretched arms askew. Suddenly, from out of the wreckage, a man was running towards us. We scattered, but he followed me and, limping, soon caught up.

"Hello," he called after me.

I stopped and turned. He was a giant. His hands were the size of Yorkshire hams and he had a jaw like the bucket we used for milking cows. There were goggles on top of his head attached to a leather cap that matched his jacket. And beneath the cap, from the murk of his face blackened with soot and grime, his eyes shone, the same blue as the sky he came from.

"I need water," he said.

He had a strange accent, one that I had never heard before.

"I'll get some."

"Wait."

He took me by the arm. I saw that his trousers were wet with blood.

"What's your name?"

"John," I said.

He pulled off the cap and wiped his brow with the back of his hand.

"John, don't tell anyone I'm here. OK?"

"OK. We have a barn. Come with me."

We walked across the field, then across the cobbled stones. No one saw us. I pointed out a bed of straw in the barn and he lay down. I brought him water and he drank it in one gulp. I went back and brought him more and stole a hunk of bread and cheese and an apple from the pantry, which he ate in silence. As darkness began to fall, I said I had to go but I would bring him breakfast the following day.

I told no one about the man. There was no one to tell because my mother had gone to bed and my father and brothers had joined some of the other villagers wandering the fields with guns and pitchforks. They had congregated around the parched and blackened plane and, from there, gone in different directions, in pairs, some with lanterns, to search the gloom for the missing pilot.

I lay awake most of the night, thinking about the man from the sky. In the morning, I brought bread and milk to the barn, but he was gone. There was an indentation where he had slept, and a stain of dark blood on the straw. First I waited. Then I walked every inch of the farm, clambering over the locked gates. I went back to Mowbray Hill and skirted the remains of his wrecked plane. Suddenly I heard a voice.

"Where is he?"

It was six-year-old Arthur climbing over the hill.

"Gone," I replied.

"Gone where?"

I looked around. From the hill you could see fields and cows and clumps of trees and the box-like buildings of the farm.

"Back to the sky," I said, and tore off a hunk of the bread in my hand.

Progress in our classrooms

If you could transport yourself back 100 years to a classroom in a British school, you would see the teacher standing at a raised blackboard, a piece of chalk in hand. He or she is lecturing and writing down large swathes of information, which the children faithfully copy onto a piece of slate. Later the children go home and memorise this information. The next day they come back to school and do it all over again. They rarely talk in class except to answer the teacher's questions, barely move a muscle, and never work in groups.

The first half of the 20th century saw the opening up of numerous new fields of understanding, among them psychology and anthropology, which led to more progressive methods in education. Educators realised that children do not necessarily learn best by copying and memorising. The development of 'hands-on' experiential learning meant that children would benefit not just from reading about how a butterfly flaps its wings but from actually seeing one; not just from reading engineering texts but from watching a bridge being built; not just from learning the rules of foreign languages but from actually trying to use them.

In time, other developments occurred. The desks were unbolted from the floor so students could move around and work in groups. Collaborative learning was born. Blackboards changed colour. They were now whiteboards, and chalk went out of fashion, much to the delight of teachers: they would no longer go home wearing clothes covered in white smudges.

Gradually, new technologies such as the cassette recorder, the video and the computer made their way into classrooms. Then, at the beginning of the 21st century, smartboards arrived. These provide access to the Internet, save everything the class has written on them, and allow users to do all sorts of things such as drag images and words around the screen. Then a hand-held device called a clicker arrived, allowing each student to answer questions in private, their answers seen only by the teacher.

So, what if we could transport ourselves 100 years into the future? What would we find in classrooms? There have been many predictions, some based on ideas that come straight out of science-fiction (brain implants, knowledge pills). Others sound less far-fetched. A few select language schools in Korea are already experimenting with robots that can teach languages. And one day smart classrooms that can track the brain movements of individual students and send messages to teachers may also become reality.

1 Look at the photo and the title of the article. What type of progress do you think it will discuss?

2 Read the article and answer the questions.

1 According to the writer, how did children learn in British classrooms 100 years ago?
2 What 21st-century technologies are mentioned?
3 What innovations does the writer think might one day become normal in children's classrooms?

3 Read the advice in the How to... box. Add more examples from the article.

How to... develop a writing style for articles

Begin by capturing the reader's attention	*If you could transport yourself back one hundred years to a classroom in a British school, you would see the teacher standing at a raised blackboard ...*
Use the present tense for an effect of immediacy	*Later the children go home and memorise this information.*
Use the active voice for more powerful sentences	*The first half of the 20th century saw the opening up of numerous new fields of understanding*
Use lists of three (for rhythm and flow) when giving examples	*They rarely talk in class ..., barely move a muscle, and never work in groups.* *... new technologies such as the cassette recorder, the video, and the computer ...*
Avoid repetition by using pronouns and reference words	*... children would benefit not just from reading about how a butterfly flaps **its** wings but from actually seeing **one*** *There have been many predictions, **some** based on ideas that come straight out of science-fiction ... **Others** sound less far-fetched.*
Use questions to involve the reader	*So, what if we could transport ourselves 100 years into the future?*
Close the article by echoing the beginning	*If you could transport yourself back 100 years ...*

4 **a** Think about how your profession, hobby or field of study has progressed in the past and might progress in the future. Plan an article for non-experts in your field.

b Now write your article.

5 | Persuasive essay

Can do write a persuasive piece

Democratic Companies: The Next Step

The people who make our shoes never wear them. Workers in sweatshops would need to save up for a year to afford a pair of $150 trainers. Imagine, then, a world in which workers maintained control of the product. Instead of seeing the results of their labour packaged and sent away to the wealthy West, the shoes would be in their hands or, rather, on their feet. The key question is this: would the world's economic system collapse if the workers became the owners?

The answer, if we look at numerous examples, is no. Worker-owned companies consistently outperform traditionally run businesses. The reason is simple: worker-owners care more. Working for themselves and for each other in small dedicated teams, they feel a sense of responsibility to their colleagues. They identify with the company and they invest more of themselves in it. One example of this is women's cooperative 'We Can Do It!' The New York house-cleaning company is owned by the immigrants who work for it, and they have an equal vote in all decisions. What's more, the company is thriving.

Perhaps the biggest argument for worker-owned companies is that they are a talent magnet. Bright, creative people want to work as equals with other bright, creative people. Generally, they are not motivated by power, but rather by achievement. And, as we all know, happy employees work more effectively than those sulking in the shadows of giant top-down organisations.

Some might say worker-ownership is a recipe for chaos. For instance, wouldn't many employees do less for the company while living off the hard work of others? Again the answer is no. The fact is that peer pressure ensures that everyone pulls their weight. Those who, at first, don't understand this generally learn it quickly or get kicked out.

So, business owners, what can you do? The first thing is to ditch the big office. Then flatten the hierarchy. Then tell everyone they are working as equals in pay, status and responsibility. Then watch your company grow.

1 Read the persuasive essay. Do you agree with the writer?

2 Look at one possible structure for an opinion essay. Does the example follow this structure?

  1 **introduction:** announces the topic (problem), prepares the reader for the argument (solution)

  2 **body (a):** gives context and evidence (anecdotes, statistics, quotes, etc.)

  3 **body (b):** gives additional arguments

  4 **body (c):** acknowledges opposing views and points out weaknesses in them

  5 **conclusion:** ends with a call to action

3 **a** Read the How to… box. Tick the expressions used in the essay.

How to… write persuasively

State your position	*I will here argue that …, the key question is …, in essence, … the fact is …*
give examples or use lists to illustrate a point	*for example, …; one example of this is …*
anticipate counter-arguments	*some might say… , the counter-argument is…, it has been argued that … (but …)*
use hedging devices (cautious language to sound less direct)	*perhaps, it can be argued, apparently, tend to, may/might/could, generally*

b Add the phrases from the box below to the How to… box.

> arguably,   for instance, …
> the main point is that …   to a certain extent,
> a common misconception is …
> the fundamental issue is …
> it has been put forward that … (but …)

4 **a** Prepare to write a persuasive essay on an aspect of work or student life. Decide on a problem that has affected you, and think of a possible solution (see below for ideas). Think about how you will persuade others to agree. Make notes.

The cost of higher education → it should be paid for by the government.

The work environment is noisy and uncomfortable → employees should be allowed to work from home three days a week.

b Now write your essay.

Pronunciation bank

English phonemes

Consonants

p	b	t	d	k	g	tʃ	dʒ
park	bath	tie	die	cat	give	church	judge
f	v	θ	ð	s	z	ʃ	ʒ
few	visit	throw	they	sell	zoo	fresh	measure
h	m	n	ŋ	l	r	j	w
hot	mine	not	sing	lot	road	yellow	warm

Vowels and diphthongs

iː	ɪ	e	æ	ɑː	ɒ	ɔː	ʊ	uː	ʌ
feet	fit	bed	bad	bath	bottle	bought	book	boot	but
ɜː	ə	eɪ	əʊ	aɪ	aʊ	ɔɪ	ɪə	eə	ʊə
bird	brother	grey	gold	by	brown	boy	here	hair	tour

Sound–spelling correspondences

Sound	Spelling	Examples
/ɪ/	i y ui e	this listen gym typical build guitar pretty
/iː/	ee ie ea e ey ei i	green sleep niece believe read teacher these complete key money receipt receive police
/æ/	a	can pasta
/ɑː/	a ar al au ea	can't dance* scarf bargain half aunt laugh heart
/ʌ/	u o ou	fun husband some mother cousin double
/ɒ/	o a	hot pocket watch want

Sound	Spelling	Examples
/ɔː/	or ou au al aw ar oo	short sport your bought daughter taught small always draw jigsaw warden warm floor indoor
/aɪ/	i y ie igh ei ey uy	like time dry cycle fries tie light high height eyes buy
/eɪ/	a ai ay ey ei ea	lake hate wait train play say they grey eight weight break
/əʊ/	o ow oa ol	home open show own coat road cold told

Weak forms

Word	Strong form	Weak form
a, an	/æ/, /æn/	/ə/, /ən/
at	/æt/	/ət/
and	/ænd/	/ən/
are	/ɑː/	/ə/ (or /ər/ before vowels)
been	/biːn/	/bɪn/
can	/kæn/	/kən/
do	/duː/	/də/
does	/dʌz/	/dəz/
has	/hæz/	/həz/, /əz/
have	/hæv/	/həv/, /əv/
than	/ðæn/	/ðən/
them	/ðem/	/ðəm/
to	/tuː/	/tə/ (before consonants)
was	/wɒz/	/wəz/

* In American English the sound in words like *can't* and *dance* is the shorter /æ/ sound, like *can* and *man*.

Stress

Stressed and unstressed words (units 1 and 4)

We usually stress the words which carry the main meaning of a sentence. These are content words (usually nouns and verbs). We are less likely to stress other words which are less essential to the meaning (for example, auxiliary verbs and prepositions).

The President arrived in Turkey today.

After the game, the manager blasted his players for their attitude.

When we use inversion, we usually stress the adverbial phrase. We do not usually stress auxiliary verbs or pronouns.

No way would I do that!

Rarely do I come late.

Emphasis (unit 5)

We can add emphasis to sentences by adding certain words (*own*, *very*, *actually*, etc.). These words are usually stressed. When we emphasise, our intonation usually rises.

I actually have my own car.

We can also add auxiliary verbs (*do*, *did*, etc.) for emphasis, which are also stressed.

You're wrong. I did see her cheating!

When we use cleft sentences, we usually emphasise different parts of the sentence.

It's David that I'm talking to, not Ben.

Connected speech

Speech units (unit 3)

When we talk for a long time, we usually divide our speech into logical parts. Between each part, we pause slightly to make it easier for the listener to follow what we're saying. The pauses have a similar function to punctuation and often occur: at the end of a sentence; between clauses linked by and, but or because; and before and after a phrase which adds extra information.

Now John told me // and I don't know if it's true // that Mary broke up with Steve, // which would amaze me. // Those two // if I'm not mistaken // are completely in love!

Contractions (units 3 and 5)

When two words make a common verb form (e.g. *I am*, *do not*, *would have*), we often contract the words so that they are pronounced as one word (*I'm*, *don't*, *would've*).

He's always saying he would've been the best if he'd had the chance

auxiliary verb *have* (unit 4)

Auxiliary verbs, modal verbs, prepositions and articles are often pronounced with a weak form.

Where have you been?

    /həv/

Audioscripts

Track 1.02

M=Mark, I=Interviewer

I: Mark, you speak seven languages.

M: That's right.

I: Can you tell us a little about your level of fluency and proficiency in the languages?

M: Well, Russian is probably my best language. I speak it pretty well because I spent a lot of time in the country, but it's a little rusty. I have quite a good ear, which is a good thing and a bad thing because my accent suggests that I know more than I really do! The other languages are mainly Latin-based: Spanish, Portuguese, Italian, but also French and Polish.

I: You learned the languages through a combination of techniques.

M: That's right. In different ways, like going to classes, travel, private study …

I: Did you use any special techniques? Any magic secrets?

M: Magic secrets, no! But I did do some interesting things, like memory training. I watched films in their original language and at some point I tried sticking lists of words around the house. But I think, with me, it was more a case of being motivated, and the biggest motivator was a love of languages and pleasure in communicating with people from other countries.

I: Would you say it's easier to learn new languages if you already know languages in that family? For example, you speak Spanish and French, so maybe it was fairly easy to pick up Portuguese.

M: I wouldn't say it was easy, but yeah, I would definitely say it's a help, although occasionally it gets confusing. You might be speaking in one language and suddenly a word from another language slips out, causing complete confusion.

I: Is there any little word of encouragement you could offer those poor souls who are trying to master a language?

M: Er … that's a tricky one. What I would say is that knowing how to read and write a language doesn't mean you can speak it. You really have to get out there and try to speak at every opportunity. Take risks. Don't be afraid to look stupid, because that's the only way you're going to learn. And you know, everyone has to start somewhere. As a young man, I went to France after years of studying French to degree level, and, to my complete embarrassment, I couldn't speak the language or understand anything. All I could do was order breakfast in my hotel!

Track 1.03

P=Presenter

P: To continue our series on famous firsts … If you ask a Brazilian who first flew an aeroplane, she'll tell you it was Alberto Santos Dumont. Ask an American and he'll answer the Wright brothers. In 1906, Santos Dumont was widely believed to have flown the first plane that was heavier than air. Others say that the Americans Wilbur and Orville Wright first flew in 1903. The truth is, we don't really know who flew first, but Santos Dumont was certainly a colourful character. He's said to be the first person to have owned a flying machine for personal use. He kept his balloon tied up outside his Paris flat and regularly flew to restaurants! Our second question … It's commonly assumed that Alexander Graham Bell invented the telephone, but now we're not so sure. Many people believe that Antonio Meucci, an Italian immigrant, got there first. And in 2003, files were discovered which suggest that a 26-year-old German science teacher, Philipp Reis, had invented the phone 15 years before Bell.

Now, who was the first to the North Pole? In 1908, Dr Frederick Cook said he'd done it, but it's commonly believed that he lied, and that a man called Robert Peary made it first. There are others who claim that neither of them reached the North Pole. The light bulb. It's widely asserted that Edison invented it, but we don't really know for sure. Edison based a lot of his inventions on other people's ideas. Also, he worked with a team, and he never shared the credit.

Moving on to our football question, it's widely assumed that South America's football glory belongs to Brazil and Argentina … but it was Uruguay that hosted and won the first World Cup in 1930. They beat Argentina 4–2 in the final in front of 93,000 people in Montevideo. The cheering of the crowd is said to have been the loudest noise ever heard in Uruguay.

Talking of sport, it is often thought that rugby and sheep are the main claims to fame for New Zealand. Not many people know that in 1893, New Zealand became the first country to allow women to vote. Now, talking of empowering women, one woman who has empowered herself is Ellen MacArthur. MacArthur is sometimes wrongly assumed to be the first woman to sail around the world. She wasn't. She was the fastest but not the first. That honour goes to another Englishwoman, Naomi James, who did it in 1979. Apparently, she got so seasick that soon afterwards she gave up sailing altogether. And our final question. The Ancient Olympic Games were of course first held in Greece. They were quite different from the Games today. Instead of money, the winners received a crown of leaves. They were also said to be allowed to put their statue up on Olympus.

Track 1.04

N=Newsreader

N: The headlines this lunchtime are …

A conservation institute in the United States has produced wild kittens by cross-breeding cloned adult cats. It is believed to be the first time that clones of wild animals have been bred. Researchers at the Audubon Centre for Research of Endangered Species say that the development holds enormous potential for the preservation of endangered species.

An American millionaire has succeeded in his long-held ambition to circumnavigate the world in a balloon. Fifty-eight-year-old Steve Fossett had already made five attempts on the record, but was frequently beaten back by the weather. In 1997 he was forced to land in Russia, in 1998 it was Australia, and in 2001 he found himself crash-landing on a cattle ranch in Brazil.

And finally, the story of a man who has entered the record books as the world's most renowned eater of burgers. It is estimated that Don Gorske has eaten over 15,000 Big Macs, and he even proposed to his girlfriend Mary in the car park of a McDonald's. In 15 years, he says, he has missed a Big Mac on only seven occasions, including the death of his mother, a snowstorm and a 600-mile drive without a McDonald's in sight.

Track 1.06

1

When I was at school, a friend of mine was injured in an accident while playing rugby. He was paralysed and needed to spend the rest of his life in a wheelchair. Together with some friends we decided to organise a sponsored bike ride to raise money for his family, and other people in a similar situation. So we set up a charity called 'One Step Ahead' and arranged to cycle from Scotland to Gibraltar. I'd never done anything like that before, so it was a fantastic learning experience. I'd always thought it would be great to cycle across a whole country, but this exceeded my expectations. There were about 20 or 30 of us on bikes, and the rest of the crew in vans with all the equipment, and camping gear. It was very tough cycling, especially in Spain where we had to battle against the heat. But we had a fantastic time, and at the end, when we arrived, there was a huge party for us, and the media came and took photos. We were even on the news! We felt we'd accomplished something quite important, and we raised lots of money for people with spinal injury too.

2

I've been doing volunteer work here in the rain forest, in Brazil, for a while now. Next week I'll have been here for three months, helping to teach English to the young children in the village. It's been an amazing experience, because I'd never even left Europe before, so you can imagine how different things are here. When I arrived, I really didn't know what to expect. It was a real culture shock, and I was here on my own for the first couple of months. Now my girlfriend has come out to join me, and things are a bit easier. I've been living with a small tribe of people right out in the forest, and I'd never done any teaching before either, so the whole thing has been quite a challenge, and I've learnt a lot. But some of the children are speaking quite good English with me now, and a few of them are starting to write little stories too, so I feel it's been quite an achievement.

3

I've run a marathon. In fact, I'm planning to run it again this year. I did it last year for the first time and it was great. It felt like a major achievement. I had to train really hard, getting up early in the morning to run before going to work. And as the distances got longer I had to get up earlier and earlier. And it was incredibly hard because I'd never done any training like that before. I've always run, but just for myself, to relax and to keep fit, but this was a chance to be more competitive, and really push myself to the limit. It is a fantastic run, because London is a beautiful city, and there's such a good atmosphere as you go along the route, with people cheering you on. My parents even came over from New Zealand to see me arrive at the finish. I couldn't move for about a week afterwards last time, but I was glad I'd done it and I'm looking forward to the next one.

Track 1.08

E=Expert

E: If you ticked mainly 'a', then you seem to be very comfortable as you are and you're not too keen on new challenges. I think you need to make an effort to get off the sofa. Go on! Take a risk – it might have a positive effect!

Now, if your answers were mainly 'b', it means you love a challenge and you take advantage of your opportunities. You seem willing to have a go at anything and everything. So, good luck, but be careful! Those of you who ticked mainly 'c', well, you obviously make a habit of checking everything before committing yourself. You are super-cautious. Well, you may live a long, safe life, but a bit of a challenge from time to time won't do you any harm!

Track 1.09

1

I'm from South Africa. I spent two and a half years, actually more like two years, living in Vancouver, Canada. Er … my wife and I were trying to set up our own business there as packagers in the publishing industry. Unfortunately, things were not going very well economically. Canada wasn't in a depression, but it was just not a very good time to try and start your own business in publishing. What did I like about Vancouver? Well, Vancouver is one of the most beautiful cities in the world. In fact, Vancouver is regularly named as the best place in the world to live. Stunningly beautiful because of mountains, sea, forests and natural beauty and for me, combined with a large city. Vancouver is a city where you can walk to the beach. Vancouver is a city where the beaches are right in the city and you can go to the beach for your lunch break. You can take a bus and go skiing in the mountains 40 minutes later. Canadian food, of course, is not at the top of the world's list of good food, but Vancouver has got a very large Chinese population, Indian population, and of course as the rest of Canada, people from all over the world, so you can eat extraordinarily good food in Vancouver. Erm … the only food that people might consider uniquely Vancouverite is what they would call 'fusion' cuisine, which is food prepared by chefs that mix their diverse background from Asia or Europe and integrate it with the local foods and in fact you can have a very good meal that way. My best memories about Canada? Well, the open spaces, the vastness and the friendly people as well.

2

I'm from Belfast originally, but over the past ten years I've been living, erm, I've lived in Spain, Austria, France and other parts of the UK. Erm, I lived in Austria for a year when I was about 22, 23. It was a gap year from university. Er, I was studying German so I wanted to spend a year there. I was a teaching assistant there. I worked in a school four days a week, so it was really great because it meant I had long weekends. Erm, I usually went travelling with my friends at the weekends. Erm, we went to Slovenia, Prague, Italy, Germany and the best thing was I pretended I was 15 so that I could get some rail discount. I got half-price train tickets which was excellent. Erm, the other great things about living there was obviously skiing and ice skating on lakes, which you can't do in Northern Ireland. Erm, obviously the scenery is beautiful. The people were lovely. The thing I didn't really like was the food, because I'm vegetarian and in Austria they tend to eat a lot of meat, but apart from that everything else was great. Erm, I think my favourite memories of Austria are the scenery, being able to go off into the mountain after school every afternoon, and go skiing or swimming in the lakes in the summer, and I'd definitely like to go back one day.

3

When I lived in Japan, actually in Tokyo, for about two years – this was about two years ago now – erm, it was, as you can imagine, a completely crazy experience for me, coming from Oxford which is a very, you know, small, provincial, very quiet kind of town. Er, I was living in Tokyo because I was working as an English-language teacher for a really tiny language school run by this lovely, lovely old lady erm, in a suburb of Tokyo. Erm, I thoroughly enjoyed Tokyo. It was such an interesting experience. It was like being, you know, dropped in the middle of a lifestyle that was completely different to my own. Erm, even going to the supermarket was a massive adventure because of course I couldn't read anything because the writing system's so different, so I'd sort of pick up a tin and think, 'Ooh that looks interesting, I'll take that take that home and, you know, I'll see what comes out' and got a few surprises of course, a few unidentifiable foods that I'd never seen before, but that's always a good thing. Erm … I think my favourite memories of the country would have to be the people. Because I was teaching English, I knew a lot of Japanese people as students, as colleagues in the school and so on, and I just found them so lovely. They were friendly, funny, really interested in what a foreigner like me was doing in Tokyo and very keen to, you know, share experiences of travelling abroad and to … to tell me all about the social customs in Japan and things like that. So it was a, it was a really rewarding experience, absolutely great.

Track 1.10

W=Woman, M=Man

M: It's made such a big difference to me. I mean, communication is miles easier than it was before. Do you remember the days when we had to go through all that hassle of writing letters?

W: Sure, I'd agree with that. But I'd still say that face-to-face communication is better. Sending an email is nowhere near as personal and meaningful as a conversation.

M: Well, it depends, doesn't it?

W: On what?

M: OK, an email is nothing like as good as seeing someone you love, or your friends or something, but I can tell you this much: rather than going to see my clients every day, or nattering on the phone, I'm much better off sending them an email. It saves time.

W: Yeah, I see what you're getting at, but I just think, the more we use email, the more we need it. It's like an addiction, with people checking their emails every five minutes even in meetings.

M: Fair enough. But I'd still rather have it than not.

W: And, well, the internet in general, there's so much rubbish on there. Do you use it to do research?

M: All the time. I think it's OK. Maybe it's not quite as good as looking in books. Well, it's not as reliable, though it's considerably faster.

W: I'd say that looking up something on the internet is marginally less reliable than shouting out of the window, 'Does anybody know the answer to this?' It's not regulated, is it? Anyone can publish anything on the internet and it may or may not be true.

M: Much the best thing about the internet is that it lets you do things more cheaply than before, like buying holidays, buying stuff on ebay.

W: I've never used eBay.

M: Or Amazon. You can get loads of cheap books.

W: Yeah, but I'd sooner go to a second-hand bookshop. I'm not into the idea of giving my bank details over the internet. No way.

M: There're lots of security measures these days …

Track 1.11

1

Erm, I'm a member of an old boys' club, erm, which is basically when when you leave school you keep in touch with your old friends and every five or ten years you have a reunion and you get together and party and remember the old days, erm … some good, some bad, obviously. Erm, we also get involved in quite a few charity events in the area where I'm from, erm … and recently we actually did some charity events to save the school that I was at, which was going to be closed. So that was something we did specially. I did it, I didn't join straight after school. Erm, I went abroad for a few years, and I found out about it through a website, er, called Friends Reunited, where you can find where your old friends are and your old school is. That was great. We probably only meet once every two years as a group. Erm, we have a big party and get to meet all the people that we remember, and some of the teachers as well, er, which is fun. What's really interesting about the group is that we've now all known each other for about 20 years, and it's so interesting to meet people every two years and see how they've changed. I'm sure that if I met some of those people in the street now after 20 years, I wouldn't recognise them, and in, in a bad sort of way, I suppose, it's, you like to measure yourself against your friends, where they've got to and how have you done in comparison. Erm, If there's something I don't like, it's that, er … it's very difficult to keep in touch when you are not meeting so regularly. Erm, and you do rely on other people to run the club and sometimes people aren't as involved as they should be, sometimes you don't hear anything for a year or two, so it is quite difficult to do. But I will definitely stick with it, because it is great to meet people and remember some of the good days.

2

Well, I'm a member of a … of a kind of society, I suppose. It's a ballroom-dancing club. Erm, it's kind of lessons, but it's also social as well. There's about … oh I suppose … it must be about 30 people in the club, and I think I'm quite unusual because I think I'm the youngest there. Erm, I go with a friend of mine, who's … who's my partner in the dancing. Erm, it's great fun, really great fun. It's kind of fun being the youngest there as well because everyone else is retired and they think we're very cool and exotic for being young. Erm, I joined about I suppose six months ago now, erm, because I just fancied giving ballroom dancing a go. I've never been terribly coordinated as a dancer and I'm not very good with choreography, but it's been absolutely great. I mean, there's quite a lot of beginners in the class so you never really feel like you know you're stuck out in the middle of all these wonderful advanced dancers. Erm, we meet once a week and sometimes we meet in a school hall, in a local suburb near to where I live. Erm, we meet in the evenings after work and sometimes it can be quite hard to get yourself out of the house again ready to do some exercise and some dancing, but it's fantastic fun. So far we've been learning … erm … the Waltz, the Foxtrot, erm … and some Latin dances like, erm, the jive and the tango. It's great fun.

Track 1.12
E=Expert
E: In 1957 a news programme called Panorama broadcast a story about spaghetti trees in Switzerland. While the reporter told the story, Swiss farmers in the background were picking spaghetti from trees. Following this, thousands of people called the show, asking how to grow spaghetti trees.
In 1998 large numbers of Americans went to Burger King asking for a new type of burger. The food company had published an ad in USA Today announcing the new 'left-handed Whopper', a burger designed for left-handed people. The following day, Burger King admitted that they had been joking all along.
Swedish technician Kjell Stensson had been working on the development of colour TV for many years when he announced in 1962 that everyone could now convert their black-and-white TV sets into colour. The procedure was simple: you had to put a nylon stocking over the TV screen. Stensson demonstrated and fooled thousands.
Pretending that it had been developing the product for some time, a British supermarket announced in 2002 that it had invented a whistling carrot. Using genetic engineering, the carrot grew with holes in it, and, when cooked, it would start whistling.

Track 1.13
1 I'd seen it before.
2 I'd prefer to go home.
3 She'd lost the opportunity.
4 Would you like to dance?
5 I didn't set the alarm.
6 What would you cook?
7 I'd have done the same.
8 Had she been there?

Track 1.14
1
My favourite fictional character has to be Philip Marlowe, the detective created by Raymond Chandler. The most famous book and movie in which he appears is, of course, *The Big Sleep*, with erm … Humphrey Bogart playing Philip Marlowe. Once you've seen Humphrey Bogart, of course it's very difficult to imagine Philip Marlowe as being anybody else other than Humphrey Bogart, because like Humphrey Bogart, Philip Marlowe is tall, good-looking, tough, very smart and a smooth talker. I suppose those are also the characteristics that I do like about Philip Marlowe. The thing about Philip Marlowe is … like … unlike most modern characters, he doesn't always say the right thing, although he always has a clever retort and he doesn't

always win. Philip Marlowe is not always on top of the situation. Philip Marlowe sounds like a real guy with real problems who's very clever, very tough and likes to get to the bottom of the problem. Erm, the sort of problems that he has to overcome, of course, as a detective in Los Angeles is generally solving murder crimes, but he's often not so much interested in who did it as to why or how. By the end of the story, you care much about, you care as much about the erm … victim as perhaps the murderer or Philip Marlowe himself. This is actually one reason why you can re-read and re-read the Raymond Chandler novels with Philip Marlowe in them, because it's not what happens in the story, it's how Philip Marlowe deals with the problems, that matters.
2
I think my favourite fictional character has to be, erm, the lead character, the heroine if you like, of, erm, Jane Austen's *Pride and Prejudice*. She's absolutely, I think, one of the best-drawn characters in, in English literature. She is of course Elizabeth Bennett. Erm, she's the heroine, she's she's sparky, she's lively, she's feisty, and when you think that this is a book that's set in the 1800s, it's really quite remarkable that you've got such a modern woman as the heroine. I mean she's, she's lippy, she talks back to all these men who are older than her and in more authority than her. Fantastic! I think it's, erm, character traits that I'd really quite like to have myself. Erm, I imagine her, and I think I'm quite influenced here by the films and so on that have been made of *Pride and Prejudice*, as being quite tall with a very lively, mobile face and possibly dark hair, as well. Erm … memorable things that she does: well, the thing that I really like about her, erm, from the story of *Pride and Prejudice* is the way that she takes control of her own life in a period of history when women really had very little power and very little control over what happened to them in the marriage market, and I think it's great that she, erm, sort of comes to a self-realisation through the events of the novel and decides to do the right thing and go for the guy that she really loves, and of course she meets lots of problems along the way: people who think she's socially unacceptable or people who, erm, have very prejudiced views about class and society and of course she succeeds and she wins the day, wins her guy in the end.
3
I think my favourite fictional character was er, the old man from *The Old Man and the Sea* by Ernest Hemingway. Er, I still have quite a strong visual image of this man. The whole story takes place in a boat off the coast of Cuba, with, with just this one character, mostly. I imagine him to be quite old. He was a lifelong fisherman. He had quite a tough life, so I imagine he had these really big strong hands that were … were cut and bruised from hauling in nets his whole life every, every night out, out in the sea. I imagine him with a little bit of grey hair, er, just old and wise, somebody who had been a fisherman his whole life, took a lot of pride in it and tried to do it as, as best he could, and he was down on his luck in the story. He hadn't caught anything for quite a long time, erm, but he still dragged himself out every night and cast his nets and hoped for, hoped that he would catch something.
In a way, he sort of reminds me of my dad, somebody who had limited opportunities in life, but found a job that he could do and did

it to the best of his ability, even though there was very little glamour attached to it, and I think this in a way the fisherman was like him. He was a fisherman and he took pride in that, and did the best job he could.

Track 1.15
W=Woman
W: Groucho Marx didn't want to be a comedian at first. He loved reading and singing, and he wanted to become a doctor. But his mother had other ideas. She got the boys to start a group called the Six Mascots. During a radio show they started making jokes, and this is when they decided to become a comedy act. Their popularity grew quickly. But in 1926 the boys' mother died, and the Great Depression began. In the 1930s a man called Irving Thalberg helped the Marx Brothers to get on television. They made their most famous films, the last of which was called *A Day At the Races*. After this, Groucho became a radio host and he also made more movies, but without his brothers. In the 70s, he toured with a live one-man show, but by now in his 90s he was getting weaker, and he died in 1977 on the same day as Elvis Presley.

Track 1.17
N=Newsreader
N: Resistance to antibiotics is on the increase. Research out today shows an increase in the number and strength of superbugs, resistant to normal antibiotics. Analysis of particularly resistant strains, kept in laboratory test tubes, shows that in the last 12 months …

A new virus, developed by hackers in South-East Asia has been crashing computer networks around the globe. The virus penetrates standard firewalls to affect computer software and eventually data stored in the microchip. Experts have warned that …

A breakthrough in genetic engineering technology means that human cloning can now enable scientists to re-build damaged organs in children. Cells taken from skin tissue are used to provide the necessary genes, which are then implanted …

The on-going budget crisis has been cited as the reason for the latest delay to the space mission. The new shuttle, Discover XVIII, which was originally due to launch last Thursday, is set to orbit Mars, scanning the surface for evidence of early life forms …

Track 1.18
I=Interviewer, S=Stan Lee
I: Legendary veteran comic writer Stan Lee co-created Spider-Man and the Fantastic Four, amongst others. We asked him how he thought of Spider-Man and this was his response:
S: When trying to create a superhero, the first thing you have to think of, or at least the first thing I have to think of, is a super power. What super power would be different, that people hadn't seen before? I had already done the Hulk, who was the strongest character on Earth; I had done a group called the Fantastic Four: one of them could fly, one was invisible, and one's body could stretch and I was trying to think, 'What else can I do?' And

I've told this story so often that for all I know it might even be true! But I was sitting and watching a fly crawling on the wall, and I thought, 'Gee – that would be great – what if a character could crawl on walls like an insect?' So I had my super power, but then I needed a name. So I thought, 'Insect-man' ... that didn't sound good. 'Crawling-man?' And I went on and on. 'Mosquito-man?' And then somehow I said 'Spider-Man' and it just sounded dramatic and mysterious to me. So that was my name.

I: When asked why he made Spider-man a scientist, he replied:

S: I had always resented the fact that in most superhero stories, or actually in most comic books, the hero is some sort of a rugged, muscular outdoorsman, a sportsman, an adventurer. And anybody who was literate or scholarly ... they were ... he was always considered to be somewhat of a nerd. And I thought, 'My gosh, people don't have enough respect for intelligence.' So again, in trying to be different, and in trying to be realistic, I thought I would make my teenage hero a scholarship student, extra-bright; he was studying science. And just to show that there's no reason why a hero couldn't also be a kid who likes science and is good in school and is smart ... and that was the thinking behind it.

I: When asked if he was at all scientific, he replied:

S: I'm not much of a scientist. I love reading science-fiction but when it comes to actual science, I'm ... I'm a dummy. But I like to make things seem scientific!

I: Our final question asked if Stan Lee thought there would ever be real superheroes.

S: I believe that they will be able, through cloning, through genetics, they will be able ... they will have to, see? Once these wars are finished with, if they ever are, we're going to want to go to the planets. They're going to want to go to Mars. Now it's such a long trip, and it will be so hard to get back again, they're going to have to make human beings able to adapt to Mars, adapt themselves. Or is it adopt? I never ... I always get those two mixed up! But at any rate, I believe that they will find a way to make people able to live in the atmosphere of Mars, through altering them genetically. Because of genetics, I think we can do virtually anything.

Track 1.21

Dialogue 1

K=Kevin, L=Lizzie

K: Hello?

L: Hi, Kevin. It's Lizzie.

K: Oh hi, Lizzie. How are you?

L: Yeah, great. You?

K: Yeah, fine.

L: I guess you're busy as usual this Saturday?

K: Erm ... sort of.

L: Yeah?

K: Well, I'm playing cricket.

L: Oh, I didn't know you played cricket.

K: I don't really. Well, once in a blue moon.

L: So that's all day Saturday?

K: Yeah, that'll be ... yeah ... more or less all day.

L: What are you up to in the evening?

K: Well, I might be free. Let me think. Mm, maybe about eight-ish. What have you got lined up?

L: Erm, we're thinking of going to Clancy's ...

K: Oh yeah? I used to go there from time to time when I was a student. Do you want me to pick you up?

L: Erm, or should I drive?

K: I don't mind driving. Do you want me to?

L: In a way, it's easier if I take my car. Yeah, don't worry. I think I'll drive ...

Dialogue 2

L=Lauren, A=Andy

L: Lauren James.

A: Hi, sweetheart.

L: Oh hi, darling.

A: Still working?

L: Yep.

A: Bit of a hard day?

L: Kind of. Nothing major ... just various bits and pieces.

A: Right.

L: Filling in forms, replying to emails, that kind of thing.

A: Uhuh.

L: Going over the accounts again, checking petty cash, etcetera etcetera. Actually, there were loads of mistakes.

A: Oh really?

L: Yep. But I'm nearly finished.

A: So, do you want me to get something ready?

L: Yeah, I'm a bit peckish actually.

A: Pasta maybe? Or we've got chicken in the fridge.

L: Chicken sounds good. Erm, I'll be home in an hour or so.

A: OK, I'll put the chicken in the oven ...

Track 1.22

1 How many phone calls do you make per day?
2 How many times do you check your emails per week?
3 How many close friends do you have?
4 How frequently do you write letters?
5 What do you do in the evening?
6 How long do you spend studying English at home?

Track 1.23

1 Not since Mozart has there been a greater genius.
2 Only after the age of three did she begin to show her gift.
3 Nowhere do the rules say you can't teach advanced subjects to children.
4 Only later did we understand the truth about our gifted child.
5 Not only was he able to write poetry when he was five years old, he also played the violin well.
6 No sooner had we given her a paintbrush than she produced a masterpiece.

Track 1.24

I=Interviewer, W=Woman

I: Can you tell us a little bit about the case and what made it so special?

W: The case concerned a pair of twins called John and Michael. They were, I suppose in their late teens, but they were absolutely tiny and they wore thick glasses. They used to get laughed at at school because, in a conventional sense, they weren't very bright or social.

I: They were outsiders.

W: Well, that's right. Outsiders. But they had an amazing gift. You could name any date in the past or future 40,000 years and they would be able to tell you what day of the week it was.

I: So I could say, for example, 5th June 1376 and they could tell me it was Sunday or whatever ...

W: That's right.

I: Or 10th July 2099, and ...

W: And they would say 'Monday!' But that wasn't all. During one interview, the psychologist dropped a box of matches on the floor and the twins immediately called out 'one hundred and eleven'. The psychologist counted the matches and there were exactly 111.

I: And the twins hadn't counted them?

W: No. There was no time. As soon as the matches hit the floor, they knew there were 111. Now another thing the twins could do was remember extremely long sequences of numbers. You could say a number of up to 300 digits, and they were able to repeat it back to you perfectly.

I: So they basically have an extraordinary ability with numbers.

W: Not only with numbers. They have another talent, which is that you can name any day of their lives since they were about four years old, and they are able to tell you what the weather was like, what they did, and other events in the wider world. They can remember absolutely everything about that day.

I: Just any ordinary day?

W: Any and every ordinary day.

I: Obviously the twins, John and Michael, were studied at length by various psychologists, educators ...

W: Yes, they were.

I: What progress did these people make in coming up with explanations of their ability?

W: I think the main thing is that we realise that John and Michael's ability is actually a visual one as well as mathematical. If you ask them how they do it, they say they can 'see' the answers. When the box of matches fell, they 'saw' 111. It wasn't a calculation. Similarly, they can 'see' themselves as five-year-olds. Somehow they have an ability to record incredible numbers of things in the mind. Of course, we have no idea how it works, but it would be very interesting to learn ...

Track 1.25

1

Great discoveries of our time ... well, in the last 100 years or so, I guess medical advances, like the use of X-rays in diagnosis, or the discovery of penicillin by Fleming. I mean, he made that discovery almost by mistake, and it changed modern medicine completely. Or perhaps the elucidation of DNA by Watson and Crick in the 50s. That paved the way for the whole area of genetics and genetic engineering ...

2

I would say that sending man to the moon was one of the greatest scientific achievements, learning about space. The man who invented the liquid-fuelled rocket, Robert Goddard, was fascinated by the idea of sending a rocket into space, and he spent years researching his ideas, until he developed the first rocket, called Nell. It was 10-feet-tall, and he fired it from his aunt's farm in the US. At first nothing happened, but when the fuel finally ignited, the rocket was launched. It only reached a disappointing 14 metres into the air though and scientists were sceptical of its success. When the newspapers got hold of the story they wrote the headlines 'Moon rocket misses target by 238,799 miles.' But later, engineers in Germany and America used his ideas, and the film footage of Nell, to develop military and space-exploring rockets. The *New York Times* had to write Goddard a public apology …

3
Computers, it has to be. Information technology and the internet. The whole way in which information is distributed and kept nowadays. It's just been revolutionised by information technology. And things have happened so quickly. I mean, the first computer was built in 1948, I think. And was so big it took up a whole room! If you think about the latest designs now, and the capacity, it's just amazing. And it has made the world a smaller place, because it is so easy now to get information about anywhere in the world. There are no secrets …

4
I don't think we should underestimate the importance of domestic appliances, like the washing machine, dishwasher, all your electrical goods. And processes like freeze-drying food. These time-saving discoveries have allowed a whole new freedom to women, who previously had to spend their whole lives in the kitchen. It's meant that they could go out to work, and that has had a huge impact on society. Or perhaps it should be the advances in travel, with the bicycle, then the car and the aeroplane. The world must have been a very different place when the fastest way to get anywhere was on a horse!

Track 1.27

P=Presenter

1 Business partners. Why not go with friends and family?
P: While we're on the subject of choosing business partners, I cringe whenever I hear that two old friends or family members are planning to start a business together as fifty–fifty partners. It isn't that doing business with friends and family is a bad idea – many very successful businesses are family-owned. It's just that being someone's friend or relative is one of the worst reasons I can think of for making that someone your business partner. One of the problems is that once someone becomes your business partner, there is generally only one way to get rid of them (legally, of course) if things don't work out. You must buy them out for the fair value of their interest in the business. And that can be an expensive proposition.

2 What type of person makes a good business partner?
P: There are a few ways to determine if someone has what it takes to be your business partner, however. Firstly, you need to decide, are you a visionary, or an operations person? Successful partnerships combine those two kinds of people. A visionary is a strategic, 'big picture' thinker who understands the business model, the market and the overall business plan. An operations person is someone who rolls up their sleeves, wades up to their hip boots in the details and executes the strategy that the visionary comes up with. You are either one or the other – it is almost impossible to be both. Once you have determined if you are a 'visionary' or an 'operations person', look for your opposite number. That way your business is more likely to strike the right balance between strategy and tactics.

3 What skills does the company need?
P: Do you have all the skills you need on board to make the business work? Perhaps you are an inventor who is excellent at product design but clueless about selling. Perhaps you have a strong marketing background but need someone to help you crunch the numbers and make sure your products or services can be delivered within budget. Your partners should complement your set of business skills, not duplicate them. Keep in mind that you can acquire someone's skills without making them a partner. If a particular skill, such as contract negotiation or bookkeeping, is not critical to the success of your business, you may be better off hiring a lawyer, accountant or consultant to do it for you and keeping ownership of your business.

4 Will communication be a problem?
P: Can you communicate directly and honestly with this person, without pulling any punches? Communication between partners can often get rough; disagreements and arguments break out all the time. It is difficult to criticise someone harshly, yet sometimes you must be cruel with your business partners in order to do the right thing for your business. Your business may well suffer if you consistently hold back important information for fear of offending your partner or jeopardising the underlying friendship or emotional bond between you. Sometimes the most successful business partnerships are those where the partners do not socialise outside the office.

5 The long-term. Will your partner stay through good times and bad times?
P: And lastly, is your business partner willing to hang around for the long haul? This is the critical test of a business partner. Many people are happy to help out with a business during its start-up phase, only to lose interest later on when something more attractive (like a job offer from a big corporation) comes along, a life-changing event (like the birth of a new child) occurs, or the going is getting tougher and the business isn't as much 'fun' as it used to be. If you are not sure if someone is committed to the long-term success of your business, make them an employee or independent contractor, with perhaps an 'option' to acquire an interest in your business at a date two or three years down the road … provided, of course, they are still working for you at that time and you continue to be satisfied with their performance.

Track 1.29

I=Interviewer, W=Will

I: 98 percent of staff working at Piranha recruitment say they laugh a lot with their team. As many as 95 percent say that they are excited about where the company is going. So what have they all got to smile about? Last month this small London-based company won a prestigious award for being one of the best small companies in the UK to work for. With us today is Will Becks, the company director. Will, first of all, tell us a little bit more about the company and what you do.

W: Good morning. Well, Piranha is more than just a normal recruitment agency. The difference is that we actually train and then place graduates in sales jobs. That means we have a lot of young people working for us, so it's a bit like a continuation of university, but with a salary. We're only a small company, with as few as 60 employees, but there's a good atmosphere in the office. There's a great deal of energy.

I: Yes, your employees have said that there is a fun atmosphere, with outgoing, like-minded people. You have regular parties, an annual skiing holiday, a present for the most-appreciated employee of the month, and plenty of other benefits too. I'm not much of an expert on these things. Why such an emphasis on staff incentives?

W: Well, our staff are young and highly qualified. They are good at what they do, and they believe in it. We have trained sales people going into companies to try and place graduates. Quite a few of them get offered the jobs themselves. If we didn't look after our staff, they would quickly get poached by other companies. So the incentives need to be good to keep people.

I: So how are your salaries?

W: Salaries are good and there are monthly, performance-related cash bonuses. Staff also set their own targets for the coming year, and for the most part they have a say in their incentives too. Our accountant has just got the new Audi A3. He chose it, and he's delighted.

I: And how about the atmosphere in the office. How do you influence that?

W: We have a company bar, where we offer free breakfasts, and cappuccino all day long. People spend an awful lot of time in there discussing ideas over coffee, but it's very productive.

I: The vast majority of your staff say that they admire their managers, and feel that they can actively contribute to the future success of the company. How did you achieve this?

W: Well, one of the things is that we help them with finding somewhere nice to live. Rent is very expensive in London, and as lots of our employees are fresh out of university, with a lot of debts, they don't have a huge budget for accommodation. So, we've bought some properties, and quite a few staff rent them from us at reasonable rates. It makes a real difference. It means that working for the company becomes a lifestyle choice. They are involved personally. Also, we like to give people a say in the company. We have monthly meetings to discuss big issues, when we all sit around and talk about things. Initially, only a handful of people would come to the meetings. So we decided to offer free food, sandwiches and pizza, so now everyone comes, and everyone has something to say.

Track 1.31

K=Keith, B=Bridget

K: Well, I'd replace these chairs for a start. No wonder I've got backache.

B: Oh come on, we can do better than that. How about blowing it all on an all-expenses-paid jaunt to the West Indies or something?

K: Erm … would you really want to go on holiday with the rest of the staff?

B: Well, no, but … erm …

K: I think it should go on day-to-day things that'll make a difference in the long term, like renovating the office.

B: God, how boring.

K: Or maybe ... what d'you mean boring?!

B: Well, it's loads of money – let's have some fun! The company could get a house by the sea that the employees could use whenever they were on holiday.

K: Yeah, but that would only be useful once every few years for each person. I mean it wouldn't make the least bit of difference really. My main priority would be to do something practical with the money ...

NEW

Total English

ADVANCED

Workbook with Key

Antonia Clare and JJ Wilson

Pearson Education Limited
Edinburgh Gate
Harlow
Essex CM20 2JE
England
and Associated Companies throughout the world.

www.pearsonelt.com

© Pearson Education Limited 2012

The right of Antonia Clare and JJ Wilson to be identified as author of this Work has been asserted by them in accordance with the Copyright, Designs and Patents Act 1988.

All rights reserved; no part of this publication may be reproduced, stored in a retrieval system, or transmitted in any form or by any means, electronic, mechanical, photocopying, recording, or otherwise without the prior written permission of the Publishers.

First published 2012
Fourth impression 2016

ISBN: 978-1-4082-8581-7

Set in MetaPlusBook-Roman
Printed in China
SWTC/04

Acknowledgements

We are grateful to the following for permission to reproduce copyright material:

Cartoons
Cartoon Unit 10.1 from Ha Ha Ha ISBN: 0-7493-9735-7, ha Ha Ha' (Roddy Doyle) Cover

Text
Article Unit 1. from http://www.telegraph.co.uk/news/main. jhtml?xml=/news/2006/05/17/wever17.xml Paul Chapman 17/05/06, copyright (c) Telegraph Media Group Limited; Article Unit 1 adapted from http://www.annieseel.com/2005Maroc. html; Article Unit 1 adapted from http://www.guardian.co.uk/ transport/Story/0,1773924,00.html, The Guardian Unlimited / Matt Seaton; Article Unit 4 adapted from http://abcnews.go.com/ US/Living/story?id=202523&page=1, ABC News Internet Ventures / Adrienne Mand 1/11/04, Adapted article ABC News;Article Unit 4 adapted from Director, 9, call shots in Bollywood, The Sunday Times, 22/01/2006, 25 (Dean Nelson); Article Unit 4 adapted from Special report: Superhero science, Focus Magazine, Issue no 141 ISBN: 9770966427074, 01/08/2004 (Caroline Green); Article Unit 5 adapted from Courtney Reid-Eaton, http://americanradioworks.

publicradio.org/features/hardtime/courtney.html, Courtney Reid-Eaton 2006; Article Unit 5 adapted from http://www.ncf. carleton.ca/~aj624/toomuch.html, National Post /Veronique Mandal/ August 19, 2000; Article Unit 8 adapted from www. futureworld.co.za/News/20050923BusinessLife.aspx, Business Life, Premier Magazines (British Airways) Wolfgang Grulke/ Sept 2005/ 26; Article Unit 9 adapted from Profile: Stephen Hawking How Stephen Hawking beat motor neurone disease and discovered how time began BBC Focus 135, 28-31 (Graham Southorn); Article Unit 10 adapted from http://www.timesonline. co.uk/article/0,2092-2261601.html, The Sunday Times / Giles Hattersley / July 09, 2006; Article Unit 10 adapted from http:// www.trans4mind.com/new_life_course/, Peter Shepherd; Extract Unit 10 from Ha Ha Ha ISBN: 0-7493-9735-7, Minerva (Paddy Clarke) 4, 5

In some instances we have been unable to trace the owners of copyright material, and we would appreciate any information that would enable us to do so.

The publisher would like to thank the following for their kind permission to reproduce their photographs:

(Key: b-bottom; c-centre; l-left; r-right; t-top)

Alamy Images: Dennis Frates 54bl, Peter Horree 16l, Sami Sarkis Travel 16c; **Ardea:** John Daniels 6c; **Art Directors and TRIP Photo Library:** Spencer Grant 16r; **Fotolia.com:** Yuri Arcurs 12tr, Mikhail Basov 63tc, CandyBox Images 63b, Mehmet Dilsiz 63bc, Eishier 55, granitepeaker 54r, Eric Isselée 22l, Marsy 12l, NMaverick 44, Tyler Olson 46, Laetitia Soustiel 63c, Tanya 17, Vaso 53, Vibe Images 66, Jan Will 22cl; **Getty Images:** Simon Fergusson 4, Popperfoto 6t, Joe Raedle 74, Time Life Pictures / Pierre Boulat 71, Ami Vitale 32; **Kobal Collection Ltd:** Marvel / Sony Pictures 28bl, Universal / Marvel Entertainment 28c, Warner Bros / DC Comics 28tr; **Pearson Education Ltd:** Corbis 54tl, Creatas 22r, Photodisc / Cybermedia 22cr; **PunchStock:** Blend Images 12br, Creatas 73; **Rex Features:** Image Source 83; **Shutterstock.com:** Dasha Petrenko 63t

All other images © Pearson Education

Every effort has been made to trace the copyright holders and we apologise in advance for any unintentional omissions. We would be pleased to insert the appropriate acknowledgement in any subsequent edition of this publication.

Illustrated by Roger Penwill, Brian Lee and Lucy Truman (New Division)

Cover images: *Front:* **Photolibrary.com:** Hill Creek Pictures BV

Contents

Reading

1 Read the article. Write true (T) or false (F).

1 Mark Inglis had both his legs amputated after a climbing accident in 1982. ☐

2 He never found the courage to return to climb the mountain where the accident happened. ☐

3 On reaching the top of Everest, Mark found he was hardly able to speak. ☐

4 Sir Edmund Hillary and the prime minister of New Zealand were among the people to congratulate Mark on his achievement. ☐

5 Mark broke one of his artificial legs when climbing down the mountain. ☐

6 Mark had taken several replacement legs with him on the climb. ☐

7 Mark's main problem during the climb was that he needed to go very slowly. ☐

8 Before his legs were amputated, Mark had also won a silver medal for cycling in the Olympics. ☐

9 The New Zealand prime minister feels that Mark is setting a good example to people with disabilities. ☐

2 a Complete the questions.

> make   daunting   set   ambition
> without   face   rising   attitude

1 How did Mark _____ achievable goals?

2 What challenges did he _____ ?

3 Did Mark succeed in _____ to the challenge?

4 How did he _____ his dream come true?

5 What couldn't Mark have done it _____ ?

6 What advice does the New Zealand prime minister give to people with a burning _____ ?

7 Do you think Mark had the right _____ ?

8 What would you consider most _____ about his challenge?

b Answer the questions (1–8) from exercise 2a.

Feeling on top of the world

The first man with no legs to climb to the top of Mount Everest was almost speechless when he reached the summit and called his wife by satellite phone.

Mark Inglis, 47 at the time, who had lost both legs in a climbing accident 24 years earlier, was suffering an attack of laryngitis and managed only to croak: 'I did it!'

Sir Edmund Hillary, who had conquered the world's highest peak in May 1953, was among the first to offer his congratulations. 'It's a remarkable effort. He's done a pretty good job,' he said.

According to members of his party, his short conversation with his wife Anne when he spoke from the summit were among the few words he was able to utter.

Asked by New Zealand television how the climb had been, he managed to say only: 'Bloody hard.'

His wife said one of his carbon-fibre artificial legs snapped on the ascent, but was quickly replaced from a bundle of spare legs and parts taken with him.

Wayne Alexander, one of three climbing companions up the 29,035-feet summit, said: 'What Mark did was

absolutely remarkable. I have never seen such human endurance.' Speaking from Advance Base Camp on the mountain, he added: 'He did so well. It was a bit like chasing a greyhound – he was gone.'

The New Zealand prime minister, said: 'To reach the summit of Everest is a once-in-a-lifetime achievement, but for Mark Inglis it will be even more satisfying. He has said it was a childhood dream to stand on the roof of the world, but he thought he had lost it when he lost his legs.'

Inglis had his legs amputated below the knees due to frostbite, suffered in 1982 while he was trapped for 14 days by blizzards on Mount Cook, the highest peak in New Zealand.

He went on to become the first double amputee to reach the mountain's summit, and followed this achievement by conquering 26,906-foot Mount Cho Oyu in Tibet, the world's sixth-highest peak. He also won a silver medal for cycling in the 2000 Sydney Paralympic Games.

The New Zealand prime minister added that Mr Inglis had sent a signal to others with disabilities 'that your ambitions should never be limited'.

Grammar | verbs/adjectives/nouns with prepositions

3 Choose the correct words in *italics*.

1 We finally opted *to/for/on* the silver colour.

2 It is a method of distinguishing cancer cells *from/between/of* normal tissue.

3 Very few people succeed *on losing/to lose/ in losing* weight and keeping it off!

4 His headaches stemmed *from/with/to* vision problems.

5 It is most likely to appeal *at/to/with* the younger generation.

6 I wouldn't bother *in/to/about* calling him now.

7 We all came to rely *on/in/with* her judgement.

8 We want him to get the maximum benefit *of/from/with* the course.

9 Can you lend me a few dollars? I'm a bit short *on/of/with* money at the moment.

10 The wall of the prison was riddled *of/in/with* bullet holes.

11 She seems to be lacking *with/on/in* confidence.

12 They weren't at all nervous *about/with/for* asking for a rise.

Vocabulary | learning languages

4 Complete the dialogues using words from the box.

> dialect slide ball overload
> garbled babbling picked master

1 A: How is your German nowadays?
   B: It's terrible. I've really let it _____ .

2 A: I didn't know you could speak Thai!
   B: I can't really. I just _____ up a few words while I was there on holiday.

3 A: How long did it take you to _____ the grammar?
   B: Years! I used to spend a lot of time cramming information from grammar books until I had complete information _____ .

4 A: Have you heard from Simon?
   B: He left a _____ message which I can't understand.

5 A: What do you enjoy most about living abroad?
   B: Everything is great, although I think I'm starting to lose my original _____ !

6 A: I can't believe how quickly she's learnt to speak.
   B: Yes, it only seems a short while ago that she was _____ unintelligibly, like all babies do.

Listening

5 🔘 2 Cover the audioscript. Listen to a radio programme and answer the questions.

1 What is different about a polyglot's brain?

2 What do scientists hope to achieve through doing the new research?

3 What did people have to distinguish between during the trial?

4 How did the researchers decide who was a 'good' language learner?

5 What is the function of fibres in the brain's white matter?

6 What can you tell from the brain scans?

AUDIOSCRIPT

Polyglots 'have different brains'. New research has shown that people with a gift for other languages could actually have different types of brains from other people. Neuroscientists at University College London say that polyglots have more 'white brain matter' in a part of the brain which processes sound. It is hoped that the research, published in a medical journal, could be used to help identify reasons for language difficulties.

During a trial involving native French speakers, people were asked to distinguish between two similar sounds from different languages. The first was the 'd' sound found in French. The second was a 'd' found in Hindi, which is pronounced in a different way. Researchers tested the speed at which participants could process the information about the different sounds. People who were successful on this task were asked to listen to other similar sounds.

Some of the fastest learners were able to tell the sounds apart within a few minutes, while the slowest learners were only able to make random guesses after 20 minutes of training.

Dr Narly Golestani from UCL's Institute of Cognitive Neuroscience said the brain's white matter was involved in the efficient processing of sound information. Its fibres are involved in connecting brain regions together. Fast language learners had a greater volume of white matter and that may mean they have more, or perhaps thicker fibres.

'We are starting to understand that brain shape and structure can be informative about people's abilities – why people are good at some things and not others is evident from these scans,' she said.

White brain matter is involved in connecting different parts of the brain together, and greater amounts of this could indicate an increased ability to process sound. Previous research suggested that having a talent for music was linked to the structure of grey matter in the brain.

'This latest research could be used in other ways,' Dr Narly said. 'We can start to make predictions regarding whether people will be good at something or not based on their brain structure, or even to diagnose clinical problems.'

Vocabulary | knowledge

1 Match the sentence beginnings (1–10) to the endings (a–j).

1	We had to learn poems by	a	doubt that this was where she wanted to be.
2	I grew up here. I know it like the back	b	head I'd say there were about 50.
3	I know next to	c	are concerned, a lot of our hotels are below standard.
4	She knew without a	d	of my hand.
5	Just off the top of my	e	David Marshall?
6	I'm pretty	f	heart when I was at school.
7	As far as the Americans	g	what time the show starts?
8	Have you ever heard of	h	sure he'll say yes.
9	Erikson knew the game	i	nothing about antiques.
10	Do you know offhand	j	inside out.

Reading and Grammar | passives: distancing

2 Read the article. <u>Underline</u> examples of passives used for distancing.

Notable lasts

1
Lillian Asplund, who died aged 99, was the last American survivor of the Titanic, and the only living person with any memory of the events of 15 April 1912. She was five years old when the ship went down in the freezing waters of the north Atlantic, taking with it her father and three of her brothers. As she was winched to safety in a lifeboat, she saw them peering at her over the ship's railing. The image is said to have haunted her for the rest of her life, and despite the world's ongoing fascination with the Titanic, it seems she rarely spoke of the tragedy.

2
Martha is thought to have been the last surviving carrier pigeon. Carrier pigeons were probably once the most common birds in the world. It is estimated that there were as many as five billion carrier pigeons in the United States. They lived in enormous flocks, sometimes up to a mile wide and 300 miles long, taking several days to pass and probably containing two billion birds. They were hunted to extinction by humans. Martha, the last of her species, died in Cincinnati Zoo in 1914. She was then frozen in a block of ice and her body was sent to The Smithsonian Institution, where she can still be seen.

3
'Ishi' was the name given to the last member of the Yahi tribe of California, and means 'man' in the Yahi language. Ishi is believed to have been the last native American in Northern California to have lived the bulk of his life completely outside the European American culture. He was thought to have left his homeland in the foothills near Lassen Peak, California, and was found when he emerged from the wild on 29 August 1911. His real name was never known, because in his society it was taboo to say one's own name. Since he was the last member of his tribe, his real name died with him.

3 Complete the sentences (1–10) using words from the article.

1 Two men were _____ out of the sinking boat by an RAF helicopter. (para 1)

2 Jimmy was _____ through the wet windscreen at the cars ahead. (para 1)

3 Clare was _____ by the fear that her husband was having an affair. (para 1)

4 Police knew of his _____ with guns. (para 1)

5 We glanced up in surprise as a _____ of wild geese flew noisily overhead. (para 2)

6 The nearest hotel might be _____ away. (para 2)

7 This rare breed was on the verge of _____ . (para 2)

8 The _____ of our clients are young professionals. (para 3)

9 We went skiing in the _____ of the Alps. (para 3)

10 There were cheers as the sun _____ from behind the clouds. (para 3)

4 Complete the texts with the correct form of the verbs in brackets. Add extra words if necessary.

It (1) _____ (say) Thomas Edison, the famous inventor, believed that taking off one's clothing caused insomnia. It (2) _____ (seem) he often slept in his clothes on newspapers beneath the stairs in his laboratory.

Alexander Graham Bell, inventor of the telephone, (3) _____ (claim) to have first answered the device by saying 'hoy, hoy' instead of 'hello'!

Joseph Gayetty invented toilet paper in 1857, and (4) _____ (think) to have had his name printed on each sheet.

Charles Goodyear, who (5) _____ (say) to have been instrumental in establishing the rubber industry in the US, (6) _____ (think) to have carried out his first experiments in jail. It (7) _____ (seem) as though he had been imprisoned for failure to pay his debts.

Leonardo da Vinci (8) _____ (think) to have designed a military tank in the 15th century. Remarkably, he (9) _____ (believe) to have also worked on designs for hot-air balloons and deep-sea diving suits.

Joseph Merlin, a Belgian musician, invented roller skates in 1760. He (10) _____ (appear) to have first demonstrated them at a ball by skating across the room playing a violin.

Listening

5 ● 3 Cover the audioscript. Listen to the news stories. For each story, do the tasks (1–4).

1 Write down the key words.

2 Listen again.

3 Choose one of the stories and try to write down the story exactly as you hear it. (Listen as many times as you need to.)

4 Check by reading the audioscript.

AUDIOSCRIPT

1 A huge hurricane has reached the east coast of the United States, forcing millions of people to flee their homes, as towns and cities have had to be evacuated. The tropical storm has been travelling north causing both damage and devastation. Thirteen states have now declared a state of emergency and flights from many US cities have had to be cancelled.

2 Officials in the Seychelles have admitted that more should have been done to warn tourists about the danger of shark attacks in the area after reports of several attacks in recent weeks. One man, Tony Felito, died from his injuries after being bitten by a large shark, whilst out swimming with his fiancée. Experts believe the shark is a Great White, which had been spotted in the waters near to where the fatal attack happened. People have now been warned not to swim in the area until the killer shark is captured.

3 Fire-fighters were called to a multi-storey car park in Manchester yesterday after a car crashed through the wall on the fourth floor. The driver lost control of the vehicle and drove through the metal barriers so that the front wheels of the car were hanging partly out of the building. The driver managed to escape with only minor injuries and no other vehicles were involved in the accident. Police closed off the road below the crash site until the car could be safely removed.

4 A woman has survived a skydive fall of over 1000m. Doctors were amazed when a female skydiver survived the huge fall, escaping with just bruises, a broken leg and concussion. Mother of one, Sam Cavendish plummeted to the ground when her parachute became entangled during a skydive.

Pronunciation | word stress

6 **a** ● 3 Read and listen to the news stories. Underline the words which carry the main stress. Are these the key words you chose in exercise 5?

b Practise reading the news stories. Try to imitate the rhythm of the speaker.

Reading

1 **a** Read the interview and answer the questions.

1 What kinds of races does Annie compete in?

2 What is her ambition?

3 How did her parents influence her?

4 What injuries has she suffered?

5 How does she cope when she is hurt?

b Match the definitions (1–12) with words from the interview.

1 long for/strongly desire (para 1)

_____

2 do on your own (para 1) _____

3 only just (para 1) _____

4 satisfy her desire for doing well (para 2) _____

5 something she really wants to achieve (para 2) _____

6 an equally strong competitor (para 2) _____

7 inspired/impressed (para 3) _____

8 be very keen to do something (para 4) _____

9 give up (para 5) _____

10 self-determination (para 5) _____

11 continued despite difficulties (para 5)

_____

c Complete the sentences (1–7). Use the correct form of words from exercise 1b.

1 He is extremely ambitious. His _____ is to take over the whole company.

2 Ellen MacArthur sailed _____ around the world.

3 My job is getting so stressful, I'm thinking about _____ .

4 They had _____ left the office when the police arrived.

5 The New Zealand team are very fit, and will prove to be a _____ for the Irish.

6 I was _____ adventure, so I signed up for a trip across Africa.

Nerves of steel

(1) She's blonde, charming, enthusiastic and above all extremely determined. If you only judge Annie Seel by her looks, you're in for the greatest of surprises. There are other women motorcyclists for sure, but how many crave extreme adventure in such a way, and how many take on single-handedly all the toughest rallies the world has to offer? Addicted early on to speed and adrenaline, the desert princess switched from horse to motorcycle races when she was barely 16.

(2) Several years and more than 20 broken bones on, she continues to try to quench her thirst for success and for new records to break, as much at home in Sweden, or up Mount Everest as on African rallies, on tarmac races as on Mexican *bajas*. Can you guess the ultimate quest for this woman of one metre 63? To be a true match in the toughest of races, the Dakar Rally.

(3) **Annie, what gave you this taste for extreme adventure?**

'I grew up next to a horse racecourse. I quickly got addicted to speed, and then at 16, I saw a motorcycle stuntman at a show. I was awed. I bought myself a motorcycle, but none of my friends liked speed the same as me. Then when I was 18 or 19, I started to compete in road racing and finished eighth in the Swedish Championships ...'

(4) **And in 2000 you raced your first rally in Dubai ...**

'I went to Morocco on a motorcycle tour and fell in love with the desert. I was desperate to do a desert rally. I ordered a DIY Husaberg 600 motorcycle and assembled it barely ten days before the start.

I rode on my own and made straight for the sand dunes. On the last day I got a fractured foot but I still got to the finish in 49th place. Since then, I've now raced 20 cross-country rallies, including five Dakar rallies, and I have finished all of them which is very unique, since only 50% of the starters actually reach the finish line. This is how difficult the rallies are. My biggest victory was in the 2010 Dakar rally when I won the Women's Trophy. But already in 2004 I had been crowned the Women's 450 Champion.'

(5) **What's most impressive about you is your determination. You've broken your bones more than 20 times, yet you've never given up.**

'No, I never quit. My father, who died when I was 16, gave me a taste for mechanical things, and my mother gave me fairly exceptionally strong will power. When I broke my hand on the fourth stage of the Dakar in 2002, I held on till the end. My left leg had gone blue all over. I'll admit, though, that I've always been lucky enough to have injuries that didn't prevent me from finishing the race. When I run into a problem, I cry a bit and then I carry on.'

Vocabulary | achievement

2 Complete the sentences (1–10) using words from the box.

> potential   greatest   persevered   pushing
> faces   pursue   heading   deal   triumphs
> believes

1 She _____ in herself – that's why she's so successful.
2 You need to keep your priorities in order if you want to _____ your dream.
3 The president _____ the difficult task of putting the economy back on its feet.
4 My tutor was always _____ me to do better.
5 Winning the championship is one of our _____ _____ .
6 He has the _____ to be a great politician.
7 We have had to _____ with a lot of unnecessary criticism.
8 She _____ in her claim for insurance, and in the end it paid off.
9 It's clear that he's _____ for the top.

Grammar | perfect aspect

3 Complete the article with the correct form of the verbs in brackets.

Round-the-world cyclist Heinz Stucke has an aura of calm about him. By the end of this year he (1) _____ (be) on the road for over 44 years. The German cyclist, who (2) _____ (travel) a third of a million miles, through 211 territories, arrived in Portsmouth last week. Within hours of getting off the ferry from France, the bicycle that (3) _____ (be) his constant companion since 1962 was stolen. But he's not bitter.

'I trust everybody,' he said, 'because if you didn't, you just wouldn't go around the world. You take a calculated risk everywhere you go.'

In fact, his bike – a unique artefact which (4) _____ already _____ (be requested) by a museum of cycling back in Germany – was returned to him little more than 36 hours after its theft. Heinz was expecting it. Before this, the bike (5) _____ already _____ (be) stolen on five previous occasions. 'The last time (6) _____ (be) in 1997 – almost every ten years it has been stolen. That's not bad in 150,000 kilometres.'

This is not the only problem Heinz (7) _____ (have) to deal with. Since 1962 – when he (8) _____ (give up) his job as a toolmaker in a small town in Germany and (9) _____ (set off) on his odyssey – Stucke (10) _____ (be attacked) twice by swarms of bees, and (11) _____ (shoot) in the foot by Zambian guerrillas. He (12) _____ often _____ (be) hungry (he makes a living by selling a book about his experiences) and exhausted. At one point, his bicycle (13) _____ (rust) because of the sweat dripping off his nose. And then there's the loneliness. 'I (14) _____ (have) many little affairs,' he says. 'But now it's more complicated: I'm 66 and on a bicycle, and I sleep in a tent …'

How to... | talk about your achievements

4 Complete the blog with the extracts (a–i).
a   I really feel I have accomplished something
b   I'd never been involved in catering before
c   exactly the kind of environment I wanted to achieve.
d   maybe in a couple of year's time
e   One of my greatest achievements
f   opened Café Mundo six months ago
g   and I've had to learn a lot very quickly
h   so we decided to buy it
i   I'd always dreamed of

(1) _____ is finally to have set up my own business with a friend. (2) _____ running a small café, with a bookshop inside. I wanted it to be a place where people can come to enjoy a coffee, read a book, listen to music, or chat to friends. I had a very clear vision in my head of (3) _____ . Last year, I found the perfect location for the café, (4) _____ . It was a big gamble as (5) _____ , but we spent a few months renovating the building and (6) _____ . It's been an incredibly hard year, (7) _____ , but it's been a great experience and (8) _____ . We're thinking of opening a second café, (9) _____ .

Writing

5 Use the model in exercise 4 to write a paragraph about a personal achievement, or about an achievement which you particularly admire.

Review and consolidation unit 1

Passives: distancing

1 Choose the correct option (A–D) to complete the sentences.

1 It is widely _____ eating too many fatty foods causes heart disease.

  A believing   B to be believed of   C believed that
  D believed to be

2 The notes from last month's meeting _____ lost.
  A are appeared   B seem to have be
  C appear that they are   D seem to have been

3 It seems _____ Mr Klein was wrong about the figures.
  A as though   B if   C as to   D as

4 Is the shipment _____ this afternoon?
  A be delivered   B being delivered   C deliver
  D to deliver

5 Smoking _____ allowed on planes for years.
  A isn't being   B isn't   C hasn't been   D doesn't

6 The governing body decided that the postponed game _____ next week.
  A must be played   B must have been played
  C will play   D will be being played

7 It _____ by various journalists that the scandal was caused by government corruption.
  A is being asserted   B has being said
  C was suggest   D did assert

8 _____ in the past that the world was flat?
  A Was there assumed   B Did it assume
  C Was assumed   D Was it assumed

9 Reuben _____ the most handsome man in London society.
  A has said to be   B was said to be   C was to be
  D was said

10 The company _____ gone bankrupt because of increased competition.
  A is thought   B is said to be   C said to have
  D is thought to have

2 Match the sentence beginnings (1–8) to the endings (a–h).

1 She is said to
2 It was widely
3 The robbers were thought
4 Judging by this map, we appear to have
5 It seems as though
6 You look as
7 The competition entry must
8 The wedding cake will have been

a made by now.
b if you've just seen a ghost.
c to have escaped.
d be a genius.
e be submitted tomorrow.
f the weather will get better.
g got completely lost.
h assumed that Dobson would inherit his father's money.

Perfect aspect

3 Complete the sentences with the perfect aspect.

1 By this time next week, we _____ school and I'll be on holiday!

2 It was only when Mariana told me her name that I _____ met before.

3 The children were all sunburned. They _____ football in the sun all day.

4 She looks exhausted because she _____ well recently. She needs a new bed.

5 Even by next July, Kazunari probably _____ writing his thesis.

6 Oh no! _____ the key in the car and it's locked!

7 Yesterday, Mr Jones finally received his visa. He _____ to get one for years.

8 Wow! Fantastic news! I _____ a scholarship by the university.

9 We went to a Mowgli concert. I _____ of them before, but they were very good.

10 By tomorrow, Don _____ here for over 50 years! He started as an office boy.

4 Which statement (A or B) do the underlined sentences reply to?

1 A We haven't been feeding the cat enough food.
  B We haven't fed the cat enough food.
  <u>I know. He's started catching mice again recently.</u> ☐

2 A How many countries will you have visited after this trip?
  B How many countries will you visit on this trip?
  <u>Eighteen if you include the one where I was born!</u> ☐

3 A We haven't been told the itinerary.
  B We hadn't been told the itinerary.
  <u>Well, I think the conference starts at 9.00 and you're speaking at 11.00.</u> ☐

4 A I've been sitting quietly, minding my own business.
  B I'd been sitting quietly, minding my own business.
  <u>And then what happened?</u> ☐

5 A Where have you put the money?
  B Where will you have put the money?
  <u>I put it where you told me to.</u> ☐

6 A I'd always wanted a place of my own.
  B I've always wanted a place of my own.
  <u>Well, congratulations! It's a really nice house.</u> ☐

Verbs/adjectives/nouns with prepositions

5 Complete the advert with the correct form of words from the box and a preposition.

> opt succeed reminiscent short appeal
> bother nervous subject rely benefit

Holiday *challenge*

Holiday Challenge is guaranteed to (1) _____ _____ your adventurous spirit. We provide a choice of parachute jumps, hang gliding, rock climbing and kayaking. You can (2) _____ _____ two sports plus board and luxury lodging for just $300 a week! If you're (3) _____ _____ cash, you can choose the economy camping option at $175.

What if you are (4) _____ _____ trying a new sport? Don't worry. You can (5) _____ _____ us to provide the best training available to ensure that you're safe. And we won't (6) _____ you _____ any 5.00 a.m. starts or boot camp horrors! Read what our customers have said about us.

'I really (7) _____ _____ my two weeks with Holiday Challenge. It was an amazing experience!'
(Cal Jones, New York)

'It was (8) _____ _____ my childhood: running around, learning new stuff, without a care in the world. The best holiday I've ever had.' **(Jill Healey, UK)**

'Don't (9) _____ _____ checking the competitors. Holiday Challenge is the one.'
(Sanath Kuppara, Sri Lanka)

'I (10) _____ _____ living my dreams! Thank you, Holiday Challenge.' **(Macarena Duval, Chile)**

6 Correct the sentences by adding or cutting one word.

1 Paulo Freire? Who's he? I've never heard him.
2 The Whorf-Sapir hypothesis? I know it like in the back of my hand.
3 Wendy's phone number? I don't know it by offhand.
4 Shakespeare's love poems? We spent years learning them by the heart.
5 Is Ronaldinho the best footballer in the world? Without but a doubt.
6 The Highway Code? Ask Susie – she's a driving instructor. She knows it inside.
7 International banking? I know next nothing about it.
8 Was Matisse the greatest painter in history? As far as I'm, he was.

Prefixes

7 Add a prefix to each word.

1 She couldn't finish the race because she's totally ___fit.
2 I read an article recently about ___paid bosses who earn millions for doing virtually nothing.
3 I just couldn't do any work because I was feeling so ___motivated.
4 Only a fool would ___estimate Thomson; she has the potential to be a great leader.
5 The workers are all ___-smokers so no one has ever asked for a smoking area.
6 He's a ___-professional footballer. He does it part-time for about £100 a week.
7 The problem was that they had ___understood the instructions, which is why the mistake occurred.
8 I'm totally ___worked. I have to organise a conference and write seven reports in two days.
9 Your excuses are completely ___relevant to me! You should have done your homework on time!
10 Davies was ___aware of the plan to fire him, which is why it was such a shock when it happened.

How to... talk about your achievements

8 Put the story in order.

a Climber Rheinhold Messner always knew that he had the   `1`
b challenge. Most doctors and scientists suggested that this was not an achievable   ☐
c come true with a successful three-day ascent.   ☐
d all expectations. After a few months' preparation, Messner pursued his dream   ☐
e something truly amazing in the mountains. However, in 1980 he exceeded   ☐
f of risk about climbing Everest, but Messner's attempt to take   ☐
g of being the first man to ascend Everest without oxygen supplies. There is always an element   ☐
h potential to accomplish   ☐
i on the world's highest mountain with the   ☐
j goal. Against all expectations, on 20th August he made his dream   ☐
k constraint of no oxygen was a truly daunting   ☐

Listening

1 **a** 🔵 4 Cover the audioscript. Listen to three speakers describing embarrassing moments abroad. Complete the table.

	Speaker 1	Speaker 2	Speaker 3
Nationality of speaker	(1) _____	(5) _____	(9) _____
Country where embarrassing moment happened	(2) _____	(6) _____	(10) _____
Main problem	(3) _____	(7) _____	(11) _____
Speaker's final thoughts about the situation	(4) _____	(8) _____	(12) _____

AUDIOSCRIPT

1

After a ten-hour journey from London I was really happy to have arrived at my host family's house in Colombia. They were extremely friendly, even though I spoke only a little Spanish, and they plied me with lemonade and made me feel comfortable. After a while, the mother asked me: 'Estas casado'? I thought she was asking me if I was tired, so I said: 'Si, un poco,' which means 'yes, a little'. Suddenly everyone laughed. Later I found out that 'casado' means married, and 'cansado' means tired. So she'd asked me if I was married and I'd said: 'Oh, a little'! That was just the first of many linguistic blunders I made! Actually, looking back, I wish I'd learned more of the language before moving there, but at the time I thought I'd just muddle through. Bad idea.

2

I'm from Colombia but I've lived in the US for ten years. When I first got a car, I needed to buy gas so I drove to a gas station and sat there waiting to be served. And I sat there, and I sat there, and no one came. Eventually, a bit perplexed, I went into the store and asked for a full tank of gas. The girl took my money, and I went back to the car and waited again. Still no one came. So I thought maybe someone had done it for me while I was in the store. So

I drove off. But then I looked at the gasometer and the tank was completely empty. I drove back to the gas station and suddenly I realised I had to fill the car myself. I've never done this before because in Colombia the people who work at the gas station do it for you. Well, I felt a bit stupid, as you can imagine.

3

This was before I could speak English properly. I was flying back to Italy and I was at Heathrow. Now, for some reason or other, I didn't have my glasses and I'm very short sighted so I couldn't see the information on the screen. So I asked someone official-looking: 'Which gate for Milan?' and he said: 'It's too early. There's no gate.' Now I got a bit confused because I thought that 'early' meant 'late', so I began to panic, thinking I'd missed my flight. So I asked someone else, and again: 'You're too early. No gate assigned. You'll have to wait.' And I was tearing my hair out and wondering why these English people were so calm when I'd just missed my flight. Eventually, a nice English man explained, very pleasantly, that the gate number would appear very soon and that I hadn't missed my flight. He was probably thinking: 'Dumb tourist.' So the moral of the story is: learn the basics. And don't lose your glasses!

b Listen again and check.

c Match the definitions (1–6) to phrases from the audioscript.

1 give someone large amounts of food or drink (speaker 1) _____

2 stupid mistakes (speaker 1) _____

3 continue doing something even though you aren't very good at it (speaker 1) _____

4 confused by something (speaker 2) _____

5 formal word for *given*, e.g. a task or a seat (speaker 3) _____

6 idiom for going crazy/getting angry (speaker 3) _____

Grammar | verb patterns (1)

2 Choose the correct words in *italics*.

1 The agency advises tourists *to take/taking/take* traveller's cheques rather than cash.
2 We look forward to *meet/meeting/have met* you in June.
3 My parents always encouraged me *that/write/writing/ to write* down my thoughts.
4 After graduating, Louise thought *of travel/of travelling/ to travel* for a year, but decided against it.
5 Mark recommended *ride/her to ride/riding* a bicycle as a good way to get fit.
6 They couldn't afford *to waste/that they waste/wasting* time on trivial matters.
7 I would urge *to reconsider/you to reconsider/ you reconsider* the offer before it's too late.
8 We've avoided *to do/that we do/doing* anything too dangerous so far.
9 I object *I have to/to having to/I have to* pay for my own travel to these conferences.
10 Chiara persuaded *us that we go/us go/us to go* on a boat trip with her.

3 Complete the article below with the correct form of verbs from the box. Add extra words where necessary.

> change   hear   make   find   object   take   live
> advise   think   afford

Culture shock

Those people thinking (1) _____ abroad will face a number of challenges including communication difficulties and settling in to a new community. But perhaps the biggest challenge is culture shock. You may find yourself (2) _____ to everything about the host culture: the way the people drive, queue, greet you, their habits and attitudes towards everything around you such as litter and personal space. This is common. People cannot avoid (3) _____ that their own culture does things 'the right way'. Everything else is therefore wrong. We urge you (4) _____ your mindset. There are no cultural rights or wrongs, only differences. What's more, if you're committed to staying in a foreign country for more than a few days, you can't (5) _____ be critical of everything around you. It'll make your life miserable.

The greatest divider of nations is ignorance, and so the first solution is knowledge. We recommend that you (6) _____ as much as you can about the host culture before you arrive – its customs, people, priorities and manners. When you've done your homework, if you really can't imagine (7) _____ a new life there, go somewhere else.

We also encourage you (8) _____ the attitude that diversity is interesting. No one would really want to live in a world in which every culture is the same, so we'd (9) _____ to observe and enjoy the differences. Eventually you will come to accept them.

We look forward (10) _____ from you about your experiences.

How to... | give advice/make recommendations about places

4 Match the sentence beginnings (1–10) with the endings (a–j).

1 The Taj Mahal really is a must- ☐
2 Disney World is superb value ☐
3 The hotel is nice, but it's ☐
4 Everyone says the museum is amazing, but in my view it's not ☐
5 If I were you, I'd ☐
6 You should try ☐
7 Make sure ☐
8 Watch out ☐
9 One thing to be wary ☐
10 Whatever you do, don't ☐

a for mosquitoes and take your malaria pills.
b backpacking because it's cheap.
c of is the number of pickpockets.
d see because it's so beautiful.
e all it's cracked up to be.
f go in April when isn't too hot.
g miss the textiles market.
h a bit overpriced.
i you go to the Eiffel Tower.
j for money.

Vocabulary | communities

5 Complete the paragraph below with words from the box.

> traffic   cosmopolitan   rate
> vibrant   areas   standard
> infrastructure   levels   life   mild

The best thing about my city is the high (1) _____ of living. It's a thriving community; there aren't high (2) _____ of unemployment and the crime (3) _____ is low. Another good thing is the cultural (4) _____ . There are lots of art galleries, cinemas and theatres, and there's also quite a (5) _____ nightlife with several good nightclubs and bars.

The city centre is very busy and there is some (6) _____ congestion during the day. The transport (7) _____ has improved but a lot of people still use cars. It's safe to walk around, though there are one or two no-go (8) _____ in the suburbs. The (9) _____ climate means you can stroll around and see people in the street cafés for ten months of the year. There are people from all over the world – it's a very (10) _____ city.

Grammar | comparatives

1 a Read the article and complete the sentence.

Part 1 is _____ positive about Wikipedia _____ part 2.

(1)

> Wikipedia has revolutionised the way encyclopaedias are compiled. Its open nature has led to a democratising process; knowledge is now not only in the hands of professors, but of the ordinary man or woman who has the interest, time and dedication to research and document facts. No wonder the establishment feels threatened. 'It's not authoritative!' they cry. 'It's too left-wing!' 'It doesn't represent the whole range of culture!' Of course it doesn't. It is a contemporary comment on the world. With time, today's contributors' views will be challenged and edited by a new generation.

(2)

> Wikipedia is a valuable resource for the amateur researcher in a hurry. If you want to find out when the Crimean War started, or what *quarks* are or when Picasso painted *Guernica*, Wikipedia will tell you, with 99.99% accuracy. But for anything more complex, Wikipedia is full of potential or real misinformation. It's not the contributors' fault; they genuinely want to get it right. But, for all we know, the contributors could be five-year-olds. Wikipedia's open-source system means that anyone – young children, obsessives and the lunatic fringe – can edit it. Because of this, no serious academic should trust Wikipedia.

b Find the mistake in each sentence and correct it.

1 Text 2 is nothing near as complimentary about Wikipedia as the other text. ☐

2 It suggests that Wikipedia is nowhere like as reliable as other encyclopaedias. ☐

3 It is more considerably positive about Wikipedia than the other text. ☐

4 The author of the text had rather let each generation question the views of the preceding generation. ☐

5 According to the text, the less we know about the contributors, less we can trust Wikipedia. ☐

6 The author of text 1 is definitely not as critical of Wikipedia to the author of the other text. ☐

7 The author probably thinks that rather for using Wikipedia for all research, you should only use it for simple facts. ☐

8 The text implies that it's a mile better to let everyone contribute to encyclopaedias. ☐

How to... | recognise features of informal language

2 a Replace the underlined words with words from the box. You don't need all of them.

> in due course   don't hesitate to contact me
> would like   concerning   Dear   be grateful
> Yours sincerely   of your attendance
> following   a previous arrangement
> look forward to hearing   take place

a We hope to hear from you <u>soon</u>. ☐

b Please <u>get in touch</u> if you have any queries. ☐

c <u>Hi</u> Mrs Dormer, ☐

d Technics Solutions <u>wants</u> to invite you to our annual investors' meeting ☐

e inform us <u>whether you will be able to come</u> by 14 June. ☐

f which will <u>be</u> at The Atrium on Rose Street at 5.00 p.m. on Wednesday 6 July. ☐

g We would <u>like it</u> if you could ☐

h <u>Best wishes,</u> ☐

b Put the sentences (a–h) in order to make a formal letter.

Reading

3 **a** Read the article. Which community did each website target?

a Fashionable people ☐

b Readers ☐

c People who have goods to sell ☐

1

Pierre Omidyar, the son of French-Iranian immigrants, was already a millionaire before launching eBay. Omidyah's electronics site, e-shop, was bought out by Microsoft in 1996, making him a millionaire before he had turned 30. With this money, he set up an online auction company which allowed people to show items they wished to sell; other users then made a bid. Omidyar wanted to name the site Echo Bay Technology Group, but this name was already owned by a Canadian mining company, so he shortened the name to 'eBay', and a legend was born. Almost immediately, eBay made a profit. The site sold goods ranging from computers to posters to underwear. The growth of eBay was phenomenal. It is now the world's most successful online business and its users consider themselves part of a distinct community. 150 million registered users buy and sell goods worth $1,050 every second. The website is used by big companies such as Vodaphone and IBM to sell off excess stock, but the majority of goods still sell for less than $50.

2

It was the early 1990s, the internet boom was just beginning, and Jeff Bezos wanted to be a part of this brave, new, forward-thinking community. After leaving his job on Wall Street, Bezos decided to set up an online bookselling business. Using his garage in Seattle as an office, Bezos created Amazon.com. The idea was to make the buying of books cheap and easy, with more choice than the traditional bookshop could provide. The site had a number of features which made it attractive to potential users: fast service, search capabilities, low costs for users, tools for comparing prices of books, and personalisation in the form of customer-written book reviews. As a 24-hour virtual bookshop, Amazon was convenient, cheap and reliable. Gradually, through word-of-mouth, the company grew in popularity. Bezos had originally handled customer orders himself, but soon he realised that the company was growing too fast for one man. By 1998, the net sales were $540 million and a whole generation of book buyers was hooked.

3

Ernst Malmsten, an events organiser, and Kajsa Leander, a supermodel, grew up in Lund, Sweden. In the late 1990s, they decided to launch boo.com, a website that would create a global fashion community by selling designer clothes all over the world.

From the beginning, there were difficulties. Clothing companies didn't trust the internet and were reluctant to sell online. Also, no one was sure that people would buy clothes without trying them on first. On 3 November 1999, the day boo.com was launched, the website had 25,000 hits, but these resulted in only eight actual orders for clothes. Worse, a well-known journalist wrote a negative article about boo.com, explaining how it had taken him 81 minutes to order a product. Other problems included viruses and a fraud detection system that rejected customers' orders. By March 2000, half of boo.com's workforce had lost their jobs. While most internet start-ups are run from garages or bedrooms, boo.com had luxurious offices in six of the world's most glamorous and expensive cities. Fresh fruit and flowers were delivered daily. Malmsten and Leander, who always travelled first-class, claimed that companies in the fashion industry needed this image. But boo.com was spending faster than it was earning and the company was doomed.

b Read the statements (1–8). Write eBay (E), Amazon.com (A) or boo.com (B).

1 The founder originally wanted a different name for the website. ☐

2 The company had a high-class, stylish image. ☐

3 Users of the site could post their own opinions of the things being sold. ☐

4 The site sold a range of goods from the beginning. ☐

5 The type of goods for sale weren't ideal for online shopping. ☐

6 The founder/founders originally ran the website alone. ☐

7 The founder/founders was/were already rich before launching the website. ☐

8 The company had some technical problems. ☐

c Match the definitions (1–7) to words in the article.

1 offer of a price for something (part 1)

_____

2 extraordinary or remarkable (part 1)

_____

3 a store of goods ready for sale (part 1)

_____

4 unwilling/not wanting to do something (part 3)

_____

5 new company (especially internet companies) (part 3)

_____

6 extremely comfortable and expensive (part 3)

_____

7 destined to end badly or in failure (part 3)

_____

Listening

1 **a** 🔘 5 Cover the audioscript. Listen to three speakers talking about their communities. What positive aspects of each community do they talk about?

Speaker 1 _____

Speaker 2 _____

Speaker 3 _____

AUDIOSCRIPT

1

People might think that because the community is poor, the people are incredibly unhappy or maybe there's nothing to do. But that's really not the case at all. All kinds of things go on within the townships, so you'd say it was a real hive of activity. For example, one of the ways we entertain ourselves is through music, and if you think about it, you'll understand that music brings people together and of course it's free. There are so many choirs here I've lost count, and they don't just sing our traditional songs; they do all sorts of other things like pop and classical music. A traveller once left us a tape of Robbie Williams and we learned these songs and sang the harmonies. Another activity that's important here is football. Again, the beauty of it is that it's free and anyone can play. The girls have a team, and there's an over-60s team. The main pitch used to be covered with broken glass and animals grazing, but we fixed it and now it's very good. And whenever *Bafana Bafana* plays, we all sit around one television and cheer and sing. So, life in a township is hard, of course, but we have a way of making the best out of the things we have. No one sits around feeling sorry for himself.

2

My grandfather once told me a saying. He said that the land doesn't belong to the people; the people belong to the land. I think this idea is one of the reasons why Vanuatu is special. The people are close to nature, and the nature here really is wonderful. Vanuatu is made up of lots of small islands, and we have beautiful coastlines and rainforests. The land is so fertile that we grow most of our own food, and this means that even the many poor people here won't starve. We are a close-knit

community. People tend to help each other perhaps more than in built-up, developed communities. I remember a few years ago, an Englishman was stranded on one of the islands with his ten-year-old son because of a problem with the airline. I think he was a researcher. There were no shops or hotels, but the people here fed them and looked after them for three weeks until they could fly out. This is quite normal in Vanuatu. We are a spiritual people, not very materialistic. We enjoy what we have and don't really seek material things. I hope that is how the world sees us, although I'm told that we are more famous for inventing bungee jumping!

3

We were fed up of the ... I guess you could call them 'annoyances' of living in a regular community, so we decided to set up our own. Four years ago, a group of 28 of us, all retired and all over 65, bought up some real estate and had the whole community designed and laid out for us. And this is the result. We have nothing at all against young people. In fact, most of us have children and grandchildren. But as a place to live, we just wanted a quiet neighbourhood without the noise and the trash, and it works incredibly well. We are all old friends and we have complementary skills, like Jack down the road knows how to service an automobile, and I used to work in property law so I deal with those issues. Reuben Barrios next door was a gardener, so he tells everyone how to grow flowers. It's everything we wanted from our old age. The grandchildren visit us on the weekend and we have a lot of fun, but come Monday they're gone and it's back to a quiet life.

b Write true (T) or false (F). Listen again to check.

Speaker 1

1 The speaker is from a rich area. ☐
2 The hobbies they do don't cost anything. ☐
3 The people of the community are probably close and they do many things together. ☐

Speaker 2

4 Vanuatu is a place of natural beauty. ☐
5 Most of the people of Vanuatu are wealthy. ☐
6 The speaker thinks that the people of Vanuatu are becoming more materialistic. ☐

Speaker 3

7 The speaker is probably quite wealthy. ☐
8 The community is made up of friends. ☐
9 The speaker wishes there were more young people in the community. ☐

c Choose the best definition for each expression (a, b or c). Check in the audioscript.

1 a real hive of activity
   a full of action and productivity
   b a place where people meet
   c an appropriate time to do something
2 *Bafana Bafana*
   a an African game
   b a football team
   c a type of music
3 fertile
   a beautiful and full of colour
   b free for everyone to use
   c good for growing plants/food
4 stranded
   a very hungry
   b in trouble with the police
   c couldn't get out
5 real estate
   a property such as houses or land
   b a very large house
   c a plan made by an architect
6 complementary (adjective)
   a saying how good something is
   b (things) go well together, though they are different
   c the best

Vocabulary | adjectives to describe places

2 Complete the article with words from the box.

> unspoilt   diverse   tranquil   side by side   vast
> run-down   stunning   packed   off the beaten track

Instead of going to the usual tourist spots, Werner and I went (1) _____ to Tallinn, capital of Estonia. I'm glad we did. The heart of the city is the Old Town. We found the architecture absolutely (2) _____ with cobbled streets and church spires, castles and beautiful ancient buildings standing (3) _____ .
We wandered for a while before stopping for lunch in a local restaurant. I ate a superb cod and potato dish while Werner tucked into a lamb cutlet.
The best thing to do in Tallinn is see the old buildings – the (4) _____ town hall, which seems to stretch for miles, and the wonderful Alexander Nevsky Cathedral. It's a great city to stroll around because everything is fairly close together and the streets are pedestrian-friendly.
We were staying in a very cheap hotel near the centre. The building was old and slightly (5) _____ and the room wasn't the biggest, but it was clean and comfortable. In the evening we went out to sample the nightlife. I was told that the clubbing scene is pretty (6) _____ , with techno, jazz, folk and disco music all available every night of the week. Tallinn is also popular with the stag-party crowd and apparently some of the nightclubs – Hollywood and Decolte in particular – are usually (7) _____ with tourists. But when we were there, the town seemed completely (8) _____ by tourism. Werner and I went for a quiet drink in a bar called Guitar Safari, and ended up listening to excellent live music all evening. Overall, after the excitement of some of the other cities, we found our experience of Tallinn extremely (9) _____ , but by no means boring.

Grammar | introductory *it*

3 Make sentences using *it* and the words in brackets.

1 There's no point handing in the paper now. You've missed the deadline. (no/use)

_____

2 I'd be grateful if you could call me on 0982 654726. (appreciate)

_____

3 I'm not surprised that Marie won the competition. She's a genius. (no/wonder)

_____

4 You have to sign the contract by 12 September. (essential)

_____

5 What a pity you can't come to the show. (shame)

_____

6 It annoys me to see people throw litter. (hate/when)

_____

Communities

1 Choose the correct words in *italics*.

1 The *price/cost/rate* of living is high in Monaco.
2 The transport *structure/facility/infrastructure* is good in London.
3 Germany has a *mild/calm/normal* climate.
4 The *health/medical/healthcare* system in Cuba used to be excellent, with many top hospitals.
5 Arguably, the highest *standard/rate/style* of living is found in Scandinavian countries.
6 For several years the crime *level/statistics/rate* in New York has been falling.
7 *Job opportunities/Job-seeking/Unemployment* among unqualified immigrants is a problem.
8 The *party life/night action/nightlife* in Poland is fantastic.
9 Hong Kong is becoming increasingly *cosmopolitan/diverse/varied*.
10 The best thing about Brazil is the sense of *liberty/freeing/freedom* as you walk around.
11 Egypt has possibly the world's most amazing *monuments/artefacts/buildings*.
12 In most city centres there's a lot of traffic *pollution/congestion/excess*.

Adjectives to describe places

2 Put the underlined letters in order.

The town where I grew up used to be absolutely (1) hcraginm. The scenery was (2) rnqtluai: there were large rolling hills and a small forest (3) fof het nebaet rktac. I used to (4) slrtol there for hours on end, and (5) azge at the trees. I went back there recently and was surprised at how much it had changed. Right in the (6) threa of the town there was a car park which stood (7) dise yb edis with a new shopping mall. I went inside the mall and it was (8) ecakpd. Then I drove to my old school, which was still (9) gutibsln with children, though the buildings looked a little (10) nru nwod. I went in, hoping to see some of my old teachers, when suddenly a security guard approached, asked who I was, and promptly kicked me out. So I drove towards the forest, assuming that some things would remain (11) poutnlsi. Unfortunately, the forest didn't exist any more: they'd built a (12) asvt block of flats there.

Phrasal verbs

3 Complete the phrasal verbs with the correct words.

1 Alexandra cycles so fast that she's extremely hard to keep _____ .
   a on with   b up to   c up with
2 The work was tough but we were able to carry it _____ .
   a out   b by   c in
3 A solution to this problem won't be easy, but we'll see what we manage to come _____ .
   a round for   b in to   c up with
4 The house was run-down so we had to do it _____ .
   a round   b up   c over
5 Hannah has just started at a new school, so I hope she fits _____ .
   a in   b up   c on
6 It'll be a great party if he turns _____ .
   a up   b on   c out
7 There was a crash on the motorway so the traffic was held _____ .
   a in   b up   c on
8 The salary is terrible. They barely pay you enough money to get _____ .
   a through   b on   c by

Verb patterns (1)

4 Complete the sentences with words from the box. Not all the words are necessary.

recommend entering being us to use
to do afford going stand to go avoids
of watching us using to pass is urge
us to enter doing to watch

1 I'm thinking of _____ to France. What's it like in April?
2 Dave can't _____ to take a holiday, so he's camping in his garden this year!
3 Can you imagine _____ an astronaut? You could go into space!
4 Mario's so lazy. He always _____ doing the washing up.
5 I tried to persuade Gail _____ a DVD tonight, but she didn't want to.
6 I can't _____ smoking. The smoke makes me ill.
7 They advised _____ traveller's cheques because they're safer.
8 I wouldn't _____ spending long in the museum. It's a bit dull.
9 My teachers always encouraged me _____ my best.
10 Libby urged _____ the competition. She was right – we won!

Comparatives (review)

5 Complete the article with eight words.

The online community is predicting that blogs will soon replace print journalism. While publishing news and views on the web is far easier /getting into print, I have my doubts about this prediction. Firstly, blogs are nowhere as reliable as print journalism. There are checks and balances for print journalists, and newspapers are far likely than websites to be prosecuted if they get the facts wrong. Reading a blog is much the same reading a diary: if it is full of lies and exaggeration, there's not a lot you can do. The advantage of blogs is that they are personal and usually unedited. But than using them as formal carriers of news, I think we'd be better having them as an alternative source of opinion. Basically, they act as a voice that cannot be silenced. The easier the web becomes to use, more diverse voices it will contain, and that's a great thing. As for me, I sooner read a newspaper any day!

[handwritten: than]

6 Do the pairs of sentences have similar (S) or different (D) meanings?

1 a It's much the same whether you buy your ticket on the Internet or at the station.
   b Buying the ticket on the internet is marginally cheaper but there's hardly any difference. ☐

2 a I'd sooner live in a quiet community than one with lots of nightlife.
   b In my view, the more nightlife, the better. ☐

3 a São Paulo is much the biggest city I've ever been in.
   b São Paulo is by far the biggest city I've ever been in. ☐

4 a The less we mix with that community, the less trouble we'll have.
   b We're much better off mixing with that community. ☐

5 a Togo is nowhere near as expensive as South Africa.
   b South Africa is nothing like as cheap as Togo. ☐

6 a Lugano is considerably prettier than my home town.
   b My home town isn't quite as pretty as Lugano. ☐

7 a Bristol is nothing like as exciting as the town where I grew up.
   b Bristol is miles more exciting than the town where I grew up. ☐

8 a I'd prefer to live in the countryside.
   b I think we'd be better off living in the countryside. ☐

How to... give advice/make recommendations

7 Complete the crossword with the missing words.

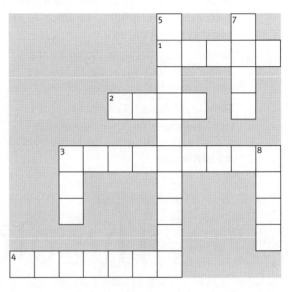

Across

1 That jacket you bought ten years ago was good _____ for money. It still looks nice.

2 When you go to the market be _____ of pickpockets. They are notorious.

3 Everyone said the film was great but I thought it was a bit _____ .

4 That statue isn't all it's _____ up to be. I thought it would be much more beautiful than it is.

Down

3 You should watch _____ for the mosquitoes. There are a lot of them at this time of year.

5 The drinks are _____ in this nightclub. They shouldn't be this expensive!

7 You can't miss the Picasso exhibition. It's a _____ !

8 The film was really _____ . I found it so boring that I fell asleep.

Reading

1 **a** Read the article and choose the best summary.

1 Some communities claim they have a secret way to stay young and healthy. The article describes how they manage to do it. ☐

2 Some communities claim that many of their people live until they are over a hundred. The article disputes these claims. ☐

3 Some researchers believe that ancient communities are healthier than modern societies. The article lists the problems of modern living. ☐

b Read the article again. Write questions for these answers.

1 It was an academic paper about the peoples he studied.

2 A local man whose stated age changed by 11 years in only four years.

3 It was lost when a church caught fire.

4 Because in these societies, the older you are, the more respected you are.

5 The condition of the people's bones, and official documents.

6 Because they were afraid of being caught.

The old-age hoax

A little old man walks the fields of Vilcabamba, Ecuador. His skin is wrinkled from exposure to the sun, and his legs move slowly, steadily. As the sky turns red, he puts down his ancient tools and walks across the valley to the mud
5 hut that he calls home. He is 140 years old.

Hard to believe? Well, Methuselah lived to be 969, according to the Bible. And, according to some, there are communities – the people of Vilcabamba, the Abkhazians of Georgia, the Hunza of Pakistan – which contain large numbers of
10 centenarians, those lucky people who live to be 100.

Let's take a trip back in time. January,1973. Dr Alexander Leaf of Harvard University publishes a report in the *National Geographic* magazine that describes his journeys to study the Hunza, Abkhazians and the Vilcabambas. He
15 calls his report *Every Day Over 100 is a Gift*. According to Leaf, there are ten times the number of centenarians found in these areas than is normal in modern Western civilisations. The article caused a minor stir in anthropology circles and one or two commercial ones
20 too: an American entrepreneur makes plans to invest in bottled water from Vilcabamba, and a Japanese company discusses building a hotel there for elderly tourists.

But then, as further studies followed Leaf's, the evidence began to point not to mythical communities with
25 ancient youth-preserving lifestyles, but rather to lies, exaggeration and the creation of a sensational myth. Although Leaf's report sounded plausible enough at first, a number of questions arose later. When Dr Leaf returned to Vilcabamba four years after his first visit, one of the
30 villagers, Miguel Carpiro, had miraculously become eleven years older. Leaf asked to see Carpiro's birth certificate, but was told that it had been destroyed in a church fire.

Indeed, birth records were one of the main problems: societies with low levels of literacy usually don't have
35 them. And in Vilcabamba names were used repeatedly within the family so that grandfathers, fathers and sons may have exactly the same name, adding to the confusion. Furthermore, old age is revered in societies such as Abkhazian, and so people exaggerate to improve
40 their social status. When the exaggeration also brings about increased attention and tourism, there is even further temptation to add a few years to your age.

After Leaf's report, two researchers, Mazess and Forman, went to Vilcabamba and checked skeletal conditions
45 as well as existing records. They found enormous inaccuracies everywhere. Miguel Carpiro, who had claimed to be 121, was actually 87. His mother was born five years after he'd claimed to be born! Another researcher, a Russian geneticist named Zhores Medvedev,
50 studied the people of Abkhazia, who had also claimed to have many centenarians. He discovered that many of them had assumed the identities of their parents. Some of these people were World War I deserters, and they had used their dead parents' names in order
55 to avoid detection.

So, myth or reality? We don't know for sure. Roger Maupin, an anthropologist, says of these peoples: 'Their lifestyle is certainly healthy. They have constant steady work, a good diet and a small community untroubled by
60 such things as war, technology and the stresses these bring. But we just have no reliable evidence about their real age. Ultimately, I don't think it matters. It's not the age you live to, it's the quality of your life that counts.'

c Match the definitions (1–8) to words in the article.

1 people who are still alive at 100 (*n*) (line 10)
2 attracted a lot of attention (*v*) (line 18)
3 believable (*adj*) (line 27)
4 deeply respected (*adj*) (line 38)
5 importance (how much a person is respected) within a community (*n*) (line 40)
6 causes (*v*) (line 41)
7 soldiers who run away from battle (*n*) (line 53)
8 being found (*v*) (line 55)

Grammar | narrative tenses (review)

2 Tick the sentence (a or b) that describes each picture.

 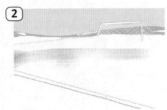

1 a At midnight, when we got back, she had already put the baby to bed.
  b At midnight, when we got back, she was putting the baby to bed.
2 a The game was cancelled because it had been snowing.
  b The game was cancelled because it was snowing.
3 a Juan had painted the bathroom.
  b Juan had been painting the bathroom.
4 a I got home and discovered that my flat had been burgled.
  b I got home and discovered that my flat was being burgled.
5 a Junichi told us he had been training for the Olympics.
  b Junichi told us he was training for the Olympics.
6 a When I saw Joan she was going to the hairdresser's.
  b When I saw Joan she had been to the hairdresser's.

3 Complete the sentences with the correct form of the verbs in brackets.

1 Who _____ to on the phone? (talk)
2 We could tell from his filthy clothes that he _____ in the garden for hours. (work)
3 I knew something was wrong because the dog _____ constantly. (bark)
4 How _____ me? I thought I was safe. (find)
5 Once I _____ her properly, I knew she was the girl for me. (meet)
6 The maid obviously hadn't come because my room _____ . (clean)
7 _____ of him before you saw the film? (hear)
8 Later, I realised that we _____ about different people! (talk)
9 I couldn't pick him up because my car _____ in the garage. (fix)
10 It was clear that he _____ anything during the lecture. (understand)

Pronunciation | differentiating tenses

4 **a** 6 Listen and tick the sentences you hear.

1 a I'd have helped you every time.
  b I've helped you every time.
2 a Why did you hit him?
  b Why had you hit him?
3 a Have we paid already?
  b Had we paid already?
4 a Would you like to play chess?
  b Do you like to play chess?
5 a I'd run ten miles.
  b I've run ten miles.
6 a She'd stopped smoking.
  b She stopped smoking.
7 a I prefer vegetables to meat.
  b I'd prefer vegetables to meat.
8 a I hadn't run for ages.
  b I didn't run for ages.

b Listen again and repeat the sentences.

Reading and listening

1 **a** 🔊 7 Read and listen to a short story. Answer the questions.

1 Who do you think had the idea to go birdwatching?

2 What type of town do Thomas and Rosie live in?

3 Is Thomas good at spelling? How do we know?

4 What type of person is Rosie? How do we know?

5 What does the father think of Thomas's description of the birdwatching trip?

6 Why was Rosie 'disgraced'?

7 How does the father feel about his children?

8 Which of these words would you use to describe the story?

> surprising   surreal   traditional
> shocking   funny

b Match the definitions (1–8) to words in the story.

1 ready and waiting (line 9) _____

2 high-pitched shout (line 20) _____

3 walking with short steps, body moving from side to side (line 32) _____

4 walking vigorously (usually through something) (line 34) _____

5 preserved in some kind of (solid) form, but no longer living/growing/used (line 35) _____

6 thrown away/abandoned (line 42) _____

7 made something uneven/messy by rubbing it (line 43) _____

8 looking at something, angrily (line 49) _____

c Find the object or person in the story that words (1–8) refer to.

1 it (line 4) _____

2 on which (line 10) _____

3 this same sound (line 25) _____

4 it (line 27) _____

5 it (line 31) _____

6 it (line 33) _____

7 he (line 47) _____

8 its (line 49) _____

Birdwatcher

At 2.32 on the afternoon of 10th July, eight-year-old Thomas Smith saw a large yellow-beaked eagle rise from the roof of the local post office. His sister, ten-year-old Rosie, didn't see it because she was busy
5   applying her mother's lipstick to her small, but very pretty, mouth, and in any case she wasn't all that keen on birdwatching.
'Rosie,' said Thomas. 'How do you spell "eagle"?' His pencil was poised above a notebook which
10 had a picture of an owl on the front and on which Thomas had written 'Burds'. B-u-r-d-s.
'Eagle?' said Rosie. 'I-d-i-o-t.'
'Very funny.'
'E-e-g-l-e.'
15 Thomas wrote it down. Eegle. 2.32, 10th July. Kingston Road Post Office.
    They crossed the street, slipping between the fat cars all stopped still in the summer heat, fingers tapping outside windows. It was at this point that
20 Thomas heard the distant shriek of seagulls and recognised the sound at once. The previous summer they had spent a week with their parents at a seaside town eating huge sausages in pools of grease and getting red-faced in the sun, and had been woken
25 every morning by this same sound.
'Rosie, how do you spell "seagull"?'
'Same as eagle but it starts with an s.'
    At 2.58 Thomas and Rosie paused for a minute while Rosie searched her handbag for the blue eye-
30 shadow that she had removed from her mother's drawer. It was called Aquamarine Dream. At this moment, Thomas noticed a penguin waddling down the High Street. Thomas watched it go by, the penguin merrily traipsing through the cigarette butts
35 and chewing gum stains fossilised on the pavement, and Thomas wrote "Pen Win" in his notebook.
    Later, while the disgraced Rosie was shut up in her room, her mother's makeup returned, Thomas sat at his father's feet and explained about the
40 eagle on the post office roof, the ostrich outside the library, the vulture in Rosemary Gardens snacking on a discarded bag of popcorn. And his father ruffled the boy's hair and laughed to himself and thought about the wonders of the child's
45 imagination. And the man felt at peace with the world and with his two naughty children, at least until 3.11 a.m. the following morning when he was woken by an enormous white swan sitting at the end of his bed, its yellow eyes glaring.

Vocabulary | books

2 Complete the book review below with words from the box.

> depicts   one-dimensional   down   base
> found   hooked   best-seller   bookworm
> gripping   avid

Meredith Johnson's new book, *Feather Man*, like her four previous novels, is a page-turner and destined to be a (1) _____ . Unusually for Johnson, she doesn't (2) _____ her plot on a true story (her last book was a fictionalised account of a failed bank robbery), though once again she brilliantly (3) _____ Edinburgh's criminal underworld, where a wrong word can earn you a slashing with a razor blade and a wrong move can get you injected with something very nasty indeed.

She soon has the reader (4) _____ . The hero, Paul Schroeder, detective and (5) _____ who spends half his life in a library, finds himself investigating a writer called Max Dowling when Schroeder realises that Dowling leaves clues to unsolved crimes in his books.

I (6) _____ the story totally (7) _____ , and if some of the characters are a little (8) _____ – for example, a rather unrealistic group of street gangsters all seem to wear raincoats, smoke a lot and have particularly unpleasant domestic pets – the pace and action more than make up for it. Frankly, I couldn't put *Feather Man* (9) _____ . I recommend it highly not only for (10) _____ readers of Johnson's work, but for new converts, too.

How to... | describe people

3 Read what these people say about their partners. Choose the correct word in *italics*.

1 She comes *across/over/around* as very kind and gentle when you first meet her.
2 Once you *become to know/get to know/seem to know* her, you realise she's really funny.
3 The thing that *strikes/hits you/strikes you* about Colin is that he's so intelligent.
4 What I really *think about/like for/like about* Susana is her sense of humour.
5 Matthew is *such a/so/a such* talented guy that you have to admire him.
6 He can be *a bit of/a bit/bit* mean sometimes, especially when he's in a bad mood.

Vocabulary | compound words

4 a Match words 1–8 to words a–h to make compound words.

1	single-	a	minded
2	self-	b	minded
3	thick-	c	offish
4	kind-	d	orientated
5	stand-	e	hearted
6	career-	f	skinned
7	level-	g	sufficient
8	absent-	h	headed

b Match the compound words in exercise 4a to the people in extracts 1–5. You may match more than compound word to each person. Two compound words are not needed.

1 Bradbury was determined to claw his way to the top of the company, trampling on whoever got in his way. He had only been in the business six months when he decided that the quickest way to get promoted would be to murder William DeFries.

_____

2 Delilah sat in the corner for the whole party. Whenever a young man approached, she immediately feigned boredom and continued sipping from her slim glass of iced water, eyes raised to the ceiling.

_____

3 My mother was the type of person who regularly left home in her slippers. She frequently forgot to turn off ovens, lights, televisions and radios. She was known to make phone calls and, on being answered, immediately forget not only why she was calling, but who she was calling.

_____

4 Being short, skinny and ugly, I have been called names since I was old enough to walk. 'Stick insect, creepy-crawly, witch, rat-face, alien, ET, lizard.' I answer the name-callers with a wink and a smile. You see, I just don't care.

_____

5 Mr Trimble had watery grey eyes and a pocket permanently stuffed full of sweets for any children he came across. He walked with the slowness of a snail, leaving no slime but a trail of happiness wherever he went.

_____

Listening

1 **a** 🔊 8 Cover the audioscript. Listen to three jokes and match them to the pictures.

 A

 B

 C

AUDIOSCRIPT

1 _____

A policeman stops a car because it is speeding. He asks the driver for his licence. 'I don't have one,' says the driver. 'And the car's not mine. I stole it. But I think I saw a driver's licence in the glove box when I put my gun in there.'

'You stole it?! You have a gun in the glove box?!'

'Yes,' says the driver. 'I put it there just before I threw the car owner's body in the boot.' The policeman calls for backup and five minutes later, four police cars arrive. The captain says, 'Sir, may I see your licence?'

'Sure,' says the driver. He opens the glove box slowly and gives him the licence. The police captain says, 'So, no gun in the glove box?'

'Gun? Of course not!'

'And no body in the boot?'

'What?!' says the driver. And the captain says: 'My police officer told me you had a gun in the glove box and a body in the boot.'

'Yeah, and I bet the liar told you I was speeding too.'

2 _____

A couple owned a cat, but the man hated it. So one day, he decided to get rid of it. He drove ten blocks and threw the cat out of the car window. But when he got home, there the cat was, lying on the doormat. So the next day he drove 20 blocks and threw the cat into a river. But, on entering his driveway the cat was there again, fast asleep by the door. So the next day he drove 15 blocks, took a left, took a right, went down the motorway, crossed a couple of bridges and threw the cat into a large hole in the ground. After driving a while, he called his wife. 'Is the cat there?' he asked.

'Yes,' she said. 'Why do you ask?'

'OK, put the cat on the phone. I'm lost and I need directions home.'

3 _____

A new manager walks into his office and finds four numbered envelopes on the desk. Number one says 'Open me first'. So he opens it and finds a letter from the previous manager. It says, 'When the company is having problems and you don't know what to do, open these envelopes in order.' So he puts the envelopes away and forgets about them. Six months later, the company is in big trouble and the manager may lose his job. Suddenly he remembers the envelopes so he opens the second envelope. In it there is a message which says, 'Blame everything on me, the previous manager.' He does this and saves his job and the company recovers. But six months after this, the company is in trouble again and losing money fast. He opens the third envelope and reads the message. It says, 'Blame everything on the government.' He does this and everyone agrees and he keeps his job. Six months later the company is in even bigger trouble, and the workers are on strike. So he opens the fourth envelope. The message says: 'Prepare four envelopes.'

b Complete the sentences from the audioscript. Listen again to check.

Joke 1

1 The driver was stopped because he was _____ .

2 There wasn't a gun in the _____ or a body in the _____ .

Joke 2

3 A man wanted to _____ of a cat.

4 The man needed _____ to get home.

Joke 3

5 The second note said '_____ everything on me'.

6 The manger's final problem was that the workers were on _____ .

c Mark the sentences that are sarcastic (SA), show surprise (S) and those which are said calmly (C).

1 'You stole it?! You have a gun in the glove box?!' ☐

2 'I put it there just before I threw the car owner's body into the boot.' ☐

3 'Sir, may I see your licence?' ☐

4 'So no gun in the glove box?' ☐

5 'Gun? Of course not!' ☐

6 'My police officer told me you had a gun in the glove box and a body in the boot.' ☐

7 'Yeah, and I bet the liar told you I was speeding, too.' ☐

Pronunciation | intonation

2 **a** 🔊 8 Listen again and answer the questions.

1 Which sentences are said loudly?

2 In which sentences does the voice rise and fall a lot? Which words are emphasised?

3 In which sentences does the tone of voice stay the same?

b Listen again and repeat.

Grammar | participle clauses

3 Six of these sentences contain mistakes. Find the mistakes and correct them.

1 Not having heard the music, I can't really judge it.
2 On been arrested by the police, Teresa admitted that she was guilty of fraud.
3 She broke her leg while to play hockey.
4 He stood there in front of us, desolate, robbed of everything he'd ever owned.
5 To help other people wasn't something that usually made Mrs Davies happy.
6 Having been given the car just the day before, Lucas promptly crashed it.
7 All of the boys, hoped to be football stars, trained for six hours every day.
8 Told by his teacher that he had the ability to pass his exam, Bill finally achieved his goal.
9 Having wake up at 4.00 a.m., we were exhausted by 11.00.
10 After being listening to the speech for four hours, Bianca eventually fell asleep.

4 Complete the stories with the correct form of verbs from the box.

> have/catch   ask   play   celebrate
> call   cheat

In the wild old days of cowboys and saloons, (1) _____ at cards was likely to get you killed. (2) _____ cheating in a saloon in 1857, Donald Blewett was shot dead. The men (3) _____ still wanted to finish their game, however, and they needed another player, so they asked a stranger to join them. This stranger then proceeded to win over $4,000. (4) _____ to the scene a bit later, the police decided to try and find Donald Blewett's nearest relative. After (5) _____ around to find out the dead man's name, they discovered that the stranger (6) _____ his $4,000 jackpot was Blewett's son, who hadn't seen his father for over ten years.

> have/place   tell   involve   bet   have/make   know

(7) _____ should never have been easier. (8) _____ elaborate plans to cheat, horse owner and politician Horatio Bottomley placed 'the perfect bet' on a horse race in Belgium. He owned all six of the horses (9) _____ in the race and he employed the six English jockeys. After (10) _____ the jockeys the order in which they should finish, Bottomley thought he couldn't lose. However, (11) _____ his bet, he got a surprise. Halfway through the race, a thick fog descended on the course. As a result, the race was declared null and void, with no winner. Bottomley, (12) _____ for his money-making ability, lost a fortune.

Vocabulary | humour

5 Complete the crossword.

1 give the impression that something is greater or larger than it really is
2 a funny drawing
3 humorous use of words that sound the same but have different meanings
4 comic moments connected to very serious subjects
5 when you say the opposite of what you mean, for a humorous effect
6 comic drama using unlikely situations and people acting stupidly
7 make something/someone seem ridiculous (often in order to laugh at people who have power)

Narrative tenses (review)

1 Complete the sentences using the correct form of verbs from the box.

> face   write   memorise   get up   read
> borrow   turn into   drive   make   leave

1 By midday I was really tired, because I _____ on the motorway since 5 a.m.

2 She said all the noise was because the building next door _____ a shopping mall. The work wouldn't be completed until the following May.

3 They desperately wanted to see Francesca, but the janitor told them that she _____ already.

4 One of the children recited the whole story. Apparently, he _____ it for weeks.

5 When I got home, the fridge _____ a weird noise, so I called the engineer.

6 He _____ his autobiography in the months before he died, so although it wasn't finished, we had a good idea of his life story.

7 My friends knew the film had a twist in the tail, but I didn't because I _____ the book.

8 Rob tried to take a photo of Lily, but she _____ the wrong way.

9 Yevgeny was searching for a book in the library, but it _____ already.

10 _____ you _____ early this morning? I thought I heard you scampering around!

Participle clauses

2 Choose the correct words in *italics*. Sometimes more than one answer is possible.

1 *To hope/Hoping/Hoped* to find a new wife, Davies settled in Paris.

2 *Restored/Having been restored/After restored* to its former glory, the painting was re-hung.

3 *Ran/To run/Running* marathons is what she does best.

4 I know the man *having sat/sat/sitting* in the blue car.

5 *While driving/Driven/Having driven* in the tunnel, keep your lights on.

6 *On hearing/Heard/Having heard* the news, he rushed over to the hospital.

7 *Buried/Being buried/Burying* in the cemetery is a famous scientist of the early 20th century.

8 *After catching/After being caught/Having been caught*, the robber put down his gun.

9 The photos *taken/being taken/having been taken* today will turn out fine. The light is perfect.

10 *After being treated/Treating/Treated* by experts, the dog began to recover.

Tales

3 Complete the sentences (1–8) with the correct words.

1 In order to avoid hurting people, I think it's OK to tell _____
   A a feeble excuse. **B** a white lie. **C** a rumour.

2 Advertising writers aren't exactly liars, but they tend to be a bit _____
   A of a gossip. **B** exaggerated.
   C prone to exaggeration.

3 The yeti is probably just a _____
   A tale. **B** myth. **C** tall story.

4 We heard the fire alarm, but it turned out to be an elaborate _____
   A rumour. **B** false. **C** hoax.

5 Whenever his results were bad, Peter made _____
   A excuses. **B** a lie. **C** a trick.

6 Joanne first told me about it, and then the rumour _____
   A went. **B** passed around. **C** spread.

7 He's always telling stories about other people – he's such a _____
   A hoaxer. **B** bareface. **C** gossip.

8 I should never have trusted her. She played a _____ on me and stupidly I was taken in.
   A joke. **B** hoax. **C** punch line.

Humour

4 Match the review extracts (1–5) to types of humour from the box. Two are not used.

> farce   puns   cartoons   black humour
> irony   exaggeration   satire

1 Comedian John Weeding spent an hour of his brilliant show doing impressions of Tony Blair and other politicians, and the audience lapped up his hilarious take on modern society.

2 We see the usual tricks of the genre in this tedious play: mistresses hiding in wardrobes, husbands caught with their trousers down, and a plot that goes from the silly to the ridiculous.

3 What animal will always keep you warm? A kangaroo, because it's a good jumper. If you like this type of humour – and most children do – *The Bumper Book of Kids' Jokes* is for you.

4 He goes way beyond what you usually find in the back pages of the newspaper. The writing and drawing are so exquisite that he's been called a mix between Leonardo and Woody Allen.

5 The whole play revolves around a search for a dead body. Somehow Lara Williams manages to wring humour out of a very dark situation.

Compound words

5 Complete the crossword.

Someone who ...

Across

1 forgets little things is _____-minded.
2 doesn't get offended easily when she is criticised is thick-_____ .
3 is difficult to talk to and not very friendly is stand-_____ .
4 is always thinking about how to get further in her career is career-_____ .
5 is very calm even when in a tricky situation is level-_____ .

Down

2 can look after herself without help is self-_____ .
6 is determined to do something is single-_____ .
7 is generous and nice to others is kind-_____ .

How to... describe people

6 Correct the sentences by adding or crossing out one word.

1 Yolanda seems be a very nice girl.
2 You're such fast swimmer, I could never keep up with you.
3 What thing I don't like about Samantha is that she's so selfish.
4 The thing strikes you about Gudrun is her determination.
5 He can be a bit of annoying sometimes, but his heart's in the right place.
6 Once you get to know of Maurice, you'll like him.

Metaphors

7 Rewrite sentences 1–10 with a metaphor using the words in brackets.

1 Your current employment has no future prospects and it won't get you anywhere. (dead-end)
It is _____ .
2 Maggie and Denis are always arguing and shouting at each other. (stormy)
Maggie and Denis have _____ .
3 That was the moment when she got promoted and became famous in the industry. (took)
That was the moment when her _____
_____ .
4 The manager is the one who takes responsibility if things go wrong. (line)
It's the manager who's in _____ .
5 They didn't seem at all pleased to see me. (frosty)
They gave me _____ .
6 I'd always wanted to do something different from my mother's work. (footsteps)
I'd never wanted to follow in _____
_____ .
7 Once you get promoted, you'll have to make all the decisions. (shots)
Once you get promoted, you'll have to _____
_____ .
8 He aims to become a fighter pilot. (sights)
He has his _____
_____
becoming a fighter pilot.
9 We'd come to the point at which we had to make a vital decision. (crossroads)
We'd _____
_____ .
10 Several of us were feeling ill that day. (weather)
Several of us were feeling a bit _____
_____ .

Vocabulary | progress

1 **a** Match the words (1–8) to their common collocations (a–h).

1	computer	a	tube
2	skin	b	company
3	genetic	c	tissue
4	rare	d	launch
5	shuttle	e	strain
6	test	f	network
7	orbit	g	the moon
8	software	h	engineering

b Complete the sentences (1–8) with collocations from exercise 1a.

1 Microsoft is a hugely influential _____ .

2 They were able to eradicate the disease through _____ .

3 We watched the _____ on the television. It was incredibly exciting.

4 They used _____ , taken from his leg, to cover the wound.

5 The plan is for the shuttle to _____ the _____ .

6 The cells were placed in a _____ for analysis.

7 Scientists have managed to isolate this very _____ of the virus.

8 I can't use my email. We are having problems with the _____ .

Reading

2 Read the article quickly and choose the best title.

1 Superheroes – too strong for their own good?

2 Real-life superheroes – inspiration for developing superhero characters

3 Making a superhero – fact or fiction?

From gamma-radiation to radioactive spiders, superheroes are born in a variety of weird and wonderful ways. But how realistic are they?

Being born on other planets, or finding cosmic lanterns requires a huge leap of the imagination. But what about the humans who develop special powers by slightly more prosaic means – how plausible are they?

Take the Incredible Hulk: Scientist Dr Robert Banner receives a huge dose of gamma rays while working on a nuclear bomb. Gamma rays are real enough, being produced by nuclear explosions, but the bad news is that the gamma-radiation that gave Robert Banner his powers would've only caused fatal radiation sickness.

Forgetting that minor point, Lois Gresh, author of *Science and Superheroes*, argues it's just about possible to create a believable version of hulk. Banner could take large amounts of (highly dangerous) anabolic steroids to produce that pumped-up look, which in real life could cause his notorious rages as they increase aggressive mood swings. As for the green skin, French genetic researchers have at least created a glowing green rabbit by genetic engineering using fluorescent protein.

Spider-Man, on the other hand, has bigger problems. While a radioactive spider could exist (spiders are tolerant to radiation), an animal does not transfer DNA via a bite. And even if it did, it couldn't fuse with our DNA. If being ingested was enough to make this happen, we'd get characteristics of, say, apples or chickens whenever we ate them.

Batman – the 'Dark Knight' – might be the most realistic of the heroes, says Gresh. It is of course possible for a person to train obsessively in martial arts and subjects such as criminology. But in this case, it's gadgets that make Batman who he is. Most of Batman's toys, from his tiny cameras to smoke grenades to superstrong ropes, exist in the 21st century. Even creating a batmobile shouldn't present modern carmakers with too much difficulty.

Grammar | future probability

3 Complete the sentences about the article with the words in brackets.

1 The _____ being born on another planet. (odds)
2 I _____ you would find a cosmic lantern. (whether)
3 Gamma rays _____ produced by nuclear explosions. (definitely)
4 There _____ that if Dr Banner had received this radiation, he would have died. (likelihood)
5 There _____ we could create a believable version of hulk in reality. (slim)
6 Giving him anabolic steroids would _____ create his pumped-up look. (almost)
7 These _____ cause him to become more aggressive and moody. (might)
8 There _____ that we could create green skin by genetic engineering. (remote)
9 A radioactive spider _____ exist. (conceivably)
10 An animal _____ of transferring DNA via a bite. (stands)
11 If it did transfer its DNA, it wouldn't _____ of fusing with our DNA. (chance)
12 If ingesting DNA was enough to change our own DNA, we _____ adopt the characteristics of chickens and apples when we ate them. (presumably)
13 Batman _____ be the most realistic of the heroes. (well)
14 There _____ that modern carmakers could even create a batmobile. (distinct)

4 Complete sentences 1–10 with words from the box.

> doubt against conceivably no likelihood slim doubtful well any chances possibility bound

1 A: Do you think there's _____ chance that we'll see Martha at the weekend?
   B: I wouldn't count on it, but there's a _____ chance that she'll turn up.
2 The odds are _____ us meeting the sales targets for this quarter, but there's a strong _____ that things will improve over the coming months.
3 Rooney stands _____ chance of being chosen for the team.
4 I _____ whether they'll finish the work by the end of the week.
5 We may _____ have the chance to explore the area in more detail later.
6 Why did you do that? It's _____ to upset her.
7 It's _____ that they could have chosen a worse time to announce the news.
8 It could _____ help us in the future.
9 There's every _____ that soon he will hand over to his deputy.
10 The _____ are that we'll beat them in the Cup Final.

Listening

5 a 🔵9 Cover the audioscript. Listen to the news story and answer the questions.

1 Why does the young boy call Leisa 'Wonder Woman'?
_____
2 Why did Nathan Peters climb up the side of the house?
_____

b Listen again and complete the summary.

Real-life superheroes

Leisa Hodgkinson of Warrington is just (1) _____ , but she lifted a (2) _____ off a seven-year-old boy (3) _____ . The boy was (4) _____ , but has since made a (5) _____ and now calls Leisa 'Wonder Woman'. She said at the time that she (6) _____ to lift the car after (7) _____ , the same age as the trapped boy.
Sussex man Nathan Peters won (8) _____ from the fire brigade for (9) _____ in 2000 after helping to (10) _____ from a burning building in a (11) _____ worthy of Spider-Man. He scaled the (12) _____ , despite minimal hand and foot-holds, and stayed (13) _____ with the two to comfort them until (14) _____ .

AUDIOSCRIPT

Leisa Hodgkinson of Warrington is just 1.7 metres tall, but she lifted a one-tonne car off a seven-year-old boy trapped underneath. The boy was severely injured, but has since made a good recovery and now calls Leisa 'Wonder Woman'. She said at the time that she found the strength to lift the car after thinking of her own son, the same age as the trapped boy.

Sussex man Nathan Peters won an award from the fire brigade for outstanding bravery in 2000, after helping to rescue a mother and child from a burning building in a daring climb worthy of Spider-Man. He scaled the front of the building, despite minimal hand and footholds, and stayed in the smoke-filled room with the two to comfort them until the fire fighters arrived.

Vocabulary | arrangements

1 Choose the correct words to complete the sentences.

1 I'm not at all sure what to do this weekend. I'm really at a loose _____ .

   a time   b end   c up

2 What are you _____ to later? We're going out for a meal.

   a up   b in   c on

3 Have you got anything _____ up for tonight?

   a straight   b going   c lined

4 We were planning to all meet for lunch next week, but the plans have fallen _____ .

   a off   b out   c through

5 I'm afraid I'm _____ up all week sorting out the accounts.

   a tied   b turned   c lined

6 Please try and come. Can't you _____ out of going to see your granny?

   a go   b come   c get

7 They've had to call _____ the wedding because she's changed her mind.

   a on   b of   c off

8 I'll let you know if anything else crops _____ .

   a up   b on   c in

9 Do you know if the meeting is still going _____ ?

   a for   b ahead   c in

10 You need to just relax and put your feet _____ .

   a on   b down   c up

Grammar | future forms

2 Choose the correct words in *italics*.

1 The traffic's worse than I was expecting. I think we *'re going to/'ll* be late.

2 *I'll/I'm going to* pick you up from the airport if you like.

3 I've got a doctor's appointment this afternoon, so *I'm leaving/I leave* work at 3 p.m.

4 What sort of job do you think you *will do/will be doing* in ten years' time?

5 By the time we get there, all the food *will go/will have gone*.

6 I'm sure you'll have a great time wherever *you decide/you'll decide* to go.

7 He asked if we *will/would* take this case for him.

8 The reception is bad in here. I *'ll/'m going to* call you back in a minute.

9 He's not coming until Thursday, and we *'ll be finishing/'ll have finished* by then.

10 The flight *leaves/is going to leave* at 21.20.

Reading

3 Read the article. Write true (T) or false (F) next to sentences 1–10.

'Slow movement' encourages less stressful living

1 Carl Honoré, a recovered 'speedaholic', had an epiphany that caused him to slow down the hectic pace of his life. A journalist based in London, Honoré read a newspaper article on time-saving tips that referenced a book of one-minute bedtime stories. He found it an appealing idea since he'd already got into the habit of speed-reading stories to his son. 'My first reaction was, yes, one-minute bedtime stories,' he said. 'My next thought was, whoa, has it really come to this? That was really when a light bulb went off in my head.'

2 He realised he had become so anxious to rush through the nightly ritual that he'd rather get seven or even eight stories done in less time than he'd normally spend reading one. He wasn't making the most of this quality time.

3 So he embarked on finding a way to address the issue of 'time poverty', the constant fast-forward motion in which many overscheduled, stressed-out people are always rushing towards their next task – work, meals, family time – rather than savouring what they consider most important.

4 Honoré's book, *In Praise of Slowness: How a Worldwide Movement Is Challenging the Cult of Speed*, has made him the unofficial godfather of a growing cultural shift towards slowing down. '[There's a] backlash against the mainstream dictate that faster is always better, which puts quantity always ahead of quality,' he said. 'People all across the West are waking up to the folly of that.'

5 For advocates of the Slow Movement, it's not about rejecting technology or changing modern life completely, but rather about keeping it all in balance – not talking on the phone, driving and checking a BlackBerry while headed to the drive-thru before the next meeting.

'I love technology. I love speed. You need some things to be fast – ice hockey, squash, a fast Internet connection,' Honoré said. 'But,' he said, 'my passion for speed had become an addiction. I was doing everything faster.'

6 **What to Do?**

To make the transition to a slower life, Honoré has several suggestions: don't schedule something in every free moment of your day – prioritise activities and cut from the bottom of the list; limit television watching; and keep an eye on your 'personal speedometer' so you can gauge when you are rushing for speed's sake rather than necessity.

7 But don't expect the change to happen immediately – or even naturally. 'You don't slow down by snapping you're fingers, "Now I'm slow"', said Honoré, who got a speeding ticket on his way to a Slow Food dinner as he researched the book. 'That happens,' he said. 'My life has been transformed by it, but I still feel that old itch.'

1 Carl Honoré came to a slow realisation that he was living life too fast. ☐

2 He was reading an article about ways to spend more quality time with your children. ☐

3 Carl initially thought that one-minute bedtime stories were a good idea, as he regularly read stories to his son. ☐

4 He reflected that he needed to re-address the priorities in his life. ☐

5 According to the article, people are stressed because they fail to think ahead to the next task. ☐

6 Carl believes that people are starting to question whether quality is better than quantity. ☐

7 People who join the Slow Movement do not use computers, travel in cars, or watch television. ☐

8 Carl thinks the change to a 'slower' philosophy can only happen slowly. ☐

9 His advice is to reduce the number of things you do by deciding what is least important. ☐

10 He says his life is not so different to before. ☐

4 **a** Match the definitions (1–8) to words from the article.

1 desperate (to do something) (para 2) _____

2 began (something long and difficult) (para 3) _____

3 enjoying (para 3) _____

4 person to whom people look to for advice or (para 4) _____

5 a strong negative reaction (para 4) _____

6 (a) silly (idea) (para 4) _____

7 to measure (para 6) _____

8 a desire to do something you should not (para 7) _____

b Complete the sentences (1–5) with words or phrases from exercise 4a.

1 We _____ on the long, difficult journey.

2 I'm _____ to speak to Phyllis before she leaves.

3 Try to _____ the views while you are here. We might never come back.

4 It was hard to _____ his reaction to the new ideas.

5 There has been a strong _____ to the changes.

How to... | be vague/imprecise

5 **a** Complete each vague expression with one word.

1 She's more or _____ finished redecorating.

2 We go camping from _____ to time.

3 I only ever see them once in a blue _____ .

4 I've got a few _____ and pieces to finish off.

5 We work mainly with textiles and _____ kind of thing.

6 We'll be arriving at _____ five-ish.

7 We were sort _____ expecting to hear from you.

8 I was kind _____ hoping you could help.

b 🔊 10 Listen and check your answers.

Pronunciation | sounding sure

6 **a** Listen again and mark the stressed word in each sentence from exercise 5a.

b 🔊 10 Listen and repeat the sentences.

Vocabulary | special abilities

1 Complete the sentences with the letters in brackets in the correct order.

1 There is a lot of pressure, and the job is very _____ . (niegmdand)
2 She is a naturally _____ piano player. (fitegd)
3 The youngsters in the area are hooligans in the _____ . (kanimg)
4 Mozart was a musical _____ . (dipogry)
5 As a film star, he was the subject of much _____ from his fans. (donulatai)
6 Staff members are trained by their _____ . (srepe)
7 People with severe disabilities used to be considered _____ . (karsef)

Reading

2 Read the article and make a list of Kishan's interests and achievements.

Nine-year-old calls the shots

(1) The director is barking orders from the edit suite as he cuts a shot featuring Jackie Shroff, a leading Indian film star. It could be an everyday scene of Bollywood folk making their movies – except the director is a nine-year-old boy.

(2) Master Kishan, as he is known, has already been in twenty-four films and appeared in more than 1000 episodes of a popular television soap opera. He is now fulfilling another dream: becoming the youngest director not just in India, but in the world. 'I am different from other children, because this is the age for children to play,' admitted Kishan, sitting in his director's seat, his feet not quite touching the floor. 'I like playing, but not as much as other children. I don't know if the film will be successful, I hope it will be. I have a good feeling about it.'

(3) Dressed in a black corduroy shirt and dark jeans, he looked like any other affluent middle-class Indian child. Later, at a local café, he ordered coffee and mysore pak, a buttery sweet pudding, while fielding approaches from admiring fans.

(4) Kishan, whose favourite actors are Arnold Schwarzenegger and Amithabh Bachchan, a Bollywood superstar, began his acting career aged four after his friends urged his parents to send him for an audition. He was given a part in *Goddess of the Village*, a fantasy adventure, before landing a leading role in *Papa Pandu*, a daily Bangalore soap. He wrote a hit song for a film at the age of six, and has sung on others.

(5) Kishan's father, Shri Kanth, a tax official, said his son had been obsessed with cameras since he was a toddler. 'We noticed that when the camera was on him his behaviour would improve,' he said. 'After he started working on the soap, the staff would complain that he asked too many questions about this shot and that shot.'

(6) Kishan's transition to director began after he talked to children selling newspapers beside a busy road in Bangalore. When he asked them why they were not at school, some replied that they were orphans, others that they would be beaten if they went home without any money. Kishan was so moved that he wrote a short story about his encounter. 'I want them to go to school, and I hope the film encourages them to want to go,' he said.

(7) With the help of local journalists, he turned his story into a screenplay, *C/o Footpath*, about a Bangalore boy drugged by a woman who uses him as a prop to beg on the streets.

(8) Ironically, Kishan's commitments mean that he has attended school for only ten days a month during filming. His secretary collects school notes to help him keep up. Kishan nevertheless shows little sign of missing classes. He speaks good English and Kanada, the local language, and understands Hindi and Tamil.

(9) Shri Kanth, however, worries that his son is missing childhood and recently invited his friends to bring their children on a beach holiday so that Kishan could play. He was surprised to see him building row after row of sand castles. 'When I asked him why he was building them in rows, he held his hands up to make a frame and said it was to give the shot depth,' he said. A child psychologist friend has reassured him his son is fine.

3 Read the article again and answer the questions.

1 What makes Kishan different from other children his age? _____

2 How did Kishan become involved in acting? _____

3 What triggered Kishan's move towards becoming a director? _____

4 What inspired Kishan's short story? _____

5 What does he hope to achieve through the film? _____

6 How does Kishan keep up with his school work? _____

7 Why does his father worry? _____

4 a Match the definitions (1–10) to words in the article.

1 shouting instructions (para 1) _____

2 wealthy (para 3) _____

3 encouraged (para 4) _____

4 think about something all the time (para 5) _____

5 be hit many times (para 6) _____

6 feel a strong emotion (sad/sympathetic) (para 6) _____

7 a meeting (para 6) _____

8 something you use to help achieve a special effect (theatrical) (para 7) _____

9 not fall behind (with work/study) (para 8) _____

10 make someone feel calmer/less worried (para 9) _____

b Underline words in the article related to films or the media.

Grammar | inversion

5 Choose the correct words in *italics*.

1 No sooner *we had heard/had we heard* the news than the police rang to tell us what had happened.

2 *Not only did she/Not only she did* break the rules, but she also lied about her behaviour.

3 Only when *everyone has arrived/has everyone arrived* can we begin the discussions.

4 Rarely *have I been/I have been* so upset about something.

5 *Not since I went/Since I didn't go* to university have I made so many new friends.

6 No way *I am going/am I going* to pay for their mistake!

7 *Only if/If only* we work day and night will we get the job finished on time.

8 No longer *you do need to/do you need to* stand in long queues at airports. You can check in yourself!

9 Only after she had left *did I/I did* realise what had happened.

10 Not only *the service is great/is the service great*, but it's the cheapest hotel in the area.

6 Complete the sentences with a suitable word or phrase.

1 _____ could be more exotic to explore than these picturesque islands.

2 _____ recently have we begun to understand how the disease spreads.

3 Not _____ the organiser phoned me did I find out about the meeting.

4 No _____ had the plane taken off than they had to make an emergency landing.

5 _____ for one minute did I think I would win the competition.

6 _____ will you find such fantastic examples of the style.

7 Never _____ have we achieved such great sales.

8 _____ when she began to sing did we realise she had a special talent.

9 _____ if you have your bags checked will you be allowed through the entrance.

10 _____ again will I ride on an elephant!

Review and consolidation unit 4

Future probability

1 Put the sentences in order.

1 winning / The / are / series / against / odds / them / the / .

_____

2 the / We're / flight / to / her / on / bound / see / .

_____

3 The / later / it / are / will / chances / that / rain / .

_____

4 It / we / everything / time / doubtful / will / that / is / finish / today / have / to / .

_____

5 competition / is / that / There / a / beat / distinct / we'll / the / possibility / .

_____

6 promotion / he'll / likelihood / is / every / get / There / that / the / .

_____

7 That / idea / to / well / excellent / prove / may / be / an / .

_____

8 There / could / catch / a / chance / is / train / that / we / slim / the / earlier / .

_____

Future tenses

2 Complete the sentences using the correct form of the verbs in brackets. There may be more than one possibility.

1 That's fine. I _____ you next week to confirm the details. (call)

2 We _____ all the work by February. (finish)

3 OK, the taxi _____ to collect us in half an hour. (come)

4 I've got no idea what I _____ next year. (do)

5 Is Anna feeling OK? She looks like she _____ sick. (be)

6 Let me help you. I _____ this pile and you deal with the rest. (take)

7 I have to leave at five o'clock. I _____ Michael to discuss finances. (meet)

8 The traffic is awful. I'm afraid I _____ late. (be)

9 It was really good to see you. Hopefully, I _____ you again soon. (see)

10 I'm stuck at work and I don't know when I _____ home. (get)

Inversion

3 There are mistakes in seven of the sentences. Find the mistakes and correct them.

1 Not only they apologised for the inconvenience, but they have refunded the money!

2 No sooner do you ask her to do a job than she has done it.

3 Only after did I repeatedly ask them, did I manage to get a response.

4 Not since 2005 there has been such a hot summer.

5 Rarely do you find someone with such great talent.

6 Never before we have been able to photograph these small creatures in such detail.

7 Only if we keep looking we will ever find the solution.

8 No way am I going to dress up as Superman!

9 Not for one minute did I thought they really meant what they said.

10 Nowhere it does say that we aren't allowed to use this room.

How to... sound vague/ imprecise

4 Complete the dialogues.

1 A: How often to you manage to see your grandmother?
   B: From _____ to time.

2 A: Send me a postcard next time you go.
   B: I would, but we only go there _____ in a blue moon.

3 A: What are you doing later?
   B: Oh, just _____ and pieces.

4 A: How long do you think the meeting will last?
   B: More or _____ all day.

5 A: Shall we get started early?
   B: OK. Shall we say about six _____ ?

6 A: What does your new job involve?
   B: There is a lot of talking to clients and that _____ of thing.

7 A: Let's split the bill.
   B: Actually, I was _____ of hoping you might offer to pay.

8 A: What time shall we meet?
   B: About eight or _____ .

Progress

5 Choose the correct words to complete the sentences.

1 One of the problems is that _____ are over-used nowadays, which creates resistance.

   A antibiotics **B** viruses **C** skin tissue

2 In the future, people will have _____ in our bodies with details of medical records.

   A missions **B** microchips **C** microscopes

3 _____ have developed a virus which can penetrate the firewall.

   A Organs **B** Genes **C** Hackers

4 Almost anything is possible with genetic _____ .

   A cloning **B** engineering
   C analyses

5 The rocket was launched into _____ .

   A orbit **B** mission **C** shuttle

Arrangements

6 Complete the crossword.

Across

4 I can't make it tomorrow. I'm a bit _____ up.

5 We've had to _____ off the trip because we are just
too busy.

7 We were both at a loose _____ , so we went out together.

8 Why don't you sit down and put your _____ up?

9 I was wondering what you were _____ to at the weekend.

Down

1 Do you know if the plans are going _____ ?

2 Have you got anything _____ up for tonight?

3 We were going to Greece for a holiday, but it has all _____ through.

5 I'll let you know if anything _____ up.

6 There's an office party that night and I can't _____ out of it.

Two-part expressions

7 Complete the two-part expressions.

1 The police don't seem to be able maintain law and _____ .

2 _____ and large, we don't come across too many problems of this type.

3 We'll have to work it out by _____ and error.

4 It's difficult to keep up with all the new rules and _____ .

5 He's always complaining of _____ and pains.

6 Don't worry. It's a _____ and tested formula.

7 The lecturer bombarded us with _____ and figures about the economy.

8 I've got no idea where he could be. He's always out and _____ .

9 We need to sort this matter out _____ and for all.

10 We are all _____ and waiting.

11 I only see my aunt now and _____ .

12 I think we have more or _____ finished, unless anyone else has something to add.

13 I'm not sure how long it's going to take. First, I need to sort out some bits and _____ in the office.

14 I get terrible headaches from time to _____ .

15 I'm sick and _____ of clearing up everyone else's mess.

5 Fortunes

Vocabulary | fortunes

1 Put the letters in brackets in order.

1 He came into a small _____ when his father died. (netourf)

2 It is common practice to _____ in the shops to bring the price down. (galgeh)

3 These young bankers make their fortunes betting on changes in the _____ market. (ctoks)

4 Let me buy everyone a drink. I got a _____ today! (sier)

5 The business is trying to attract _____ families. (ghih-monice)

6 Her ideas are unique, so her work is absolutely _____ . (crisepels)

7 It doesn't affect our salary as we're paid on _____ . (smocsimino)

8 They have done really well considering their last business went _____ . (knaptrub)

Vocabulary | business

2 Complete the sentences.

> fringe   start-up   break even   recruited
> profit share   bail   profit   make a living
> publicity   launch   hands-on

1 It's a wonderful opportunity for him to get some _____ work experience.

2 A competitive salary with _____ benefits will be offered.

3 Many government officials were _____ from private industry.

4 Local businesses have offered to _____ out the museum.

5 They have applied to the bank for some _____ funds for the new business.

6 The firm struggled to make any profit, but it managed to _____ after three years.

7 The new drugs company hopes to _____ in September.

8 The couple decided that running a bed and breakfast from their house could provide them with a way to _____ .

9 Igor worked incredibly hard to make a success of the business, not least because it was run on a _____ system.

10 The current high standards of education are good _____ for the school.

11 It will be difficult for the company to make a _____ in the current economic climate.

Grammar | emphasis

3 Rewrite the sentences with the words in brackets.

The average house price in the UK is now £170,000 making it difficult for people to buy a home. (own)

The average house price in the UK is £170,000 making it difficult for people to buy their own home.

1 The fact that 1 in 10 children in the UK are suffering from a mental health disorder is worrying. (indeed)

_____

2 Americans are not very interested in soccer. They prefer to watch baseball. (all)

_____

3 It isn't certain that giving aid is the best way to help poorer countries. (means)

_____

4 Kandinsky abandoned his law studies in order to train as an artist in Munich. (even)

_____

5 The most popular soap opera in South American history, *I Am Betty The Ugly*, was so successful because the woman who played Betty was incredibly beautiful. (reason)

_____

6 Marco Diacono planted the UK's first ever olive grove in 2006. He hoped that global warming would help the trees to survive. (person)

_____

7 We went to the Pantanal, in Brazil, to enjoy the wildlife, but I got a shock when I found an eight-foot-long caiman alligator outside my tent. (did)

_____

8 I would suggest you stay in Amalfi. (place)

_____

Pronunciation | emphasis

4 **a** Put the sentences in order.

1 unlocked / leaving / the / own / It's / car / fault / for / her / .

2 I / bit / the / least / in / carpet / buying / wasn't / in / the/ interested / .

3 was / The / to / office / means / easy / find / by / no / .

4 mistake / company / was / to / sell / It / a / complete / the / .

5 need / and / do / is / What / to / the / we / discuss / sit / options / down / .

6 The / to / did / them / to / driver / time / airport / manage / on / get / the / taxi / .

b 11 Listen to check. Which words are stressed? Repeat the sentences.

Reading and listening

5 🔵 12 Read and listen to the story. Answer the questions.

1 What memories does the writer have of her father at home? _____

2 Why do you think she particularly remembers the sound of the electronic gates? _____

3 What would happen to her mother when they arrived at the prison? _____

4 How did the young girl react to this? _____

5 How was she able to make physical contact with her father during the visits? _____

6 What things did she notice about him during the trips? _____

Child of the incarcerated

(1) I have only a small child's handful of memories of life with my father. At home after my tap dancing debut at four; a heated argument between him and my mother around the same time. And mostly and most vividly, the trips to visit him once he was serving time in Greenhaven State Penitentiary in Stormville, New York.

(2) I remember the long ride to get there. Along the way was an Indian gift shop with a teepee outside. We stopped there once, on our way home, to look at moccasins and coin purses. When we arrived at the prison, there was a series of electronic gates to pass through, papers to show. My mother was fingerprinted. They looked through her purse and patted her body down. We didn't talk while this went on. I was good at reading signals. This was serious stuff. I felt hot and sad.

(3) The visiting room was a big, bright white and steel institutional space. Guards sat at a desk, at one end of the room, taking in the exchanges between inmates and guests. We chose seats on opposite sides of a giant stainless-steel counter, accessible to him from the inside, through a barred electronic door. From counter surface to floor was solid wall, from counter to ceiling a chain link fence with one-inch square openings, large enough to fit your fingers through, for a touch, or your pursed lips, for a kiss. We talked in low murmured tones on our visits, for privacy. Sometimes the room would be full and there'd be a buzz like a hive. We tried not to sit close to anyone else. He wore greenish-gray pants and a matching shirt with buttons. He always smiled and sauntered over. He was so handsome and fit and tall. I don't remember what we talked about, or how often I went to see him. The visits were a chance to make contact – to hear his voice, to see the color of his skin, his smile, the shape of his fingernails. To imprint his stride on my memory. To notice things I probably wouldn't if I saw him every day.

6 Match the definitions (1–10) to words in the story.

1 the first time she danced this style (para 1) _____
2 an angry discussion (para 1) _____
3 an Indian tent (para 2) _____
4 Indian shoes (para 2) _____
5 prisoners (para 3) _____
6 a large metal surface (para 3) _____
7 the noise of bees (para 3) _____
8 the place where bees live (para 3) _____
9 walked casually (para 3) _____

Vocabulary | finance and philanthropy

1 Choose the best option to complete the sentences.

1 People who make large _____ to political parties expect to gain influence and shape future policy.

   A money   **B** donations   **C** fortunes

2 Chinese banks have invested _____ in New York City.

   A heavily   **B** grandly   **C** huge

3 Billionaires are under increasing pressure to be seen to give money _____ .

   A for charity   **B** in charity   **C** to charity

4 When a payment is late, companies have the right to _____ interest.

   A seek   **B** pay for   **C** charge

5 Firms across the world have decided to _____ less money to IT (information technology)

   A dedicate   **B** spend   **C** invest

6 The funds will _____ the welfare of children in the school.

   A help   **B** promote   **C** provide

7 The program aims to _____ malaria from Africa.

   A eradicate   **B** take   **C** improve

8 The young music star managed to _____ a fortune in just two years.

   A become a   **B** success   **C** amass

Grammar | conditionals (review)

2 Complete the sentences with the correct form of the verbs in brackets.

1 If I _____ my car here, I _____ you a lift. (have) (offer)

2 I _____ some coffee if everyone _____ eating. (make) (finish)

3 If it _____ for Jamie, we _____ for ages. (not be) (wait)

4 If you _____ carefully to what I said, this _____ ! (listen) (not happen)

5 Provided that she _____ all the right injections, she _____ fine. (have) (be)

6 If only they _____ us ten minutes earlier, we _____ the order. (ring) (cancel)

7 Unless Graham _____ his strategy, the business _____ bankrupt. (change) (go)

8 Should you happen _____ in Oxford, you _____ and stay. (be) (come)

9 Supposing they _____ her the job, would she _____ it? (offer) (accept)

10 I _____ how much it costs, so long as the job _____ by Sunday. (not mind) (finish)

3 Complete the first half of the sentences with a suitable word. Then choose the correct second halves.

1 _____ that the team keep playing as they are at the moment,

   a we had a good chance of winning the cup. ☐

   b we have a good chance of winning the cup. ☐

2 Should you _____ to see Martin on your travels,

   a could you tell him I've been trying to contact him? ☐

   b you could have told him I'd been trying to contact him. ☐

3 If it _____ been for Kate telling us,

   a we never realised what they were planning. ☐

   b we never would have realised what they were planning. ☐

4 If you _____ like to see the rest of the house,

   a I could have left the key and you could show yourself around. ☐

   b I can leave you the key and you can show yourself around. ☐

5 _____ we hadn't bought the tickets already,

   a then we could change our plans. ☐

   b then we changed our plans. ☐

6 As _____ as Sheila still works there,

   a she should be able to give you all the information you need. ☐

   b she could be able to give you all the information you need. ☐

Vocabulary | words that are verbs and nouns

4 **a** Complete the sentences with words from the box.

> charge   launch   fund   experience   profit
> recruit   share   benefit

1 A _____ was set up to try and save the school.

2 I gave them my _____ of the profits.

3 They are working together to _____ the whole community.

4 The _____ of the new company was well attended.

5 There is a _____ of 50 euros for this service.

6 Children need to _____ things for themselves in order to learn from them.

7 Some companies will clearly _____ financially from the decision.

8 The plan is to _____ workers from developing countries.

b Decide if the word you used is a noun or a verb in each case.

Instant millionaires need help

1 The high-tech world is making thousands of very young people very rich, but according to psychologists it is also creating a new illness – sudden wealth syndrome.

2 Some seek help because they are too rich and cannot handle their wealth, others because they crave more money or feel guilty. Dr Stephen Goldbart, a psychologist, runs the Money, Meaning & Choices Institute near Silicon Valley, where sixty-four new millionaires are reportedly created every day. Most of them are people in their twenties and thirties who find themselves suddenly rich, a group Dr Goldbart calls the 'Siliconaires'.

3 He noticed a change about ten years ago when people from middle-class backgrounds started coming into large sums of money. With the dot.com trend of recent years, his client numbers have steadily increased. In April, Merrill Lynch reported that the number of millionaires in the United States and Canada has risen almost forty percent since 1997 to 2.5 million.

4 Becoming unexpectedly rich has its drawbacks, Dr Goldbart says, and there should be some amount of sympathy for those who cannot handle sudden wealth. 'It can ruin their lives, rip their families apart and lead them on a path of destructive behaviour,' he says. 'Money does not always bring peace and fulfilment. They lose balance. Instead of money solving all their problems it often brings guilt, stress and confusion.'

5 People who are used to working 80 to 100 hours a week on their fledgling enterprise suddenly find they no longer need to work and are able to retire at the age of 30. However, the newfound leisure puts them into a premature, mid-life crisis. Some experience panic attacks, severe depression and insomnia, Dr Goldbart says. Others withdraw from society or go on maniacal shopping sprees.

6 Some newly rich feel guilty about having so much money and feel they are not entitled to it, or that they do not deserve it. Others become paranoid, thinking they will be exploited because of their wealth, or they become obsessed with making even more money. People most affected are the 'new rich', for whom wealth was not part of their upbringing and who expected to spend their lives working. Anxiety and depression can also come from 'ticker shock' as they watch the vagaries in the stock market, particularly a plunge when they have not exercised their stock options.

7 Part of Dr Goldbart's cure for the unhappy rich is to get them involved in the community and not just writing cheques to charities. British Columbia's Rory Holland, executive vice-president of Itemus, made his millions when the company he was involved in for eight years was sold for US$103-million in 1998. He now devotes much of his time to four non-profit groups, serves on their boards and helps raise money.

8 Dr Goldbart believes he is the only psychologist, along with family counsellor Joan DiFuria, providing therapy for the rich, and would like to see more colleagues provide the service. 'These people [the rich] are sensitive to how people feel and are reluctant to use our kind of service,' he says. 'But we help them regain the balance they've lost.'

Reading

5 Read the article quickly. What is the significance of these numbers?

1	64	5	80–100
2	30s	6	30
3	10	7	$103 million
4	2.5 million		

6 Read the article again and answer the questions.

1 What has caused the increase in the number of millionaires?

2 What feelings can someone who comes into sudden wealth experience? How can these feelings affect them?

3 Who might be particularly affected?

4 What might be the cause of these feelings?

5 What does Dr Goldbart suggest as a cure?

6 How does Dr Goldbart feel the public should treat sudden millionaires?

7 Complete the sentences (1–8) with words from the article.

1 I've got so much work on at the moment, I just can't _____ it. (para 2)

2 I've given up caffeine, but I still _____ coffee first thing in the morning. (para 2)

3 For me, the advantages outweigh the _____ when you're living in a city like London. (para 4)

4 The effect of the earthquake was literally to _____ the whole community. (para 4)

5 The plans aren't very advanced yet. It's just a _____ idea. (para 5)

6 He's given up his job, taken up jogging and started dancing classes. I think he's having a _____ . (para 5)

7 She took all the credit for the ideas, even when she is not strictly _____ to. (para 6)

8 My father died when I was young, so we had a rather difficult _____ . (para 6)

Vocabulary | describing a job

1 Complete the crossword.

1 The offices are modern and spacious, and there are lots of like-minded people, so it's a really good working _____ .

2 We attend conferences and workshops as part of our professional _____ .

3 One of the best things about working here is the _____ of the location.

4 Glenco is an international company so there are plenty of travel _____ .

5 One of the _____ of the job is this fantastic company car!

6 As a boss, he is very _____ of his staff.

7 It's a good job with excellent promotion _____ .

8 The staff received bonuses in recognition of their _____ .

9 The pay is $39,000 a year, which is a good _____ .

10 I enjoy the _____ of working for myself.

11 It's a great job if you have children because of the _____ working hours.

12 The company invests in a private _____ plan on your behalf.

13 We get strange requests from our clients, so some of our tasks can be quite _____ .

14 Most of the workers enjoyed a high degree of job _____ .

How to... | express priorities

2 **a** Put the sentences in order.

1 to / for / work / is / to / walk / essential / to / me / able / The / thing / be / .

_____

_____

2 absolutely / prospects / Having / promotion / vital / is / good / .

_____

_____

3 major / a / flexible / isn't / Having / hours / priority / working / .

_____

4 job / is / main / priority / satisfaction / My / .

_____

_____

5 couldn't / supportive / without / I / colleagues / do / .

_____

_____

6 pension / really / about / a / not / plan / I'm / having / bothered / .

_____

_____

b ⊕ 13 Listen and check your answers.

AUDIOSCRIPT

1 The essential thing for me is to be able to walk to work.

2 Having good promotion prospects is absolutely vital.

3 Having flexible working hours isn't a major priority.

4 My main priority is job satisfaction.

5 I couldn't do without supportive colleagues.

6 I'm not really bothered about having a pension plan.

Pronunciation | stress

3 **a** ⊕ 13 Listen again and underline the words that carry the main stress. Circle the syllable that is stressed.

b Repeat the sentences, copying the rhythm.

Grammar | sentence adverbials

4 Rewrite the sentences with the words in brackets.

As far as I can see, there is nothing we can do to stop the plans going ahead. (seemingly)

There is seemingly nothing we can do to stop the plans going ahead.

1 You may be surprised to hear that sales figures were up on last year. (believe)

_____

2 Everyone says that the company is losing a lot of money. (apparently)

_____

3 For the most part the management have a good relationship with the rest of the staff. (broadly)

_____

4 In my opinion, the conclusions of the report are wrong. (fundamentally)

_____

5 I'd like to say no to the extra work but I need the money. (hand)

_____

6 What you say is true, but only in part. (point)

_____

7 I travel a lot for my job. On the whole I enjoy it although it can be exhausting. (large)

_____

8 Looking back, we should probably have approached them earlier. (with)

_____

9 Unexpectedly, the results of the survey indicate that there could be a good market for the new product. (enough)

_____

Listening

5 **a** 🔘 14 Cover the audioscript. Listen to the interview and answer the questions.

1 What is Rachel Stanmore's job?

2 What kind of company is MediaCom?

b Listen again and make notes on the topics below.

- Creative ideas and strange food
- Inspiring the workers
- Number of employees/average age of workers
- Schemes and new ideas

Vocabulary | expressing quantity

6 Complete the audioscript with words from the box.

| little | deal | few | plenty | vast | most |
| awful | not | many | | | |

AUDIOSCRIPT

A: Crocodile curry and cheesy worms may not be everybody's idea of snack food, but MediaCom, rated number 28 in the *Sunday Times* listing of 'Top 100 companies to work for', wants to encourage a creative and original take on the world. So they offer chocolate ants to their workers at break times and have (1) _____ of other interesting ideas, too. With us this morning is Rachel Stanmore, a business expert who has spent some time in this innovative media company. And she's here to tell us more about it. Good morning, Rachel.

B: Good morning.

A: Now I'm (2) _____ much of an expert in these things, so what is it, Rachel, that the company's trying to achieve with these rather strange ideas?

B: Erm... well, the philosophy is that the company will do better if the workers are inspired. They don't want people coming to work thinking: 'Oh – it's just another day at the office.' So they've hired a 'Director of Freshness'. Er... it's her responsibility to make the workplace more inspiring, so she spends an (3) _____ lot of time thinking up ideas such as working in the park on a sunny day, or having magicians in the office. They want people to be on tenterhooks, wondering what's going to happen next, hence the assaults on their senses, like crocodile curry for lunch, or foot spas in the afternoon.

A: Can you tell us a (4) _____ bit more about the company?

B: Erm... sure. It's the UK's largest billing media agency, with 389 employees based in London and Edinburgh. The (5) _____ majority of the workers are young professionals, under 35, who may be earning a great (6) _____ of money, but more importantly they like to feel appreciated, and constantly motivated. For the (7) _____ part they are fully behind the business, with as (8) _____ as eight out of ten of the staff feeling excited about where the company's going. And that's because they have control – they know what it's like to run things. Quite a (9) _____ of them have had their own ideas brought into operation. Last year, for example, there was a scheme called: 'If I ran the company', and as a result a company bar was introduced, which provides free breakfasts in the morning, is also open until 11.30 at night, and has the boss working behind it.

A: Free breakfasts – now that's a better idea, although it's not chocolate ants, I hope! And what about other incentives? What other kinds of incentive are there?

Review and consolidation unit 5

Conditionals (review)

1 Complete each sentence by adding a word from the box.

> don't   would   you   as   only   were   for

1 If it hadn't been _____ the weather, we would have had a wonderful holiday.

2 You can use my phone provided that you _____ speak for too long.

3 If _____ I had listened to her advice!

4 Should _____ happen to be in Rome, you should call my sister.

5 Supposing we _____ to call the police, that might help.

6 If you _____ let us know as soon as the parcel arrives.

7 As long _____ he lives in that house, I'm not going back there.

Sentence adverbials

2 Choose the words which are <u>not</u> possible, or have a different meaning.

1 We try to support each other, and _____ it seems to work.
   A by and large   **B** however
   C broadly speaking

2 Transcil always deal with the problem quickly. _____ , they do charge a lot for their services.
   A Essentially   **B** On the other hand
   C However

3 We cut our prices by nearly 50 percent and _____ we managed to increase our profits.
   A believe it or not   **B** surprisingly enough
   C with hindsight

4 They moved the factory to China to cut costs. _____ it was the right decision.
   A With hindsight   **B** Looking back
   C However

5 The business is _____ a technical marketing company.
   A essentially   **B** looking back
   C fundamentally

6 She is working for herself, and _____ doing very well.
   A on the other hand   **B** apparently
   C seemingly

Emphasis

3 Choose the correct words to complete the sentences.

1 The main reason _____ is that I didn't enjoy the atmosphere.
   A why leaving
   B why I left
   C for I left

2 Whatever _____ when she told us there was no alternative?
   A she did mean
   B she means
   C did she mean

3 I _____ him take the money.
   A actually saw
   B saw actually
   C actual saw

4 They were so relieved to finally buy _____ house.
   A their own
   B on their own
   C own their

5 The journey was _____ .
   A by means no easy
   B by no means easy
   C no means by easy

6 _____ impresses me about them is that they are so efficient.
   A The most thing that
   B The thing that most
   C Most the thing that

7 The main ideas are _____ .
   A very indeed interesting
   B interesting very indeed
   C very interesting indeed

8 It's incredible! He's not _____ .
   A interested all at football
   B interested in football all at
   C interested in football at all

Business

4 Match the sentence beginnings (1–10) to the endings (a–j).

1   She hasn't had to worry about money since they sold the business and she came ☐
2   We are paid a fixed salary, plus a ten percent commission ☐
3   He managed to bring the price down by ☐
4   His internet business went ☐
5   It was a great business idea. Now she is waiting to get the ☐
6   If you know what you are doing, there is plenty of money ☐
7   The house is filled with priceless ☐
8   I'm not sure how they manage to make a ☐
9   The bank manager left them without a glimmer ☐
10 Ana is helping in the office to gain some work ☐

a   start-up funds.
b   bankrupt a few years ago.
c   living at all.
d   antiques.
e   on any sales we agree.
f   of hope.
g   experience.
h   to be made on the stock market.
i   into a fortune.
j   haggling with the owner.

Describing a job

5 Complete the sentences with the correct form of the words in brackets.

1   My work gives me a lot of job _____ . (satisfy)
2   Luckily, my boss is very _____ . (support)
3   The pay isn't very good initially, but there are good _____ prospects. (promote)
4   Working to deadlines can be quite _____ . (challenge)
5   The company helps with your personal and professional _____ . (develop)
6   My role was changed in _____ of my abilities. (recognise)
7   Having worked nights for so long, it is great to have such _____ working hours. (flex)
8   One of the benefits of the apartment is the _____ of its location. (convenient)

Idioms (1)

6 Add a word to each sentence.

1   He sold his business for $14 million. He's _____ a fortune.
2   As a student I lived _____ the money I earned from waitressing jobs.
3   Since my husband lost his job, we're not very well _____ financially.
4   I have spent this month's salary, so now I _____ completely broke.
5   You don't need to pay for everything. Let's split _____ bill.
6   You should treat _____ to something special at least once a month.
7   It's a beautiful dress, and the best thing about it is that it was dirt _____ .
8   Let's splash _____ on a meal in an expensive restaurant.
9   I shouldn't worry about paying back the money. She's rolling _____ it.
10 My wage brings us more than enough to get _____ on.
11 I'm glad you like the carpet. It cost me an _____ and a leg.
12 It's very expensive to buy it on my own, but perhaps we could go _____ .

Answer key

Unit 1 Challenges

Lesson 1.1

Reading

1
1 T 2 F 3 T 4 T 5 F 6 T 7 F 8 F 9 T

2a
1 set 2 face 3 rising 4 make 5 without 6 ambition 7 attitude
8 daunting

2b
1 Mount Everest was his lifetime ambition. However, first he climbed
Mount Cook, the highest peak in New Zealand. Then he chose
26,906ft Mount Cho Oyu in Tibet, the world's sixth highest. And
finally, he climbed Mount Everest.
2 He lost both his legs in an earlier climbing accident. He then broke
one of his artificial legs on the way up and had to replace it. He was
also suffering with laryngitis.
3 Yes, he replaced the broken leg with a spare one, and continued to
climb.
4 His 'childhood dream' was to 'stand on the roof of the world'. He
managed to climb Mount Everest, despite his disability.
5 He couldn't have managed without a spare leg and parts.
6 She advises that they should never be limited in their ambitions.
7 Suggested answer: Mark seems to have the right attitude in that he
persevered even when things got very tough.
8 Suggested answer: Climbing the highest mountain in the world, in
sub-zero temperatures, without the use of your own legs is all very
daunting. Perhaps the fact that he had to overcome his disability was
the most daunting challenge.

Grammar | verbs/adjectives/nouns with prepositions

3
1 for 2 from 3 in losing 4 from 5 to 6 about 7 on 8 from 9 of
10 with 11 in 12 about

Vocabulary | learning languages

4
1 I've really let it **slide**.
2 I just **picked** up a few words when I was there on holiday.
3 A: How long did it take you to **master** the grammar?
   B: Years! I used to spend a lot of time cramming information from
     grammar books until I had complete information **overload**.
4 He left a **garbled** message which I can't understand.
5 Everything is great, although I think I'm starting to lose my original
   dialect!.
6 Yes, it only seems a short while ago that she was **babbling**
   unintelligibly like all babies do.

Listening

5
1 Polyglots have more 'white brain matter' in a part of the brain which
processes sound. And their brains could also be less symmetrical
than others. 2 It is hoped the research could be used help to identify
reasons for language difficulties. 3 People were asked to distinguish
between two similar sounds from different languages. 4 Good
language learners were those who identified more than 80 percent of
the sounds correctly, within a few minutes. 5 The fibres of the brain's
white matter are involved with the efficient processing of sound by
connecting the brain's regions together. 6 The brain scans could be
used to diagnose clinical problems, or to predict whether someone
has the ability to be good at something or not.

Lesson 1.2

Vocabulary | knowledge

1
1 f 2 d 3 i 4 a 5 b 6 h 7 c 8 e 9 j 10 g

Grammar | passives: distancing

2
image is said to have haunted her
Martha is thought to have been
It is estimated that
Ishi is believed to be
He was thought to have left

3
1 winched 2 peering 3 haunted 4 fascination 5 flock
6 up to a mile 7 extinction 8 bulk 9 foothills 10 emerged

4
1 is said 2 seems 3 is claimed 4 is thought 5 is said
6 is/was thought 7 seems 8 is thought 9 is believed 10 appears

Lesson 1.3

Reading

1a
1 Extreme motorcycle races and rallies. 2 To be a true match for her
male colleagues in these extreme races. 3 Her father helped her
develop an interest in mechanics, and her mother gave her strong will
power. 4 Broken bones, including her hand. 5 She cries a bit and
carries on.

1b
1 crave 2 single-handedly 3 barely 4 quench her thirst for success
5 ultimate quest 6 a true match 7 awed 8 desperate
9 quit 10 will power 11 held on / carry on

1c
1 ultimate quest 2 single-handedly 3 quitting 4 barely
5 true match 6 craving

Vocabulary | achievement

2
1 believes 2 pursue 3 faces 4 pushing 5 greatest triumphs
6 potential 7 deal 8 persevered 9 heading

Grammar | perfect aspect

3
1 will have been 2 has travelled 3 has been (had been) 4 has/been
requested 5 had/been 6 was 7 has had 8 gave up 9 set off
10 has been attacked 11 shot 12 has/been 13 was rusting
14 have had

How to... | talk about your achievements

4
1 e 2 i 3 c 4 h 5 b 6 f 7 g 8 a 9 d

Review and consolidation unit 1

Passives: distancing

1
1 C 2 D 3 A 4 B 5 C 6 A 7 A 8 D 9 B 10 D

2
1 d 2 h 3 c 4 g 5 f 6 b 7 e 8 a

Perfect aspect

3
Suggested answers
1 will have left/finished 2 realised we had 3 had been playing
4 hasn't been sleeping 5 won't have finished 6 I've left 7 had been
trying 8 have been given/offered 9 hadn't heard 10 will have been
working/will have worked

4
1 A 2 A 3 A 4 B 5 A 6 B

Verbs/adjectives/nouns with prepositions

5
1 appeal to 2 opt for 3 short of 4 nervous about 5 rely on
6 subject/to 7 benefited from 8 reminiscent of 9 bother about
10 succeeded in

6
1 Paulo Freire? Who's he? I've never heard ~~of~~ him. 2 The Whorf-Sapir
hypothesis? I know it like ~~in~~ the back of my hand. 3 Wendy's phone
number? I don't know it ~~by~~ offhand. 4 Shakespeare's love poems?
We spent years learning them by ~~the~~ heart. 5 Is Ronaldinho the best
footballer in the world? Without ~~but~~ a doubt. 6 The Highway Code?
Ask Susie – she's a driving instructor. She knows it inside **out**.
7 International banking? I know next ~~to~~ nothing about it. 8 Was
Matisse the greatest painter in history? As far as I'm **concerned**,
he was.

Prefixes

7

1 unfit 2 overpaid 3 unmotivated 4 underestimate 5 non-smokers
6 non-/semi-professional 7 misunderstood 8 overworked
9 irrelevant 10 unaware

How to... talk about your achievements

8

1 a 2 h 3 e 4 d 5 g 6 f 7 i 8 k 9 b 10 j 11 c

Unit 2 Community

Lesson 2.1

Listening

1a

Speaker 1 1 English 2 Colombia 3 Confused *cansado* and *casado*
4 wish I'd learned more of the language before moving
Speaker 2 5 Brazilian 6 US 7 Cultural difference at gas station
8 felt a bit stupid
Speaker 3 9 Italian 10 England 11 Confused early and late
12 learn the basics

1c

1 ply 2 blunders 3 muddle through 4 perplexed 5 assigned
6 tearing my hair out

Grammar | verb patterns (1)

2

1 to take 2 meeting 3 to write 4 of travelling 5 riding 6 to waste
7 you to reconsider 8 doing 9 to having to 10 us to go

3

1 of living 2 objecting 3 thinking 4 to change 5 afford to
6 find out 7 making 8 to take 9 advise you 10 to hearing

How to... | give advice/make recommendations about places

4

1 d 2 j 3 h 4 e 5 f 6 b 7 i 8 a 9 c 10 g

Vocabulary | communities

5

1 standard 2 levels 3 rate 4 life 5 vibrant 6 traffic
7 infrastructure 8 areas 9 mild 10 cosmopolitan

Lesson 2.2

Grammar | comparatives (review)

1a

Part 1 is more positive about Wikipedia than part 2.

1b

1 Text 2 is **nowhere** near as complimentary about Wikipedia as the
other text. 2 It suggests that Wikipedia is **nothing** like as reliable
as other encyclopaedias. 3 It is **considerably more** positive about
Wikipedia than the other text. 4 The author of the text **would** rather
let each generation question the views of the preceding generation.
5 According to the text, the less we know about the contributors, **the**
less we can trust Wikipedia. 6 The author of text 1 is definitely not
as critical of Wikipedia **as** the author of the other text. 7 The author
probably thinks that rather **than** using Wikipedia for all research, you
should only use it for simple facts. 8 The text implies that it's **miles**
better to let everyone contribute to encyclopaedias.

How to... | recognise features of informal language

2a

a We look forward to hearing from you **in due course**. b Please **don't
hesitate to contact me** if you have any queries. c **Dear** Mrs Dormer,
d Technics Solutions **would like** to invite you to our annual investors
meeting e inform us **of your attendance** by 14 June. f which will
take place at The Atrium on Rose Street at 5.00 p.m. on Wednesday
6 July. g We would **be grateful** if you could h **Yours sincerely,**
Nicholas Spicer, Chairman, Technics Solutions

2b

1 c 2 d 3 f 4 g 5 e 6 b 7 a 8 h

Reading

3a

a 3 b 2 c 1

3b

1 E 2 B 3 A 4 E 5 B 6 A 7 E 8 B

3c

1 bid 2 phenomenal 3 stock 4 reluctant 5 start-up 6 luxurious
7 doomed

Lesson 2.3

Listening

1a

Speaker 1 says it's 'a hive of activity', e.g. music, football. They cheer
and sing when Bafana Bafana plays.
Speaker 2 says the people are close to nature. The nature is
wonderful, beautiful rainforests and coastlines. They grow their own
food, so no one starves. People help each other. They are spiritual
and not materialistic.
Speaker 3 says it's quiet. They are all old friends and have
complementary skills.

1b

1 F 2 T 3 T 4 T 5 F 6 F 7 T 8 T 9 F

1c

1 a 2 b 3 c 4 c 5 a 6 b

Vocabulary | adjectives to describe places

2

1 off the beaten track 2 stunning 3 side by side 4 vast 5 run-down
6 diverse 7 packed 8 unspoilt 9 tranquil

Grammar | introductory *it*

3

1 It's no use handing in the paper now. You've missed the deadline.
2 I'd appreciate it if you could call me on 0982 654726.
3 It's no wonder that Marie won the competition. She's a genius.
4 It's essential that you sign the contract by 12 September.
5 It's a shame you can't come to the show.
6 I hate it when people throw litter.

Review and consolidation unit 2

Communities

1

1 cost 2 infrastructure 3 mild 4 healthcare 5 standard 6 rate
7 Unemployment 8 nightlife 9 cosmopolitan 10 freedom
11 monuments 12 congestion

Adjectives to describe places

2

1 charming 2 tranquil 3 off the beaten track 4 stroll 5 gaze
6 heart 7 side by side 8 packed 9 bustling 10 run down
11 unspoilt 12 vast

Phrasal verbs

3

1 c 2 a 3 c 4 b 5 a 6 a 7 b 8 c

Verb patterns (1)

4

1 I'm thinking of going to France. What's it like in April? 2 Dave can't
afford to take a holiday so he's camping in his garden this year!
3 Can you imagine being an astronaut? You could go into space!
4 Mario's so lazy: he always avoids doing the washing-up.
5 I tried to persuade Gail to watch a DVD tonight, but she didn't want
to. 6 I can't stand smoking. Cigarette smoke makes me ill.
7 They advised us to use traveller's cheques because they're safer.
8 I wouldn't recommend spending more than an hour or two in that
museum. It's a bit dull. 9 My teachers always encouraged me to do
my best. 10 Libby urged us to enter the competition. She was right
- we won!

Comparatives (review)

5

The online community is predicting that blogs will soon replace
print journalism. While publishing news and views on the web is far
easier **than** getting into print, I have my doubts about this prediction.
Firstly, blogs are nowhere **near** as reliable as print journalism.There
are checks and balances for print journalists, and newspapers are
far **more** likely than websites to be prosecuted if they get the facts
wrong. Reading a blog is much the same **as** reading a diary: if it is full
of lies and exaggeration, there's not a lot you can do. The advantage
of blogs is that they are personal and usually unedited. But **rather**
than using them as formal carriers of news, I think we'd be better **off**
having them as an alternative source of opinion. Basically, they act as

a voice that cannot be silenced. The easier the web becomes to use, **the** more diverse voices it will contain, and that's a great thing. As for me, I **would** sooner read a newspaper any day!

6
1 S   2 D   3 S   4 D   5 S   6 D   7 D   8 S

How to... give advice/make recommendations

7
Across: 1 value   2 wary   3 overrated   4 cracked
Down: 3 out   5 overpriced   7 must   8 dull

Unit 3 Tales

Lesson 3.1

Reading

1a
2

1b
1 What was *Every Day Over 100 is a Gift*?   2 Who was Miguel Carpiro?   3 What (according to the local people) happened to Carpiro's birth certificate?   4 Why might people in societies such as Abkhazia and Hunza lie about their age?   5 What did Mazess and Forman check (in Vilcabamba)?   6 Why did some World War 1 deserters use their dead parents' names?

1c
1 centenarians   2 caused a minor stir   3 plausible   4 revered   5 social status   6 brings about   7 deserters   8 detection

Grammar | narrative tenses (review)

2
1 a   2 a   3 b   4 b   5 b   6 a
3
1 were you talking   2 had been working   3 was barking   4 did you find   5 had met   6 hadn't been cleaned   7 Had you heard   8 had been talking   9 was being fixed   10 hadn't understood

Pronunciation | differentiating tenses

4
1 a   2 b   3 b   4 a   5 b   6 a   7 b   8 a

Lesson 3.2

Reading and listening

1a
1 Thomas   2 A normal town, with a post office and High Street.   3 No, he spells 'birds' incorrectly.   4 Naughty (she stole her mother's make-up and she lies about the spelling of birds).   5 That it's funny and not true, but it shows the child's imagination.   6 Because she had stolen her mother's make-up and been caught.   7 He feels proud of them because they have good imaginations, even though they are naughty.   8 Suggested answers: surprising, surreal, funny

1b
1 poised   2 shriek   3 waddling   4 traipsing   5 fossilised   6 discarded   7 ruffled   8 glaring

1c
1 a large yellow-beaked eagle   2 a notebook   3 sound of seagulls   4 seagull   5 eyeshadow   6 penguin   7 Thomas's father   8 swan

Vocabulary | books

2
1 best-seller   2 base   3 depicts   4 hooked   5 bookworm   6 found   7 gripping   8 one-dimensional   9 down   10 avid

How to... | describe people

3
1 across   2 get to know   3 strikes you   4 like about   5 such a   6 a bit

Vocabulary | compound words

4a
1 single-minded   2 self-sufficient   3 thick-skinned   4 kind-hearted   5 stand-offish   6 career-orientated   7 level-headed   8 absent-minded
4b
1 single-minded and career-orientated   2 stand-offish   3 absent-minded   4 thick-skinned   5 kind-hearted

Lesson 3.3

Listening

1a
A 1   B 3   C 2
1b
1 The driver was stopped because he was speeding.   2 There wasn't a gun in the glove box or a body in the boot.   3 A man wanted to get rid of a cat.   4 The man needed directions to get home.   5 The second note said 'blame everything on me'.   6 The manager's final problem was that the workers were on strike.
1c
1 S   2 C   3 C   4 C   5 S   6 C   7 SA

Pronunciation | intonation

2a
1 sentences 1 and 5   2 sentences 1, 5 and 7. The emphasised words are stole, gun, glove box (1) and gun, course (5) and bet, liar, speeding (7)   3 sentences 2, 3, 4 and 6

Grammar | participle clauses

3
1 ✓   2 On being arrested by the police, Teresa admitted that she was guilty of fraud.   3 She broke her leg while playing hockey.   4 ✓   5 Helping other people wasn't something that usually made Mrs Davies happy.   6 ✓   7 All of the boys, hoping to be football stars, trained for six hours every day.   8 ✓   9 Having woken up at 4.00 a.m., we were exhausted by 11.   10 After listening to the speech for four hours, Bianca eventually fell asleep.

4
1 cheating   2 Having been caught   3 playing   4 Called   5 asking   6 celebrating   7 Betting   8 Having made   9 involved   10 telling   11 having placed   12 known

Vocabulary | humour

5
1 exaggeration   2 cartoon   3 pun   4 black humour   5 irony   6 farce   7 satire

Review and consolidation unit 3

Narrative tenses (review)

1
1 had been driving   2 was being turned into   3 had left   4 had been memorising   5 was making   6 had been writing   7 hadn't read   8 was facing   9 had been borrowed   10 Did/get up

Participle clauses

2
1 Hoping   2 Restored/Having been restored   3 Running   4 sat/sitting   5 While driving   6 On hearing/Having heard   7 Buried   8 After being caught/Having been caught   9 taken/being taken   10 After being treated/Treated

Tales

3
1 B   2 C   3 B   4 C   5 A   6 C   7 C   8 A

Humour

4
1 satire   2 farce   3 puns   4 cartoons   5 black humour

Compound words

5
Across: 1 absent   2 skinned   3 offish   4 orientated   5 headed
Down: 2 sufficient   6 minded   7 hearted

How to... describe people

6
1 Yolanda seems **to** be a very nice girl.   2 You're such **a** fast swimmer I could never keep up with you.   3 **The** thing I don't like about Samantha is that she's so selfish.   4 The thing **that** strikes you about Gudrun is her determination.   5 He can be a **bit annoying** sometimes but his heart's in the right place.   6 Once you **get to know** Maurice, you'll like him.

Metaphors

7

1 It is a dead-end job. 2 Maggie and Denis have a stormy relationship. 3 That was the moment when her career took off. 4 It's the manager who's in the firing line. 5 They gave me a frosty reception. 6 I'd never wanted to follow in my mother's footsteps. 7 Once you get promoted, you'll have to call the shots. 8 He has his sights set on becoming a fighter pilot. 9 We'd reached a crossroads. 10 Several of us were feeling a bit under the weather.

Unit 4 Progress

Lesson 4.1

Vocabulary | progress

1a

1 f 2 c 3 h 4 e 5 d 6 a 7 g 8 b

1b

1 software company 2 genetic engineering 3 shuttle launch 4 skin tissue 5 orbit / moon 6 test tube 7 rare strain 8 computer network

Reading

2

Making a superhero – fact or fiction?

Grammar | future probability

3

1 The odds are against being born on another planet. 2 I doubt whether you would find a cosmic lantern. 3 Gamma rays are definitely produced by nuclear explosions. 4 There's every likelihood that if Dr Banner had received this radiation, he would have died. 5 There's a slim chance we could create a believable version of hulk in reality. 6 Giving him anabolic steroids would almost definitely/certainly create his pumped-up look. 7 These might well cause him to become more aggressive and moody. 8 There is a remote possibility that we could create green skin by genetic engineering. 9 A radioactive spider could conceivably exist. 10 An animal stands no chance of transferring DNA via a bite. 11 If it did transfer its DNA, it wouldn't stand a chance of fusing with our DNA. 12 If ingesting DNA was enough to change our own DNA, we would presumably adopt the characteristics of chickens and apples when we ate them. 13 Batman may/might well be the most realistic of the heroes. 14 There is a distinct possibility that modern carmakers could even create a batmobile.

4

1 any/slim 2 against/possibility 3 no 4 doubt 5 well 6 bound 7 doubtful 8 conceivably 9 likelihood 10 chances

Listening

5a

1 Because she was able to lift the heavy car off the boy like the superhero Wonder Woman. 2 To comfort a mother and child trapped in the house by a fire.

5b

1 1.7 metres tall 2 one-tonne car 3 trapped underneath 4 severely injured 5 good recovery 6 found the strength 7 thinking of her own son 8 an award 9 outstanding bravery 10 rescue a mother and child 11 daring climb 12 front of the building 13 in the smoke-filled room 14 the firefighters arrived

Lesson 4.2

Vocabulary | arrangements

1

1 b 2 a 3 c 4 c 5 a 6 c 7 c 8 a 9 b 10 c

Grammar | future forms

2

1 're going to 2 I'll 3 I'm leaving 4 will be doing 5 will have gone 6 you decide 7 would 8 'll 9 'll have finished 10 leaves

Reading

3

1 F 2 F 3 T 4 T 5 F 6 F 7 F 8 T 9 T 10 F

4a

1 anxious (to do something) 2 embarked 3 savouring 4 godfather 5 backlash 6 folly 7 gauge 8 itch

4b

1 embarked 2 anxious 3 savour 4 gauge 5 backlash

How to | be vague/imprecise

5a

1 less 2 time 3 moon 4 bits 5 that 6 about 7 of 8 of

Lesson 4.3

Vocabulary | special abilities

1

1 demanding 2 gifted 3 making 4 prodigy 5 adulation 6 peers 7 freaks

Reading

2

obsessed with cameras as a toddler
starred in *Goddess of the Village* – aged four
role in Papa Pandu – soap opera
wrote a hit song for a film – aged six
appeared in 24 films and more than 1,000 episodes of the soap opera
wrote a short story about Bangalore street kids
later turned the story into a screenplay *C/o Footpath*
director of his own film – aged nine, youngest director in the world.

3

1 He has always been involved in film. He enjoys playing, but not as much as other children. He doesn't go to school very often. 2 He was 'obsessed with the camera' even as a toddler. His behaviour would improve when his parents were filming him. He won an audition for his first film part aged four. 3 He was always asking staff on the set of the soap about the various shots. When he wrote his own short story, he turned it into a screenplay, and then decided to direct the film himself. 4 He met some street children who were selling newspapers on a busy road. Talking to them he discovered that they were orphans who would be beaten if they didn't return home with money. He was moved by the encounter. 5 He would like the children to watch it and want to go to school. He also wants to be the youngest director in the world. 6 His secretary collects notes for him when he misses lessons. 7 His father worries that his son is missing out on his childhood, because he doesn't play like other children.

4a

1 barking orders 2 affluent 3 urged 4 (be) obsessed with 5 beaten 6 be moved by 7 encounter 8 prop 9 keep up 10 reassure

4b

director, edit suite, cuts, a shot, leading film star, scene, making movies, be in films/appear in episodes of a soap opera, the director's seat, be successful, fans' favourite, actors, Bollywood superstar, acting career, an audition, given a part, fantasy adventure, land a lead role, daily soap, wrote a hit song, obsessed with cameras, camera 'was on him', this shot/that shot, journalists, screenplay, during filming, frame, give the shot depth

Grammar | inversion

5

1 had we heard 2 Not only did she 3 everyone has arrived 4 have I been 5 Not since I went 6 am I going 7 Only if 8 do you need to 9 did I 10 is the service great

6

1 Nowhere 2 Only 3 until 4 sooner 5 Not 6 Nowhere 7 before 8 Only 9 Only 10 Never

Review and Consolidation unit 4

Future probability

1

1 The odds are against them winning the series. 2 We're bound to see her on the flight. 3 The chances are that it will rain later. 4 It is doubtful that we will have time to finish everything today. 5 There is a distinct possibility that we'll beat the competition. 6 There is every likelihood that he'll get the promotion. 7 That may well prove to be an excellent idea. 8 There is a slim chance that we could catch the earlier train.

Future tenses

2

1 'll call 2 will/'ll have finished 3 is coming 4 'm going to do/'ll do/'m doing 5 is going to be 6 'll take 7 'm meeting 8 'm going to be 9 'll see 10 'll get/'m going to get

Inversion

3

1 Not only **did they apologise** for the inconvenience, but they have refunded the money! 2 ✓ 3 Only after **I repeatedly asked them**, did I manage to get a response. 4 Not since 2005 **has there been** such a hot summer. 5 ✓ 6 Never before **have we been** able to photograph these small creatures in such detail. 7 Only if we keep looking **will we** ever find the solution. 8 ✓ 9 Not for one minute **did I think** they really meant what they said. 10 Nowhere **does it say** that we aren't allowed to use this room.

How to... sound vague/imprecise

4

1 time   2 once   3 bits   4 less   5 ish   6 sort   7 kind   8 so

Progress

5

1 A   2 B   3 C   4 B   5 A

Arrangements

6

Across: 4 tied   5 call   7 end   8 feet   9 up
Down: 1 ahead   2 lined   3 fallen   5 comes   6 get

Two-part expressions

7

1 order   2 By   3 trial   4 regulations   5 aches   6 tried   7 facts   8 about   9 once   10 ready   11 again   12 less   13 pieces   14 time   15 tired

Unit 5 Fortunes

Lesson 5.1

Vocabulary | fortunes

1

1 fortune   2 haggle   3 stock   4 rise   5 high-income   6 priceless   7 commission   8 bankrupt

Vocabulary | business

2

1 hands-on   2 fringe   3 recruited   4 bail   5 start-up   6 break even   7 launch   8 make a living   9 profit share   10 publicity   11 profit

Grammar | emphasis

3

1 The fact that 1 in 10 children in the UK are suffering from a mental health disorder is very worrying indeed.   2 Americans are not very interested in soccer at all. They prefer to watch baseball.   3 It is by no means certain that giving aid is the best way to help poorer countries.   4 Kandinsky even abandoned his law studies in order to train as an artist in Munich. OR Even Kandinsky abandoned his law studies in order to train as an artist in Munich.   5 The reason why the most popular soap opera in South American history, *I Am Betty The Ugly*, was so successful is because the woman who played Betty was incredibly beautiful.   6 The person who planted the UK's first ever olive grove in 2006 was Marco Diacono. He hoped that global warming would help the trees to survive.   7 We went to the Pantanal, in Brazil, to enjoy the wildlife, but I did get a shock when I found an 8ft-long caiman alligator outside my tent.   8 The place I would suggest you stay is Amalfi.

Pronunciation | emphasis

4b

1 It's her own fault for leaving the car unlocked.
2 I wasn't in the least bit interested in buying the carpet.
3 The office was by no means easy to find.
4 It was a complete mistake to sell the company.
5 What we need to do is sit down and discuss the options.
6 The taxi driver did manage to get them to the airport on time.

Reading and listening

5

1 She remembers him being at home when she did her first tap debut, aged four and her parents having an argument.   2 Because they were frightening to a small child in this difficult situation.   3 She had her fingerprints taken, searched, and had her bag searched.   4 The girl was quiet and serious, nervous (hot), and sad.   5 She could touch him through the fence with her fingers, or with a kiss.   6 The way her father dressed, how he walked, talked and smiled.

6

1 tap dancing debut   2 a heated argument   3 a teepee   4 moccasins   5 inmates   6 giant stainless-steel counter   7 buzz   8 hive   9 sauntered

Lesson 5.2

Vocabulary | finance and philanthropy

1

1 B   2 A   3 C   4 C   5 A   6 B   7 A   8 C

Grammar | conditionals (review)

2

1 If I had my car here, I would offer you a lift.   2 I'll make some coffee if everyone has finished eating.   3 If it hadn't been for Jamie, we would have waited for ages.   4 If you had listened carefully to what I said, this wouldn't have happened!   5 Provided that she has all the right injections, she will (or should) be fine.   6 If only they had rung us ten minutes earlier, we would have cancelled the order.   7 Unless Graham changes his strategy, the business will (or could) go bankrupt.   8 Should you happen to be in Oxford, you should (or must) come and stay.   9 Supposing they offered her the job, would she accept it?   10 I don't mind how much it costs, so long as the job is finished by Sunday.

3

1 Supposing, b   2 happen, a   3 hadn't, b   4 would, b   5 If, b   6 long, a

Vocabulary | words that are nouns and verbs

4a and b

1 fund (noun)   2 share (noun)   3 benefit (verb)   4 launch (noun)   5 charge (noun)   6 experience (verb)   7 profit (verb)   8 recruit (verb)

Reading

5

1 There are 64 new millionaires reportedly created everyday in Silicone Valley.   2 Many of the people who find themselves suddenly rich are in their 20s and 30s.   3 He noticed a change about ten years ago, when people from middle-class backgrounds started coming into money.   4 The number of millionaires in the United States and Canada at the time of the article.   5 The number of hours a week that people would work on their new business until they became rich.   6 The age at which many of these millionaires can retire.   7 The amount of money Rory Holland made when he sold his company in 1998.

6

1 The rise in internet-based businesses.   2 They may feel guilt, stress and confusion. These feelings may make them experience panic attacks, feel depressed, suffer insomnia, etc.   3 The 'new' rich, who grew up without wealth, and expected to spend their lives working are likely to suffer.   4 Anxiety and depression may be caused by watching the stock market.   5 He suggests becoming involved in the community through fundraising projects, etc.   6 He feels that they should be treated with sympathy.

7

1 handle   2 crave   3 drawbacks   4 rip apart   5 fledgling   6 mid-life crisis   7 entitled   8 upbringing

Lesson 5.3

Vocabulary | describing a job

1

1 environment   2 development   3 convenience   4 opportunities   5 perks   6 supportive   7 prospects   8 achievements   9 salary   10 autonomy   11 flexible   12 pension   13 challenging   14 satisfaction

How to | express priorities

2a

1 The essential thing for me is to be able to walk to work.   2 Having good promotion prospects is absolutely vital.   3 Having flexible working hours isn't a major priority.   4 My main priority is job satisfaction.   5 I couldn't do without supportive colleagues.   6 I'm not really bothered about having a pension plan.

Pronunciation | stress

3

1 The essential thing for me is to be able to walk to work.   2 Having good promotion prospects is absolutely vital.   3 Having flexible working hours isn't a major priority.   4 My main priority is job satisfaction.   5 I couldn't do without supportive colleagues.   6 I'm not really bothered about having a pension plan.

Grammar | sentence adverbials

4

1 Believe it or not, sales figures were up on last year. 2 Apparently, the company is losing a lot of money. OR The company is apparently losing a lot of money. 3 Broadly speaking, the management have a good relationship with the rest of the staff. 4 In my opinion, the conclusions of the report are fundamentally wrong. 5 I'd like to say no to the extra work, but on the other hand, I need the money.
6 What you say is true, but only up to a point. 7 I travel a lot for my job. By and large I enjoy it although it can be exhausting.
8 With hindsight, we should probably have approached them earlier.
9 Surprisingly enough, the results of the survey indicate that there could be a good market for the new product.

Listening

5a

1 She is a business expert. 2 It is an innovative media company.

5b

Creative ideas and strange food: To encourage their staff to be more creative they offer chocolate ants to their workers, and serve crocodile curry for lunch.
Inspiring the workers: There is a Director of Freshness who comes up with new ideas like working in the park on a sunny day, or having magicians in the office.
Number of employees/average age of workers: 389 employees, most under 35 years old
Schemes and new ideas: There was a scheme called 'If I ran the company' where workers could give their ideas. They introduced a bar which serves free breakfasts and stays open at night.

Vocabulary | expressing quantity

6

1 plenty 2 not 3 awful 4 little 5 vast 6 deal 7 most 8 many
9 few

Review and consolidation unit 5

Conditionals (review)

1

1 If it hadn't been for the weather, we would have had a wonderful holiday. 2 You can use my phone provided that you don't speak for too long. 3 If only I had listened to her advice! 4 Should you happen to be in Rome, you should call my sister. 5 Supposing we were to call the police, that might help. 6 If you would let us know as soon as the parcel arrives. 7 As long as he lives in that house, I'm not going back there.

Sentence adverbials

2

1 B 2 A 3 C 4 C 5 B 6 A

Emphasis

3

1 B 2 C 3 A 4 A 5 B 6 B 7 C 8 C

Business

4

1 i 2 e 3 j 4 b 5 a 6 h 7 d 8 c 9 f 10 g

Describing a job

5

1 satisfaction 2 supportive 3 promotion 4 challenging
5 development 6 recognition 7 flexible 8 convenience

Idioms (1)

6

1 He sold his business for $14 million. He's worth a fortune.
2 As a student I lived on/off the money I earned from waitressing jobs.
3 Since my husband lost his job, we're not very well off financially.
4 I have spent this month's salary, so now I am completely broke.
5 You don't need to pay for everything. Let's split the bill.
6 You should treat yourself to something special at least once a month.
7 It's a beautiful dress, and the best thing about it is that it was dirt cheap.
8 Let's splash out on a meal in an expensive restaurant.
9 I shouldn't worry about paying back the money. She's rolling in it.
10 My wage brings us more than enough to get by on.
11 I'm glad you like the carpet. It cost me an arm and a leg.
12 It's very expensive to buy it on my own, but perhaps we could go halves.